Christ in East
and West

Christ in East and West

edited by
Paul Fries
and
Tiran Nersoyan

introduction by
Jeffrey Gros, F.S.C.

PEETERS

MERCER

ISBN 0-86554-267-8 (casebound)
ISBN 0-86554-277-5 (perfectbound)

Library of Congress Cataloging-in-Publication Data

Christ in East and West.

Papers from a consultation of the Commission on Faith and Order,
National Council of the Churches of Christ in the U.S.A.,
with the Oriental Orthodox churches and other churches,
26-27 April 1985, New York, New York
Includes bibliographical references and index.
1. Oriental Orthodox churches—Doctrines—Congresses.
2. Jesus Christ—Person and offices—Congresses.
3. Jesus Christ—History of doctrines—Congresses.
4. Oriental Orthodox churches—Relations—Congresses.
I. Fries, Paul. II. Nersoyan, Tiran. III. National Council
of Churches of Christ in the United States of America.
Commission on Faith and Order.
BX106.2.C46   1987   232'.09   87-7699
ISBN 0-86554-267-8 (alk. paper)
ISBN 0-86554-277-5 (pbk. : alk. paper)

Contents

Part II
Protestant Views

Appendixes

Communiqué

A Consultation
Commission on Faith and Order, NCCCUSA, with the Oriental Orthodox Churches on Christological Concerns and the Apostolic Faith
26, 27 April 1985, New York, New York

Background

Participants included members from the Armenian Orthodox Church, the Ethiopian Orthodox Church and the Syrian Orthodox Church, the Disciples of Christ, the Episcopal Church, the Lutheran Church in America, the Mennonite Church (and the General Conference Mennonite Church), the Presbyterian Church (USA), the Reformed Church in America, the Southern Baptist Convention, and the United Methodist Church.* Observers from the Orthodox Church in America and the Roman Catholic Church were also in attendance.

During the past twenty years, four dialogues have taken place between the Oriental Orthodox Churches (Armenian, Ethiopian, Coptic, Indian, and Syrian Orthodox Churches) and the Eastern Orthodox Churches (Greek, Russian, and Antiochian). In addition, during the 1970s a series of four discussions took place in Vienna at the Pro Oriente Foundation between Oriental Orthodox and Roman Catholic theologians. Out of both of these series of dialogues significant unofficial Agreed Statements and Communiqués have been issued which were considered by the present Consultation. The Consultation commends these statements, encourages their study in ecumenical discussion, and looks forward to their forthcoming publication.

---

* PARTICIPANTS: Dr. Roberta Bondi (United Methodist Church), Dr. Thomas Finger (Mennonite), Dr. Paul Fries (Reformed Church in America), Dr. Patrick Henry (Presbyterian Church [USA]), Dr. E. Glenn Hinson (Southern Baptist Convention), Dr. Michael P. Kinnamon (Christian Church [Disciples of Christ]), Dr. William G. Rusch (Lutheran Church in America), Dr. Robert Wright (Episcopal Church), Father Arten Ashjian, Father Garabed Kochakian, Archbishop Tiran Nersoyan (Armenian Church of America), the Very Rev. Chorepiscopus John Meno, Archbishop Mar Athanasius Samuel (Syrian Orthodox Church of Antioch), Bishop Paulos (Ethiopian Orthodox Church), John Breck (Orthodox Church in America), Brother Jeffrey Gros, Carol Thysell (Staff: Commission on Faith and Order).

Presenters of papers from the several Reformation traditions reflected on how the above-mentioned Agreed Statements and Communiqués and their own traditions intersect with issues of particular concern to Oriental Orthodox Churches, both theologically and in the life of their churches.

The participants examined the understanding of the person of Jesus Christ in their traditions. While the traditions represented vary in their approaches to issues of Christology, authority, and ecclesiology, all those present concluded that their own traditions affirm the teaching of the early Councils that Jesus Christ is truly divine and truly human.

A number of areas of convergence were identified and a recommendation was made to pursue issues relating to questions of Christology and authority in the churches in the context of the study "Towards the Common Expression of the Apostolic Faith Today," within the Faith and Order Commission of the NCCCUSA. This study seeks to provide an expression of a common theological basis for unity among the Christian churches in our time, and follows the recently published study on *Baptism, Eucharist, and Ministry* of the World Council of Churches.

* * *

Dedication

This volume is dedicated to Sister Ann Patrick Ware, S.L., whose careful work in the Faith and Order movement through the fledgling days of Roman Catholic participation, and a wider inclusiveness in all of our churches' lives, enabled us to understand more deeply that "what is not assumed is not redeemed" in the Godhead. Her commitment to the "truly human and truly divine" orthodoxy of the Christian faith and its full inclusiveness has been a witness to all of us who have benefited from her leadership.

Introduction

*In the beginning was the Word, and the Word was with God, and the Word
was God. The Word was in the beginning with God; all things were made
through him, and without him was not anything made that was made. In
him was life, and the life was the light of humanity. The light shines in the
darkness, and the darkness has not overcome it. . . . And the Word became flesh and dwelt among us, full of grace and truth; we have beheld
his glory, glory as of the only Son from the Father.*

(John 1:1-5, 14)

In the course of the two millennia since Jesus lived and taught in the
world, his followers have become divided from one another. *The purpose
of this volume is to contribute to a deeper understanding of the centrality
of Jesus Christ in the quest for Christian unity (ecumenism), and to assist
Christians who confess his true humanity and true divinity to understand
and transcend controversies that have kept their churches separated for
over 1,500 years.* The very center of the Christian mystery is the person
and work of Jesus Christ, the Word of God. While the New Testament witness to the humanity and divinity of Christ as understood by the apostles
is very rich, the verbal expression of this revealed reality has been the focus of controversy and theological reflection through the centuries. Christ
is the center of Christian unity for those who confess Jesus as the foundation of their faith and who see the message embodied in the community
he left behind—the church.

For seventy-five years representatives of Christian churches have joined
in a movement commonly called Faith and Order, searching the Scriptures
and Christian history to discover a common understanding of the biblical
faith handed down through the apostles. Initiated in the United States by
members of Episcopal, Southern Baptist, and Disciples churches, this
movement has been sponsored in the World Council of Churches' Commission on Faith and Order, which includes representatives from Eastern
and Oriental Orthodox, Roman Catholic, Anglican, and most Protestant
churches. The goal of the council as enunciated in its first purpose is:

To call the churches to the goal of visible unity in one faith and in one
Eucharistic fellowship expressed in worship and in common life in Christ,
and to advance towards that unity in order that the world may believe.[1]

An underlying assumption of this book is that as divided Christians
come closer to Jesus Christ in spirituality, mission, and theology, they come
closer to being that Body of Christ they are called to be. Understanding the
person and nature of Christ is intimately connected to understanding the
church and its mission in the world.

Church Unity

As the church emerged from the catacombs and began to face Greco-
Roman culture, it became necessary to mediate disputes over the definitions of the apostolic faith in terms that went beyond the Scriptures. The
divinity of Christ and the triune character of the Godhead were debated and
written about for almost a century. In the Councils of Nicea (325) and
Constantinople (381), formulations were produced to explain the Incarnation and the Trinity that have served the Christian community for centuries, not only for teaching but also for mission.[2] The fifth century brought
further discussion and disagreement over definitions of the nature of Christ.
Christians agreed to speak of Mary as the *Theotokos,* the birthgiver of God,
at a Council held in Ephesus (431). And at Chalcedon (451) they con-
curred on definitions on the relationship between the humanity and the divinity of Christ.[3] In this latter Council we encounter the emergence of the
differences with which this book deals. Churches of Armenia, Antioch,
and Alexandria rejected the Council's pronouncements—supported by the
churches of Rome and Constantinople—about the nature of the unity between the humanity and the divinity of Jesus Christ. This marks one of the
oldest divisions still persisting among living communities of believers.[4]

This division is one among many in which the Faith and Order Commission hopes to provide reconciliation. It is important to comprehend the larger

---

[1]David Gill, ed., *Gathered for Life* (Geneva: World Council of Churches and Grand
Rapids: Wm. B. Eerdmans, 1983) 326.

[2]E. Glenn Hinson, *The Evangelization of the Roman Empire: Identity and Adaptability*
(Macon GA: Mercer University Press, 1981).

[3]Aloys Grillmeier, *Christ in Christian Tradition: From the Apostolic Age to Chalcedon
(451),* trans. J. S. Bowden (London: A. R. Mowbray, 1965; New York: Sheed and Ward,
1965); John Meyendorff, *Christ in Eastern Christian Thought* (Crestwood NY: St. Vladimir's Press, 1975).

[4]Karekin Sarkissian, *The Council of Chalcedon and the Armenian Church* (New York:
The Armenian Church Prelacy, 1965).

vision of unity proposed by Faith and Order to see the significance of this consultation. Faith and Order dialogues have produced historic results, bringing churches of Protestant, Anglican, Orthodox, and Roman Catholic convictions to recognize common approaches to scripture and to their traditions as well as to *the* Tradition, which is Jesus Christ himself.[5] Building on this work, theologians of the World Council Commission have suggested to the churches that they consider the unity of the church proposed in Acts 15—Christians gathered in council—as the model for this unity:

> The one Church is to be envisioned as a conciliar fellowship of local churches which are themselves truly united. In this conciliar fellowship, each local church possesses, in communion with the others, the fullness of catholicity, witnesses to the same apostolic faith, and therefore recognizes the others as belonging to the same Church of Christ and guided by the same Spirit.[6]

Recognizing the many years of division and sincere convictions over theological differences experienced by the churches, the World Council has proposed three marks necessary for the realization of such a Conciliar Fellowship:

> (1) The churches would share a common understanding of the Apostolic Faith, and be able to confess this message together in ways understandable, reconciling and liberating to their contemporaries. Living this Apostolic Faith together, the churches help the world to realize God's design for creation.

> (2) Confessing the Apostolic Faith together, the churches would share a full mutual recognition of baptism, the Eucharist and ministry and be able through their visible communion to let the healing and uniting power of these gifts become more evident amidst the visions of humankind.

> (3) The churches would agree on common ways of decision making and ways of teaching authoritatively and be able to demonstrate qualities of communion, participation and corporate responsibility which could shed healing light in a world of conflict.[7]

The *Baptism, Eucharist and Ministry* document (1982) of the World Council is meant to contribute to the discussions of the second of these

---

[5]*The Bible: Its Authority and Interpretation in the Ecumenical Movement*, Faith and Order Paper no. 99 (Geneva: World Council of Churches, 1980).

[6]Cf. David M. Paton, ed., *Breaking Barriers: Nairobi 1975* (London: SPCK, and Grand Rapids: Wm. B. Eerdmans, 1976) 60.

[7]Gill, *Gathered for Life*, 45.

marks.[8] The work of the churches in responding to the document, currently in process, will undoubtedly contribute to the theological reflection on the third.[9]

This book will contribute to understanding the first mark and attempt to clarify the doctrinal basis needed for agreement. The Faith and Order Commission of the World Council has undertaken a major study, "Towards the Common Expression of the Apostolic Faith Today." This consultation is placed in the context of this study of the trinitarian and incarnational basis for unity, bringing Oriental Orthodox and other Christians into dialogue on the problem.[10]

Oriental Orthodox Churches

The Oriental Orthodox Chuches are a family of Christians—Syrian, Egyptian (Coptic), Ethiopian, Indian, and Armenian—who claim apostolic origin and whose fidelity to the gospel reaches to the most ancient period of Christian history. While joined in the common faith of the Scripture and the first three Councils, and recognized by Catholics, Anglicans, and Eastern Orthodox as having the fullness of the apostolic ministry and sacramental life, full communion has not yet been restored between these and other churches.[11] The Armenian Church, with its center in Etchmiadzin (in present-day Soviet Armenia), was the first established national church, with Christianity being accepted by the king at least as early as 314. Jude Thaddeus and Bartholomew are the apostolic patrons of this church, which numbers over 5,000,000 members in the world, 600,000 of

---

[8]Geoffrey Wainwright, *The Ecumenical Moment: Crisis and Opportunity for the Church* (Grand Rapids: Wm. B. Eerdmans, 1983); Jeffrey Gros, ed., *The Search for Visible Unity* (New York: Pilgrim Press, 1984).

[9]Max Thurian, *Churches Respond to BEM,* Official Responses to the "Baptism, Eucharist and Ministry Text," vol. 1 (Geneva: World Council of Churches, 1986); Gennadios Limouris and Nomikos Vaporis, eds., *Orthodox Perspectives on Baptism, Eucharist and Ministry* (Brookline MA: Holy Cross Orthodox Press, 1986); Michael Fahey, ed., *Catholic Perspectives on Baptism, Eucharist, and Ministry* (New York: University Press of America, 1986); *Towards a Church of England Response to BEM and ARCIC: A Study Guide* (London: Church of England, 1985); *Initial Reaction from the Roman Catholic Dioceses in the U.S.* (Wheeling WV: NADEO, 1986).

[10]Hans-Georg Link, ed., *Apostolic Faith Today* (Geneva: World Council of Churches, 1985); Thomas Best, ed., *Faith and Renewal: Commission on Faith and Order, Stavanger, 1985* (Geneva: World Council of Churches, 1986).

[11]A. S. Atiya, *A History of Eastern Christianity* (South Bend: University of Notre Dame Press, 1963); *Oriental Orthodox Churches in the United States* (Washington DC: United States Catholic Conference, 1986).

whom are in the United States. The Coptic Church of Alexandria, Egypt, which counts St. Mark as its founder, has given rise to Christian monasticism through the desert fathers and contributed the great catechetical school of Alexandria. Pope Shenouda III, the present patriarch, has only recently been released from preventive detention in Egypt. The Ethiopian Church is a daughter of the Coptic Church and represents centuries of acculturation to its African environment, with legends linking the nation with Solomon and the Queen of Sheba. The Syrian Church of Antioch, founded by the apostle Peter, according to Acts, still worships in a language derived from the Aramaic of Jesus' time. The Indian Syrian churches or Orthodox "Thomas Christians" share their form of worship with the Syrian church and claim Thomas the apostle as their patron.

All of these churches have been involved in the ecumenical movement for many years and now have significant numbers living in the United States.[12] Indeed, events in the Middle East, refugees and relief in Ethiopia, and new immigrants in the United States make the living presence of these vital Christian communities an important ecclesial reality, of historical interest and theological significance.

Since the 1960s there have been very productive bilateral dialogues between the Oriental Orthodox Churches and the Eastern Orthodox Churches, published in full in the *Greek Orthodox Theological Review*[13] and summarized in the volume *Does Chalcedon Divide or Unite?*[14] In the 1970s a similar series of bilateral discussions between Roman Catholic and Oriental Orthodox theologians took place in Vienna at the Pro Oriente foundation, and were published in the series *Wort und Wahrheit*.[15] These European discussions, involving participants from the Eastern and Roman Churches, have not yet been received at the highest levels of the three communities involved, or found popular understanding in the United States. While the Oriental churches have been participants and even leaders in the conciliar movement both in the United States and in the World Council,

---

[12]"The Churches and the Middle East," *One World,* no. 106 (June 1985).

[13]*The Greek Orthodox Theological Review* 10:2 (Winter 1964-1965); 13:2 (Fall 1968); 16:1,2 (Spring and Fall 1971).

[14]Paulos Gregorios, William Lazareth, and Nikos Nissiotis, eds., *Does Chalcedon Divide or Unite? Towards Convergence in Orthodox Christology* (Geneva: World Council of Churches, 1981).

[15]*Wort und Wahrheit* [in English], *Revue for Religion and Culture,* Supplementary Issues no. 1 (December 1972), 2 (December 1974), 3 (December 1976), 4 [December 1978).

the understanding of these great traditions has not been strong among the United States churches.

If the World Council study "Towards the Common Expression of the Apostolic Faith Today" is to be effective it must discover modern resolutions of the ancient problems which divided the churches of the Roman Empire from the churches located on the periphery of its territories to the east and to the south, in Armenia, Egypt, Ethiopia, Syria, and India. Likewise, there will need to be a deeper understanding by the non-Oriental churches of these traditions, their life of worship, their spirituality, their theological tradition and their understanding of the faith today. *For this reason, this book focuses especially on the Christological concerns that gave rise to these divisions, the social and political contexts in which these concerns have emerged, and the separate histories that have kept the faith alive in our different traditions since the 5th century.* Not only the specific questions of the Council of Chalcedon, but also the wider issues of how the church decides and acts and confesses the faith, become issues for churches which have lived separately for so many centuries.

In discussing ecumenical methodology, it is important to note the differences between two styles of discourse. One style clarifies the historic divisions and the technical issues that lead to the division. In this particular case, for example, the issues of the fourth- and fifth-century Christology, their language, and content, have to be clarified and the difference reconciled or transcended by biblical and historical research. The essays among the Roman Catholic, Eastern, and Oriental Orthodox in the first half of this volume give particular attention to this methodology. In these essays, the classical historical and biblical methodology is augmented by more contemporary contextual approaches which clarify the political, historical, and economic forces which contributed to the initial division.

The second style of discourse in ecumenical methodology is to be in dialogue with one's own communion in order to help one's fellow believers understand the progress implied by the research. Both the first part, with its attention to the classical details and debate, and the second set of Anglican and Protestant essays are committed to that task. The reader may find it easier to read the summary report (appendix 2) and the second set of essays as a beginning. The first set of essays presumes a knowledge of the fifth-century Christian history and its Christological controversies.

While the first part may seem more formal than the second, which is more characteristic of the style of theological writing used in the United States theological context, both parts challenge the ecumenical partners and the members of their own communions towards deeper understanding and reformed attitudes about the other churches. The common statement, the working paper (appendix 2), and the record of the discussions of the papers included in the first part show the member churches the progress made by this research. The interested student of this question will be well advised to investigate in more depth the discussions of the papers included in the first part.

Christology in Dialogue

The Commission on Faith and Order of the National Council of Churches has provided an opportunity for a group of Anglican and Protestant scholars to review the European work in order both to evaluate its relevance for their own churches and to move forward the understandings reached elsewhere. Within the context of its study "Towards the Common Expression of the Apostolic Faith Today," the Commission's purpose is both educational and theological. We hope the enclosed essays will enable the *discussion of the common basis for unity in Christ* to enrich and broaden the fellowship among the churches. We also hope they will *provide resources for introducing theologians and ministerial students to the issues involved in the life* of these historic churches in relation to the churches in the United States *If we can state the centrality of Christ in the movement for Christian unity, and if in the discussion of the faith in the divinity and humanity of Christ we can find a common ground, our common witness to the world will have moved forward by another step.* If one more step in the reconciling love of Jesus Christ can be taken in witnessing to a divided world as we move forward towards unity in truth, our efforts will not have been in vain.

To achieve this goal, the Commission brought together twenty theologians of various traditions. The Roman Catholic, Oriental, and Eastern Orthodox papers included in the first part of the volume were used for the purpose of the discussion.[16] In these essays the strong historical commitments of Catholic and Orthodox to tradition is in evidence by the care given to historical research and exegesis of conciliar texts. While historical weight is given to social and political factors (de Vries, Nersoyan, Gregorios), primary weight is given to linguistic and conceptual misunderstandings and reinterpretations (Grillmeier, Samuel, Romanides, George). In some of the essays, and more so in the discussions not included, contemporary Christologies and New Testament scholarship are brought to bear on the issues

---

[16]Permission to reprint these papers and communiqués, which were originally published in English, has been given by the Pro Oriente Foundation, A-1010 Wien I, in der Burg, Saulenstiege II/54, Vienna, Austria, and from the Commission on Faith and Order, World Council of Churches, 150, route de Ferney, 1211 Geneva 20, Switzerland.

(Gregorios, George, Nersoyan). Indeed, as the United States discussion indicates, the relationship of ecclesiology, authority, conciliarity, and anthropology is central in reconciling these divisions in the Body of Christ (Gregorios, Florovsky, de Vries).

In the second part of the book we have included the seven Protestant papers prepared specifically for the consultation. These evaluate the agreements and the accounts given in Europe and further expand the discussion into areas of mission, authority, and church unity in such a way as to serve the United States church experience. The historic distance from the Oriental churches and the Christological controversies are taken into account (Hinson, Bondi, Kinnamon, Finger) as a challenge both to the theological enterprise and ecumenical dialogue. The essays emerging from confessional traditions (Rusch, Henry) emphasize the continuity between elements of Christology in the Reformation traditions and the ancient church. The essays by Rusch and Kinnamon also demonstrate how the Faith and Order discussions build upon and are enriched by the bilateral dialogues, for example, those recorded in appendix 1 and the first series of essays.[17]

The essays of the second part, as they contrast and complement the first part, point to fundamental, but not irreconcilable differences in ecumenical methodology which must eventually be dealt with as the ecumenical movement looks more closely at what is demanded for a full conciliar fellowship. The Protestant and Anglican experience of constitutionalized ecclesial life, with full roles for laity, appreciation of the interplay of praxis and theory in theological method, and the need for continual renewal for the apostolic faith to be again appropriated by the mass of the faithful is now in full and fruitful dialogue with the Orthodox and Catholic traditions. These churches are no less diverse than their Reformation partners, but for them definable continuity with the apostolic faith comes more easily than the sorting out of essential from ephemeral elements in the tradition, giving contemporary structure to collegial communion, and finding an appropriate social ethic in the modern world.

The working paper (appendix 2) gives some hints of the mutual learnings that are occurring among these several traditions, and the rich ecumenical road ahead as issues of authority, social ethics, church order, the limits of diversity, and structures of conciliar fellowship emerge on the dialogue agenda.

----

[17]The Anglican paper written for this consultation was withdrawn from publication in this volume and can be found in J. Robert Wright, "The Authority of Chalcedon for Anglicans" in *Christian Authority: Essays in Honor of Henry Chadwick,* ed. Gillian R. Evans (London: Oxford University Press, 1987).

This consultation is one of several which have been, and we expect will be carried out as elements in the United States contribution to the World Council study. Consultations on the Holy Spirit,[18] on Gender and Language in the Creed,[19] and on the Black Church perspective[20] have already been published. Underway are discussions that focus on the concerns of Pentecostal and Peace churches in the ecumenical movement, as well as exploration of the nature of the apostolic faith,[21] its diverse understandings in the United States context, and how the free churches can relate to this study in its focus on the Niceno-Constantinopolitan creed.

Thanks are in order to Dr. E. Glenn Hinson, chairperson of the Apostolic Faith Study as this project was designed, to Dr. Paul Fries and Father Arten Ashjian for their careful planning and chairing of the consultation, to Ms. Carol Thysell from the Faith and Order staff for facilitating, drafting and interpreting the consultation and to Archbishop Tiran Nersoyan who brought the seniority, wisdom, and experience to the project without which it would have been impossible.

Brother Jeffrey Gros, F.S.C.
Director, Commission on Faith and Order
National Council of the Churches of Christ in the USA

---

[18]Lukas Vischer, ed., *Spirit of God, Spirit of Christ,* Faith and Order Paper no. 103 (London: SPCK, and Geneva: World Council of Churches, 1981); *Credo in Spiritum Sanctum,* Atti del Congresso Teologica Internazionale di Pneumatologia, vols. 1 and 2 (Vatican City: Libreria Editrice Vaticana, 1983).

[19]*Union Seminary Quarterly Review* 40:3 (August 1985) (special issue on Language and the Creeds).

[20]*Midstream* 24:4 (October 1985).

[21]Hans-Georg Link, ed., *The Roots of Our Common Faith: Faith in the Scriptures and in the Early Church* (Geneva: World Council of Churches, 1984).

Part I

Catholic and Orthodox Views

The Reasons for the Rejection
of the Council of Chalcedon
by the Oriental Orthodox Churches

Wilhelm de Vries

The Council of Chalcedon had been summoned by the emperor Marcian with the consent of Pope Leo.[1] The purpose of the Council was to restore the unity and peace of the church which had been disturbed by the dispute over the formulation of the mystery of Christ. It must be pointed out that this purpose was not achieved. In spite of the decrees of the Council the dispute continued with unabated intensity. The outcome was that about half the Antiochene patriarchate, almost the entire Alexandrian patriarchate, and the entire Armenian and Ethiopian churches repudiated the Council and have not changed their attitude to this day. The East Syrian church of Persia hardly took note of the Council. The attitude of this church toward Chalcedon was ambiguous, but generally also unfavorable although for quite different reasons than those of above-mentioned churches.

Let us now examine the reasons for the relative failure of the Council. In my opinion they may be attributed first of all to the way in which the Council itself proceeded. In Chalcedon there was no true discussion, no real dialogue between the disputing parties. Perhaps it is asking too much of the people of those days to expect such a dialogue. Nevertheless it must be said that this absence of a true dialogue was responsible for the failure. It is our task today to make up for this omission.

---

[1]See Wilhelm de Vries, "Die Struktur der Kirche gemass dem Konzil von Chalkedon," *Orientalis Chr. Periodica* 35(1969): 63-122. The Council was summoned by the emperor on 17 May 451; cf. *Acta Conciliorum Oecumenicorum*, ed. Schwartz (=ACO) 2/1,1:27; J. D. Mansi, ed., *Sanctorum Conciliorum Nova et Amplissima Collectio* (=Mansi), 55 vols. (Florence, Venice, Paris, Leipzig, 1759-1962) 6:552; regarding Leo's consent in *Epistolae* (=Ep.) 89-90, 24 and 26 June 451, see J. P. Minge, ed., *Patrologia Latina* (=PL), 221 vols. (1844-1864) 54:950-54; ACO 2/4: 47-48.

On the face of things, the problem to be discussed in Chalcedon appeared undecided; in reality, the outcome was certain from the start. Formally the two parties—the opponents of Eutyches and his supporters—were equal partners. In front of the altar rails of the church of St. Euphemia the imperial commissioners were seated in the middle; to their left, in the place of honor, there were the papal legates, then Anatolius of Constantinople, Maximus of Antioch, and others. To the immediate right of the imperial commissioners Dioscorus of Alexandria was seated, followed by Juvenal of Jerusalem and Illyrian bishops.[2]

Formalities were thus observed. However, considering the political situation of the church at the beginning of the Council these were nothing but formalities which, moreover, were immediately violated: on the demand of the papal legates Dioscorus was deprived of his seat as a Father and was admitted to the sessions only as the accused. For the time being, however, his supporters retained their seats.

There were no doubts as to the outcome of the Council. After the emperor Theodosius II had been killed on 28 July 450, when falling from his horse, the situation changed radically. In 449 at Ephesus Theodosius had been persuaded by Dioscorus to vindicate Eutyches and condemn Flavian of Constantinople. Theodosius was succeeded by his sister Pulcheria, who was favorable to Pope Leo. She married the old general Marcian, thus making him emperor. Marcian shared her views so that this was one occasion where pope and emperor were of quite the same opinion. Therefore it was absolutely certain right at the beginning of the Council that the decision would be in keeping with the Tomus Leonis ad Flavianum whose reading at Ephesus (449) Dioscorus had prevented. For the pope the dogmatic question was settled in his letter. He requested the Council to accept it without discussion.[3] The emperor, on the other hand, wanted to maintain the semblance of a free discussion; at the same time he took care that the Tome of Leo was included in the doctrinal definition of the Council in spite of the strong opposition of a sizable minority of the fathers. The Illyrian and Palestinian bishops, who at the second session raised objections to Leo's Tome, were given the opportunity at the instance of the imperial commissioners to resolve their difficulties in a commission meeting with Anatolius of Constantinople and to arrive at an officially satisfactory so-

---

[2]ACO 2/1,1:65; Mansi 6: 580; cf. de Vries, "Chalcedon," 67.

[3]Ep. 82, PL 54:917-18; ACO 2/4: 41; Ep. 90, PL 54:933-34; ACO 2/4:90.

lution. In reality, however, they were not satisfied—as may be seen from the course the council subsequently took.[4]

Contrary to the pope's will, the imperial commissioners made Leo's Tome a formal subject of the discussion. In spite of the objections of the papal legates, they called upon the bishops during the fourth session to individually give their opinions on whether the creeds of Nicea and Constantinople were in accordance with Leo's letter or not. The minutes include the "*sententiae*" of the bishops on this question.[5] Thus Leo's Tome was judged according to the generally recognized dogmatic standards. The outcome could not be doubtful. At the fifth session, however, it became evident how strong opposition to Leo's theology still was among the participants in the Council, and only by concentrated pressure were the imperial commissioners able to break this opposition. It is here that the inherent weakness of Chalcedon lies, and it is the true reason why the Council was later on rejected by a considerable part of Christendom.

A commission headed by Anatolius of Constantinople had worked out a dogmatic formula which did not take into account the Tome. Unfortunately the text is not extant. However, it must have contained the words "from two natures" and not Leo's version "in two natures." When Anatolius asked whether the Council approved of the definition worked out by himself and his commission all the bishops excepting only the Roman and some Oriental bishops (those from the civil diocese "Oriens" whose capital was Antioch) exclaimed, "We all approve of the definition. . . . Whoever does not agree be cursed. . . . Expel the Nestorians!" Quite obviously the general sentiment was in favor of a dogmatic definition excluding Leo's Tome. The papal legates protested and threatened to depart and summon a council in Italy.[6] The imperial commissioners, according to the instructions of the emperor, demanded the inclusion of the pope's letter into the dogmatic definition of the Council and supported the legates with a compromise proposal: the institution of a new commission which would include the Roman legates.[7] The emperor was asked to make a decision. He approved the proposal of his commissioners, but the opposition was not yet satisfied. The Illyrian bishops exclaimed, "Whoever is against it (the proposed dogmatic definition without Leo's Tome) is a Nestorian!

---

[4]Charles Joseph Hefele and H. Leclercq, *Histoire des Conciles* 2/2:688ff., 690.

[5]ACO 2/1,2:94ff.; Mansi 7:9ff.

[6]ACO 2/1,2:123; Mansi 7:589-92.

[7]Ibid.

Whoever is against it ought to go to Rome.'' Now it became quite obvious that this opposition was directed against Leo and his letter. In this critical situation the imperial commissioners took action by confronting the opposing bishops with the decisive choice: either you are for Dioscorus or for Leo. There is no middle course. Dioscorus said, ''from two natures,'' Leo ''in two natures.'' Whom do you want to follow? In this situation the bishops could hardly do anything but decide for Leo. Dioscorus had already been condemned by the Council, and moreover was in disfavor at the imperial court. In the end the bishops—many of them reluctantly—approved the new dogmatic definition which had been worked out by the new commission and contained Leo's Tome.[8]

From these discussions it is clear that many of the Fathers of Chalcedon suspected Leo's Tome of Nestorian tendencies. Later on this was to be one of the main charges of the opponents of the Council against the decree of Chalcedon. The bishops, used to the language of St. Cyril of Alexandria who had spoken of the ''one incarnate nature of God the Word,'' were bound to take exception to the language used by Leo, who speaks of two natures. What is more, the Council vindicated the bishops Theodoret of Cyrrhus and Ibas of Edessa, who had been suspected of Nestorianism. Right at the beginning of the first session a number of Fathers had protested vigorously against the intention of the imperial commissioners to admit Theodoret to the Council. Theodoret had been condemned at Ephesus (449) but he had been vindicated by Leo in the meantime. These protests had the result that the bishop of Cyrrhus was admitted only as a plaintiff but not as a full-fledged participant.[9] It was only at the eighth session that the case of Theodoret was finally settled. The Council vindicated him after he had reluctantly pronounced anathema upon Nestorius.[10] The case of Ibas was discussed at the ninth and tenth sessions. His letter to the Persian bishop Maris in which Ibas had vehemently attacked Cyril and had praised Theodore of Mopsuestia was at least by some Fathers acknowledged to be orthodox doctrine and Ibas was vindicated.[11] Later, this was to constitute another important charge against Chalcedon.

---

[8]ACO 2/1,2:124ff.; Mansi 7:104, 105, 108.

[9]ACO 2/1,1:69-70; Mansi 6:588-92.

[10]ACO 2/1,3: 10; Mansi 7:189.

[11]Cf. Pierre Thomas Camelot, *Ephèse et Chalcédoine* (Paris: Editions d'Orante, 1961)154-155; Hefele-Leclercq *Histoire,* 2/2:749ff. On vindication of Theodoret see ACO 2/1,3:3-11; Mansi 7:185-96. On Ibas see ACO 2/1,3:32-34; Mansi 7:241-49; on the recognition of the orthodoxy of Ibas and his letter by the legates see ACO 2/1,3:39; Mansi 7:261.

In view of these events it is not surprising that after Chalcedon resistance against the decrees of the Council set in. Right from the beginning, this resistance was most virulent in Egypt. Dioscorus, the renowned bishop of Alexandria, had been deposed by the Council. The language of the great Father of Alexandria, Cyril, had not been accepted by the Council, although his second letter to Nestorius, which had been solemnly approved at Ephesus (431) was read and the agreement of Leo's Tome with Cyril's doctrine was acknowledged.[12]

The attitude of the Egyptian bishops at the Council boded ill for the future. During the fourth session they presented a creed of their own in which no mention was made of a condemnation of Eutyches. When requested by the papal legates to accept Leo's Tome and anathemize Eutyches, they remained evasive: if Eutyches' doctrine was not in accordance with their creed he was to be condemned. As far as Leo's letter was concerned they were unable—or so they said—to arrive at a decision as long as there was no archbishop in Alexandria. After all, Dioscorus had been deposed and a new archbishop had not as yet been nominated. Moreover, they declared that there were too few of them—thirteen altogether—to speak on behalf of all Egyptian bishops. No doubt they would be killed in Egypt if they gave in to the Council's demands. They would rather die on the spot than be killed at home. Other bishops called out, "The Egyptians are heretics!" Finally they were permitted to wait with their decision and to remain in Constantinople until a new archbishop of Alexandria had been installed.[13] Indeed the decrees of Chalcedon encountered violent resistance in Alexandria immediately after the Council. Dioscorus was replaced by his follower, the archpriest Proterius, who accepted the Council and Leo's Tome. The entire population was against him; they did not want any bishop other than Dioscorus. An open revolt broke out which was brutally suppressed. After the emperor Marcian's death (457) the opponents of the Council elected Timotheus Ailurus archbishop. Proterius was killed in a popular tumult when saying mass in his church. All this serves to show the violent passions released by the Council. It is impossible to tell the entire story of the struggle against the Council in Egypt. The whole population was united in its rejection of Chalcedon. When the official church, which defended Chalcedon, lost the support of the imperial government after the Arab invasion, it practically collapsed.

---

[12]Hefele-Leclercq, *Histoire,* 2/2:687, 700, 701.

[13]Ibid., 703, 704.

The main reasons for the repudiation of Chalcedon put forward in the Coptic literature are the following: the "lawless" Council of Chalcedon vindicated Nestorius, who had been condemned by the holy synod of Ephesus (431).[14] According to one Coptic fragment, the bishops of Chalcedon destroyed the creed of the unity and inseparability of Christ and divided him. "Instead of confessing to one single nature of the incarnate *Logos* they divide it into two natures in their deceitfulness. They trample the law under foot."[15] The biographer of Peter the Iberian speaks of the "time of the apostasy and outrage of Chalcedon . . . , when the denial of the Scriptures by all those faithless bishops, the approval of Leo's godless letter and the restoration of the shameful teachings of Nestorius were proclaimed."[16] Zacharias Rhetor calls Dioscorus a "peaceloving man" who was deposed not for reasons of faith, but because he refused "to go along with the high priest, Leo" and declined "to adore the idol with the two faces."[17] These examples should suffice to illustrate the reasons for the repudiation of the Council by the Coptic church. The Ethiopian church followed the Coptic mother church in its rejection of Chalcedon, although it is difficult to determine with any certainty the exact time when this took place.

In Palestine the monk Theodosius spread general unrest even before the bishop Juvenal had returned. By deposing Dioscorus, the bishops in Chalcedon had betrayed Cyril's teachings and had approved Nestorius' heresy by vindicating Theodoret. The bishop of Jerusalem, Juvenal, was said to have betrayed the true faith.[18] Upon his return Juvenal, who during the Council had changed from Dioscorus' party to that of his opponents, barely escaped being murdered. He fled to Constantinople and was restored to his see only by the forcible intercession of the government. In the long run, however, the attitude of the patriarchate of Jerusalem towards the Council was favorable so that unlike in Antioch and Alexandria no schism occured here.

---

[14]Cf. Maria Cramer and Heinrich Bacht, "Der Antichalkedonische Aspekt im historisch-geographischen Schrifttum der Koptischen Monophysiten," in *Das Konzil von Chalkedon: Geschichte und Gegenwart,* ed. Aloys Grillmeier and Heinrich Bacht, 3 vols. (Wurzburg: Echter-Verlag, 1951-1954) 2:315-38.

[15]Coptic fragment, ibid., 325.

[16]"Vita Petri iberi," 52, Raabe, ed., ibid.

[17]Ahrens Kruger, ed., Zacharias Rhetor, *Hist. Eccl.* 3.1, quoted ibid., 325-26.

[18]A. Fliche, V. Martin, *Histoire de l'Eglise depuis les Origines jusqu' à nos Jours,* (Paris, 1937) 4:276.

The bishops of the civil Diocese of Oriens, the patriarchate of Antioch (excepting the Palestinians), were opposed to Dioscorus from the very beginning of the Council. They upheld the tradition of the Antiochene school which could more easily identify with Leo's theology than with Cyril's anathemata. However, in Syria the ideas of the Alexandrian school had also spread considerably, notably among the monks. Yet there is no evidence of any popular resistance against Maximus and the other bishops who returned from Chalcedon. It was only around 470 that the anti-Chalcedonian party succeeded in installing one of its adherents, the Greek Peter the Fuller, as patriarch of Antioch. Peter was under the protection of the then *magister militum Orientis,* the later emperor Zeno. Not long afterward, Peter was driven out again, but returned when Zeno—now emperor—had proclaimed his well-known formula for unity, the "Henoticon" (482). The patriarch Calendion refused to sign the Henoticon because under this formula the Council of Chalcedon was practically dropped. In 484 Calendion was replaced by Peter the Fuller, who died in 488.

Later on, the Syrian Philoxenus, who had been installed by Peter the Fuller as bishop of the important see of Mabboug (Hierapolis), became one of the fiercest opponents of Chalcedon in the patriarchate of Antioch. During the reign of the emperor Anastasius (491-518), an opponent of Chalcedon, anti-Chalcedonian sentiments also prevailed in the patriarchate of Antioch. As a result, in 512 the Greek monk Severus of Pisidia, who was decisively opposed to the Council, became patriarch. He may really be called the father of moderate monophysitism which—as has been convincingly shown by Joseph Lebon[19]—is hardly distinguished from the Catholic creed. It is well known that Eutyches, who had been condemned at Chalcedon, had no following worth mentioning. Severus frequently repudiated Eutyches' teachings in his letters and homilies.[20] He objected to the Council and Leo's Tome because in his opinion they had helped to introduce the teachings of Nestorius into the church and had thus split the one Christ.[21] Moreover he accused the Council of having proclaimed a new dogmatic definition, thus running counter to the decrees of Ephesus (431)

---

[19]Joseph Lebon, *Le monophysisme sévèrien: étude historique littéraire et théologique sur la résistance monophysite au concile de Chaldédoine jusqu' à la constitution de l'église jacobite* (Louvain: J. Van Linthout, 1909; Lebon, "La Christologie du monophysisme syrien," in Grillmeier-Bacht, eds., *Das Konzil von Chalkedon,* 1:425-508.

[20]Cf. Wilhelm de Vries, *Der Kirchenbgriff der von Rom Getrennten Syer* (Rome, 1955) 68.

[21]Ibid., 69.

and going beyond the definition of Nicea.[22] Philoxenus rejected the Council because it had condemned Dioscorus, the "adherent of the orthodox faith."[23] For these and similar reasons the Council and Leo's Tome are again and again denounced as "godless," "Jewish," "criminal," "blasphemous" and even as summoned and conducted by the devil.[24]

Moreover, the Council of Chalcedon was repudiated out of the spontaneous conviction that its teachings ran counter to the tradition of the church. Severus, for example, quoted St. Paul to explain his opposition, "If any man preach any other gospel unto you than that we have received, let him be accursed" (Gal 1:9).[25] Philoxenus did not hesitate to say that the bishops of Chalcedon had been heretics and therefore had no authority, so their decision was invalid.[26] According to Philoxenus the acceptance of a council by the church as a whole determines whether the Fathers are heretics or not. The first three Councils had been accepted by the whole church, whereas the Council of Chalcedon was repudiated.[27]

The reasons for the repudiation of the Council of Chalcedon by the Armenian church are given in a new, thorough, and factual analysis by Karekin Sarkissian,[28] whose results I should like to sum up here. According to this analysis the repudiation of the Council by the Armenians was no sudden and precipitate decision, but the result of the general theological orientation of the Armenian church.[29] In Ephesus it had been the Antiochene school rather than Nestorius that had been condemned. The language of the West, Leo's language included, was related to that of the Antiochene school—hence the opposition against Leo of all those who clung to the theology of Cyril and the Alexandrian school. Chalcedon condemned Nestorius, but not the Antiochene school with its dualistic Christology. Theodoret and Ibas were even vindicated in Chalcedon.[30] Contrary to Inglisian,

---

[22]Ibid., annot. 4.

[23]Ibid., annot. 5.

[24]Ibid., annots. 6, 7.

[25]Ibid., 70.

[26]Ibid., 71.

[27]Ibid., annot. 23.

[28]K. Sarkissian, *The Council of Chalcedon and the Armenian Church* (London: Oxford University Press, 1965).

[29]Ibid., 19, 20.

[30]Ibid., 30, 31.

Sarkissian is of the opinion—and I tend to agree with him—that in spite of the political unrest in Armenia at the time of the Council the Armenian church very soon had knowledge of the Council's decision and was able to participate in the Christological debate. There was no Great Wall between the Byzantine empire and Armenia.[31]

Ever since they adopted Christianity, the Armenians had tended towards the Greeks. Even though they were politically dependent on Persia—especially after the abolition of the national monarchy in 428—and therefore exposed to the Nestorian influence which slowly gained ground among the Persian Christians, they were saved from adopting Nestorianism by their political antagonism towards Persia. In 485 they were granted political autonomy under the Armenian governor, Vahan Mamikonean.[32] Politically, the Armenians had sufficient freedom in making their religious decisions. Their contact with the Greeks strengthened them in their opposition against any duality in Christ. In this context the correspondence between Katholikos Sakak and the Armenians on the one hand and Akakius of Melitene and Proklus of Constantinople on the other is of particular importance. The letters were written between 432 and 438. The Greeks warned the Armenians against Nestorianism and the acceptance of any sort of duality in Christ.[33]

After the Council of Chalcedon, most probably between 480 and 484, the writings of Timotheus Ailurus against Chalcedon reached Armenia and were translated into Armenian.[34] However, in the fifth century there was as yet no condemnation of the Council by the Armenian church. It was only at the Council of Dowin (506) under Katholikos Babgen that this step was finally taken. Here mention must be made of two letters addressed by the Armenians to the "orthodox believers in Persia," that is, the opponents of the council of Chalcedon in Persia. In these letters Babgen and his bishops claim that the teachings of the heretic Nestorius were confirmed in Chalcedon. Moreover, Eutyches is also repudiated as a heretic.[35] The letters contain the doctrine of the Council of Dowin which is summed up by Sar-

---

[31]Ibid., 150, 151; V. Inglisian, "Chalkedon und die Armenische Kirche," in Grillmeier-Bacht, eds., *Das Konzil von Chalkedon*, 2:361-417; regarding Inglisian's opinion on this matter, 362.

[32]Sarkissian, *Chalcedon*, 69.

[33]Ibid., 113, 115, 119.

[34]Ibid., 167.

[35]Ibid., 211.

kissian as follows: the creed of Nicea is all that is needed. Three Councils are accepted and Cyril's teachings are approved, including those contained in the anathemata. The Henoticon is adopted and the Council of Chalcedon is expressly rejected.[36]

Finally, I should like to add a few words concerning the attitude of Persia's East Syrian church toward Chalcedon. As is well known, this church adopted the Nestorian Christological formulas as its official doctrine at the Council of Seleukeia-Ctesiphon in 486.[37] There are only a few express evaluations of the Council of Chalcedon by East Syrian writers. Contrary to J. Labourt's opinion, however, they are generally unfavorable.[38] Nevertheless, Babi the Great († c. 628), probably the most eminent East Syrian theologian and the true founder of their Christology, praises the "admirable Leo who occupied the see of St. Peter," because he eliminated Dioscorus.[39] Katholikos Iso'yahb III (647-658), however, objected to the Council because it proclaimed the unity of the *hypostasis* in Christ.[40] Thus for him Chalcedon insists too much on the unity in Christ. A comprehensive though unfavorable evaluation of the Council is contained in the book *Proof of the Orthodoxy of Faith* by Elias of Nisibis (975-1049). According to him, some of the Fathers of the Council of Chalcedon defended the teachings of the heretic Cyril but encountered vigorous resistance. In order to arrive at a solution the disputing parties addressed themselves to the emperor, who decided, "It should be assumed that there are neither two persons as taught by Nestorius nor one nature as proclaimed by Dioscorus and his followers, but two natures and one person." The emperor forcibly effected the acceptance of his formula. The Melkites were also forced to adopt the teachings of the heretic Cyril. The Orientals (the East Syrians in Persia) rejected the emperor's formula as blasphemous.[41] Ebedjesu († 1318) gives an unbiased account of the Council and states that it taught the unity of the

---

[36]Ibid., 213.

[37]Cf. W. de Vries, "Die Syrisch-Nestorianische Haltung zu Chalkedon," in Grillmeier-Bacht, eds., *Das Konzil von Chalkedon,* 1:603-35.

[38]Jérôme Labourt, *Le Christianisme dans l'Empire Perse sous la Dynastie des Assanides* (Paris: V. Lecoffre, 1904) 260.

[39]De Vries, "Chalkedon," 65.

[40]Ibid., annot. 17.

[41]Ibid., 66.

hypostasis in Christ because the Greek language did not differentiate between *hypostasis* and *prosopon*.[42]

We must admit as a matter of fact that the Council of Chalcedon did not
fulfill the expectations placed in it. Not only did it fail to restore peace in the
universal church, it even caused a schism which has unfortunately continued
to our day. It is a tragic fact that the attempt to express the unfathomable mystery of Christ in human terms resulted in an implacable struggle of Christians
against Christians. And yet they all really wanted the same thing: to attest that
there is only one Christ who is true God and true man at the same time. The
dispute arose from the basic human inability at that time to believe that the
same truth may be expressed in different words which may even be apparently contradictory. We are better able to understand this today than the people of the fifth century; therefore, it should be possible for us to overcome the
schism caused by the Council of Chalcedon.

---

[42]In ''Liber Margeritae''; de Vries, ''Chalkedon,'' 67.

St. Cyril's
"One *Physis* or *Hypostasis*
of God the Logos Incarnate"
and Chalcedon*

John S. Romanides

Both Chalcedonian and non-Chalcedonian Orthodox accept St. Cyril as the chief patristic exponent of orthodox Christology. Yet both accuse each other of not remaining completely faithful to Cyril.

The non-Chalcedonian Orthodox reject the Council of Chalcedon and accuse it of Nestorianism because it accepted the Tome of Leo and "two natures after the union," and allegedly omitted from its definition of faith such Cyrillian expressions as "one nature of God the *Logos* incarnate," "hypostatic or natural union," and "from two natures" or "from two one Christ." The failure of Chalcedon to make full use of Cyril's Twelve Chapters, to condemn the Christology of Theodore, and its acceptance of Theodoret and Ibas throw suspicion on it. Then there is the weighty accusation that the very act of composing a new definition of the faith contradicted the decision of Ephesus (431) which decreed that "It is unlawful for anyone to bring forward or to write or to compose another Creed besides that determined by the Holy Fathers assembled with the Holy Spirit in Nicea."[1]

The Chalcedonian Orthodox, on the other hand, believe that it was Cyril's Christology which was not only fully accepted at Ephesus, but served as the basis of all judgments concerning Christology at Chalcedon in 451 and especially at Constantinople in 553. In spite of its obvious deficiencies the Tome of Leo is adequately orthodox, definitely not Nesto-

---

*See my article, "Highlights in the Debate over Theodore of Mopsuestia's Christology," *The Greek Orthodox Theological Review* 5:2 (1959-60) 157-61.

[1] J. D. Mansi, ed., *Sanctorum Conciliorum Nova et Amplissima Collectio* (= Mansi), 55 vols. (Florence, Venice, Paris, Leipzig, 1759-1962) 4:1361.

rian, and was accepted only as a document against Eutyches, but again only in the light of and in subordination to the synodical letters (especially the Twelve Chapters) of Cyril to Nestorius and John of Antioch, as we shall see. The terminology and faith of Cyril were fully accepted, although the Eutychian heresy, the chief concern of the Council, called for some adaptation to the new situation. One may point out that the acceptance of the Chalcedonian definition was no different from the acceptance of Cyril's letters at Ephesus. Neither the one act nor the other can be considered as a composition of a new creed. They are both interpretations and clarifications of the Nicean faith in the light of modern circumstances. It is noteworthy that even Cyril had to defend himself against the accusation that he accepted a new creed in his reconciliatory correspondence with John of Antioch.[2] Theodoret and Ibas were restored to the episcopacy because they accepted Ephesus I and especially the Twelve Chapters, which acceptance is in itself a condemnation of what they had written about and against Cyril and his anathemas. The Fifth Ecumenical Council of 553 anathematized the writings of Theodoret and Ibas against Cyril, and the very person of Theodore, the Father of Nestorianism.

The non-Chalcedonian Orthodox have been for centuries accusing the Chalcedonian Orthodox of being Nestorians. On the other hand, the Chalcedonians have been accusing the non-Chalcedonians of either being monophysites (which for them means believers in one *ousia* in Christ) or of a one-sided insistence on Cyrillian terminology to the exclusion of Cyril's own acceptance of two natures in the confession of faith of John of Antioch which brought about the reconciliation of 433. This one-sidedness was adopted by the Ephesine Council of 449 and rejected by the Council of Chalcedon. It should also be noted that the Flavian Endemousa Synod of 448 was one-sided in its use of and insistence on the Cyrillian terminology of the 433 reconciliation to the near exclusion of Cyril's normal way of speaking about the Incarnation. From Chalcedon and especially from Constantinople II it is clear that the Chalcedonians without compromise allow for variations in terms which express the same faith. On the non-Chalcedonian side Severus of Antioch seems to be the only one who comes close to Cyril's acceptance of two natures *tei theoriai monei* after the union, a position adopted at Chalcedon and clearly stated in the definition or anathemas of the Fifth Ecumenical Council.

The purpose of this paper is to discuss a few terms against the historical background of circumstances which called them up to serve as a test of

---

[2]J. P. Migne, ed., *Patrologia Graeca* (= PG), 162 vols. (1857-1866) 77:188.

correct faith. Especially important are the circumstances surrounding the Councils of 449 and 451. Undoubtedly a key figure which conditioned Dioscorus's exasperation with all talk of two natures was its extremely clever use by Theodoret to hide what one may call a clear case of crypto-Nestorianism. Leo's support of and failure to see through Theodoret made him guilty by association, as in some measure happened with Dioscorus's support of Eutyches. This explains a good deal of the negative attitude toward Leo's Tome, not only from Egyptian quarters, but also from the Palestinian and, of all people, the Illyrian bishops, who were within Leo's own sphere of ecclesiastical influence.

The key to the approach of this paper is (1) to define Nestorianism as seen by Cyril in order to determine why Cyril could accept *tei theoriai monei* two natures in Christ after the union and John's confession of faith. and then (2) to examine very briefly in the light of this definition Leo's Tome and the attitude toward and use of it by Chalcedon. In Part II we will examine what is clearly a case of crypto-Nestorianism in the person of Theodoret, and in the light of this we will survey some of the important aspects of the Chalcedonian and non-Chalcedonian encounter with this issue. Throughout the paper we will be concerned with the place of Cyril, and especially his Twelve Chapters, at Chalcedon, thereby determining whether or not the Fifth Ecumenical Council is really a return to or rather a remaining with Cyril.

Part I

(1) Nestorius rejected the fact that he who was born of the Virgin is consubstantial with the Father according to divinity and thus by nature God. Another way of saying this is that he rejected the fact that he who before the ages is born from and is consubstantial with the Father was in the last days born according to his own and proper humanity from the Virgin Mary having become thus by nature man and consubstantial with us. On the basis of this rejection, Nestorius distorted the true significance of the title *Theotokos* which he in reality denied to the Mother of God. The most Nestorius could say is that Christ is the one person of the union of two natures, the one nature being by nature God and the other by nature man. The name Christ is not properly predicated of the *Logos,* but is the name of the person of union born of Mary and in whom the *Logos* dwells and who was assumed by the *Logos.* Nestorius fanatically insisted that the *Logos* was not born of the Virgin according to his humanity and did not, therefore, become by nature man. On the basis of this he divided the natures and predicates of Christ, attributing the human to the assumed man and the divine to the *Logos.*

Nestorius denied the two births of the *Logos* and the double consubstantiality of the one and the same *Logos,* Son of God and the self-same also son of Mary, and thus of the true meaning of the title *Theotokos*. Thus Nestorius' insistence that he does not divide Christ into two persons, but only the natures and names, was judged a mockery of the faith. On this basis he was condemned by the Third and Fourth Ecumenical Councils and rejected by John of Antioch and Leo of Rome.

I have indicated elsewhere[3] that the reconciliation of 433 between Cyril and John was brought about by the Antiochene's confession of the double birth and consubstantiality of "our Lord Jesus Christ, the only-begotten Son of God," the very doctrine rejected so violently by Nestorius and even by Theodoret, as we shall see shortly. In his confession John clearly declares that the only-begotten Son of God was:

> Before the ages begotten from the Father according to his Divinity, and in the last days the *Self-same* [*ton auton*] for us and for our salvation, (begotten) of Mary the Virgin according to his Humanity, the Self-same [*ton auton*—note that he is here speaking clearly about the only-begotten Son and not the Nestorian and Theodoretan *prosopon* of the union of two natures] consubstantial with the Father according to Divinity and consubstantial with us according to Humanity."[4]

For Cyril this confession of faith meant that the title *Theotokos* and the Incarnation were accepted in their full and true significance, in spite of the fact that John spoke of "a union *of two natures,* whereby we confess One Christ, One Son, One Lord."

In his letter to Acacius of Melitene,[5] Cyril is quite emphatic about the fact that this Antiochene confession of the double birth and double consubstantiality of the one and the same *Logos* cannot be suspected of Nestorianism since this is exactly what Nestorius denies.[6] To the objection that two natures after the union means a predication of two separate kinds of names, divine and human, to two separate natures, Cyril replies that to divide names does not mean necessarily a division of natures, *hypostases,* or persons, since all names are predicated of the one *Logos*. The division of names is considered as a safeguard against Arians and Eunomians who

---

[3]Romanides, "Christology."

[4]Mansi, 4:292.

[5]PG 77:184-201. See also *Ep. ad Eulogium*, PG 77:224-28; and *Ep. ad Successum I and II*, PG 77:228-45.

[6]PG 77:189-92, 197.

by confusing them sought to demonstrate the creatureliness of the *Logos* and his inferiority to the Father. The names, and not the natures, are divided in order to distinguish the real difference of the natures or things out of which Christ is composed, and not to divide them, since they can be distinguished after the union in contemplation only.[7]

Of course Cyril prefers to speak of "one nature or *Hypostasis* of God the *Logos* incarnate" and become man, since this better safeguards the union and the attribution of all things pertaining to Christ to the *Logos* as the subject of *all* human and divine actions. For Cyril *physis* means a concrete individual acting as subject in its own right and according to its own natural properties. Thus the one nature of God the *Logos* incarnate, having by his second birth appropriated to himself a perfect, complete, and real manhood, has as his own both the *ousia* and natural properties common to all men. It is therefore the *Logos* himself who is Christ and lives really and truly the life of man without any change whatsoever in his divinity, having remained what he always was. To speak about two natures in Christ would be somewhat equivalent to a Chalcedonian speaking about two *hypostases* in Christ. In this respect a Chalcedonian would accept and does accept everything Cyril says but would use Cyril's "one *hypostasis* of God the *Logos* Incarnate, since for him *physis* means *ousia*.

The one very essential point which Cyril makes and which some day may be given adequate consideration by the non-Chalcedonian Orthodox is that whatever one's insistence on theological accuracy in expression may be, it is sheer caricature to accuse anyone of being Nestorian who accepts the double birth and double consubstantiality of the Logos as the basis for the title *Theotokos,* as well as for the predication of all human and divine attributes and energies to the *Logos* who is the sole subject incarnate, and acting both according to his divinity and his own appropriated Manhood. This is what Theodore, Nestorius, and Theodoret denied and this is the essence of Orthodoxy. St. Cyril saw this clearly and it is our duty to place this at the center of our discussions.

(2) There is no doubt that Leo tended to separate or distinguish the acts of Christ in such a way that the two natures seem to be acting as separate subjects, a tendency explainable by what he imagined Eutyches was teaching and by his Latin formation wherein Greek trinitarian terms used in Christology were not available to him. He so obviously failed to understand how the term "one nature" was being used in the East, and especially during the Endemousa Synod of 448. This is why a non-Chalcedonian

---

[7]PG 77:193-97.

reading the Tome should read *ousia* upon coming across *natura,* since Leo was dealing with the information he had received that Eutyches denied Christ's consubstantiality with us. His expression of utter amazement that the judges did not severely censure Eutyches when making such a statement as, ''I confess that our Lord was from two Natures before the Union, but after the Union I admit but one Nature,'' confirms the confusing of his own *natura* and the Greek *ousia* with *physis.* Then Eutyches' own confusion of the terms *ousia* and *physis* did not help the matter any.

Nevertheless, Leo is very clear in his acceptance of the anti-Nestorian standard of Orthodoxy accepted by Cyril. Leo declares clearly in his Tome that:

> the Self-Same, who was the Only-begotten and Everlasting One of the Everlasting Parent, was born of the Holy Spirit and the Virgin Mary. And this birth in time takes away nothing from that divine and eternal birth, nor does it add anything to it. . . .[8]

The definition of Chalcedon is also clear in this respect:

> Following, then, the holy Fathers, we all unanimously teach that our Lord Jesus Christ is to us One and the same Son, the Self-same of a rational soul and body; consubstantial with the Father according to the Godhead, but in the last days, the Self-same, for us and for our salvation (born) of Mary the Virgin *Theotokos* according to the Manhood. . . . ''[9]

Returning to Leo's Tome, it is important to point out that at Chalcedon it was accepted only as a document against the heresy of Eutyches, in spite of the fact that both Leo and his legates believed it to be a good statement against Nestorius also. It is even more important to keep in mind that during its reading at Session II the three now famous Nestorian-sounding passages were each one challenged as the document was being read. During each interruption it was attacked and defended by the use of parallel passages from Cyril.[10] After what must have been a somewhat stormy and long debate, bishop Atticos of Nikopolis in Old Epirus, Greece, made the motion that time out be taken to give the assembly the opportunity to carefully compare Leo's Tome with the Twelve Chapters of Cyril in order to make sure of what they were approving.[11] The imperial representatives chairing

---

[8]Bindley, *Documents,* 224.

[9]Mansi, 7:116.

[10]Ibid., 6:972-73.

[11]Ibid., 973.

the meeting gave the bishops five days in which to do this and suggested the formation of a committee under the presidency of Anatolius, Patriarch of Constantinople.[12] The committee reported back at the fourth session, at the beginning of which the imperial and senatorial representatives declared the unswerving faith of the emperor in the expositions of Nicea, Constantinople, and Ephesus with its approval of the "two canonical letters of Cyril," (the Second and Third to Nestorius).[13] This profession of the imperial faith had been made also at the end of Session I,[14] and now in anticipation of the committee's report on the question of Leo's agreement with Cyril's Twelve Chapters it was repeated. The committee report[15] was included in the minutes in the form of a listing of the individual opinions of its members, all of whom expressed their belief that Leo's Tome agreed with Nicea, Ephesus, and *the letter* of Cyril. Most of the bishops mentioned *the* (one) *letter* of Cyril,[16] which cannot be any other than the Twelve Chapters since this was the one the Illyrians and Palestinians were concerned about. This is clear from the motion of the Illyrian Atticos which initiated the careful comparison of Leo's Tome with the letter of Cyril. Some of the members mentioned their belief that the Tome agreed with the two letters of Cyril, clearly referring to the ones of Ephesus mentioned as part of the imperial faith. It is extremely interesting to note that among the similar individual opinions given by the rest of the assembly and recorded in the minutes is that of none other than Theodoret of Cyrus,[17] who claims that he finds the Tome of Leo in agreement with the letters of Cyril and the Council of Ephesus, certainly a tremendous leap from his position just before the Council. In the light of his strong hesitation at Session VIII to anathematize Nestorius, a hesitation which infuriated the assembly, one wonders about his sincerity, especially since he tried to defend his former acts by an exposition of how he never taught two sons. He was interrupted by shouts of "Nestorian."[18]

The acceptance of Leo's Tome in the light of and in subordination to the letters of Cyril is also clearly contained in the Chalcedonian definition

---

[12]Ibid.

[13]Ibid., 7:8.

[14]Ibid., 6:937.

[15]Ibid., 7:48.

[16]Ibid., 36-45.

[17]Ibid., 20.

[18]Ibid., 188-92.

itself.[19] It is declared that the Council accepts the Synodical (the Third Letter to Nestorius is titled "synodical," or since this is in the plural it could be a reference to the two letters of Ephesus, which in the minutes are called canonical, plus the one to John) letters of Cyril to Nestorius and to those of the East, "and to which (epistles) it reasonably *adapted* the letter of Leo . . . (*epistolas . . . hais kai ten epistolen tou Leontos . . . eikotos synermose . . .*)." This is not a case of a balance between Cyril and Leo, as many scholars would have us believe. Leo became very sensitive about the doubts raised about his Tome. Especially disturbed did he become over determined opposition in certain quarters like Palestine, where Juvenal was deposed for accepting the Tome. In a letter to Julian of Cos (CXVII 3) in which he shows much concern with accusations of heresy against himself, he writes:

> If they think there is any doubt about our teaching, let them at least not reject the writings of such holy priests as Athanasius, Theophilus and Cyril of Alexandria, with whom our statement of the faith so completely harmonizes that anyone who professes consent to them disagrees in nothing with us.

No one can doubt the sincerity with which Leo wanted to be in agreement with those Alexandrine Fathers, but his defense of Theodoret compromised him. In a letter to the now restored Bishop of Cyrus, he chides Theodoret for the tardy way in which he anathematized Nestorius (CXX, 5). Yet in his opening remarks of this very same letter he speaks of "the victory you [Theodoret] and we together had won by assistance from on high over the blasphemy of Nestorius, as well as over the madness of Eutyches." Dioscorus's relationship to Eutyches may have some parallels.

The Chalcedonian definition also speaks of itself as "preserving the order and *all* the decrees concerning the Faith passed by the Holy Synod held formerly at Ephesus. . . ."[20] From Ibas's *ad Marim Persam* and from the minutes of the Johannine Council of Ephesus, we learn that the Antiochenes rejected the Cyrillian Council of Ephesus and damned Cyril because the heretical Twelve Chapters had been accepted.[21] In this same letter Ibas was under the impression (as were many of Cyril's friends and Theodoret)[22] that Cyril abandoned his Ephesine position in his reconciliation with

---

[19]Ibid., 113.

[20]Ibid., 109.

[21]Ibid., 4:1365ff.; 7:244-45.

[22]*Ep. CLXXI*, PG 83:1484.

John in 433.[23] However, Ibas stated at his trial in Byretus in 449 that Paul of Emessa had accepted the Alexandrine bishop's interpretation of the Twelve Chapters as Cyril had accepted the confession of the Easterners.[24] It is in the light of this that one should read the letter of John to the bishops of Rome, Alexandria, and Constantinople (the order of the letter) in which he announces Antioch's acceptance of Nestorius' excommunication and the Council of Ephesus.[25] It is impossible to accept the opinion of many that Cyril laid aside his Twelve Chapters for the sake of a reconciliation with John. As an individual he had no authority whatsoever to modify the decisions of an Ecumenical Council, and there is no evidence to substantiate this supposition. Although the Endemousa Synod of Constantinople seems to have overemphasized the Cyrillian allowances of 433, it accepted the Twelve Chapters as part of Ephesus which it approved *in toto*.[26]

In the light of the evidence, it is clear that Cyril's Third Letter to Nestorius, including the Twelve Chapters, was not repudiated by Chalcedon as many claim. On the contrary, the Twelve Chapters were used as the very basis of the Council's attitudes toward Nestorianism and Leo's Tome. It is too bad that the Chalcedonians themselves present at the Council of 531 in Constantinople did not fully realize the crucial role played at Chalcedon by Cyril's Twelve Chapters. Their answer to Severus' accusation that the Twelve Chapters were laid aside in 451 was that it was accepted and approved as part of Ephesus I. This, of course, is incontestable, but not anywhere near the reality of the matter. The significance of the use made of the Twelve Chapters at Chalcedon should be obvious enough to those who claim that they fail to find the terms characteristic of Cyrillian Christology in the definition. Groundless also are the theories (brought forward by many Protestant and Roman Catholic scholars embarrassed by the Cyrillianism of the Fifth Ecumenical Council) concerning an alleged neo-Chalcedonian movement which was supposed to have put Leo's Tome aside and returned to the Twelve Chapters of Ephesus I, especially to the Twelfth Anathema. The truth of the matter is that in pronouncing anathema on those who do not accept the Twelve Chapters of Cyril, the Fifth Ecumenical Council of 553 is simply repeating what was done at Ephesus in 431 and again at Chalcedon in 451.

---

[23]Mansi, 7:248.

[24]Ibid., 240.

[25]Ibid., 5:285.

[26]Ibid., 6:665.

II

Now we must turn to the Crypto-Nestorianism of Theodoret, a type of Christology which in some measure can hide itself behind the language used in the formulary of reunion of 433, without, however, adopting its exact wording and meaning. It was undoubtedly his exasperation with this type of Antiochene Christology more than anything else which goaded Dioscorus into setting aside Cyril's act of 433 and returning to what may be called Alexandrine exclusiveness as the only sure means of uprooting the new form behind which Nestorianism hid itself.

In the course of the Christological controversies, Theodoret learned to modify some of his opinions—without, however, changing his basic vision and presuppositions. For example, he rejected Cyril's suggestion that the *Logos* himself became by nature man,[27] but by the time he wrote his *Eranistes* he had adapted, to some degree, his language to that of Cyril. In some contrast to Nestorius he claims that "the Truth is both God by nature and man by nature."[28] In another work he says that "the Same is by nature God and man."[29] He who was born of the Virgin, according to Theodoret, is consubstantial with the Father according to his godhead and consubstantial with us according to his manhood. Christ was born, says the bishop of Cyrus, before the ages from God the Father and in our own time the selfsame Christ was born from the Virgin *Theotokos*.[30] These expressions are not those of Nestorius, yet they are not completely Orthodox. The name Christ, for Theodoret, is predicated of the *Logos* because the only-begotten Son of God assumed a man or manhood which was born from the Virgin.[31] Until his acceptance of the Third and Fourth Ecumenical Councils, Theodoret could not say that the *Logos* himself, being by nature God, became according to the flesh by nature man, or consubstantial with us, by his second birth in time from the Virgin Mary, while remaining immutably what he was. Such a double birth and the double consubstantiality must be predicated of Christ alone and not the *Logos*. Only divine names can be predicated of the *Logos*.[32] Yet all names, both human and divine, can be

---

[27]*Ep. de XII Capitulis*, PG 76:388A.

[28]PG 83:121B.

[29]*Demonstrations*, PG 83:328A.

[30]Ibid., 1420.

[31]Ibid., 264B, 280-81.

[32]Ibid.

predicated of Christ because of the union in him of the two natures.[33] Thus, when Theodoret says that he who was born of the Virgin is consubstantial with God the Father, he does not mean that he who is consubstantial with the Father was born of Mary in the flesh.

The name Christ seems to be the only one Theodoret allows to be predicated of the *Logos* in the flesh, and by means of this he avoids saying with Nestorius that Christ is the son of David and Son of God united in his (Christ's) one person. Yet he clearly follows Nestorius by distinguishing the only-begotten Son and Christ in the creed by insisting that the name Jesus Christ, and not the title of only-begotten Son, is the recipient of the things human such as birth, suffering, death, burial, and resurrection.[34] His attempt to explain why only the name Christ of all things human should be predicated of the *Logos* in the flesh is a Nestorian failure. Thus it was the *prosopon* of Christ who suffered, died, and was buried in the tomb, not the impassible *Logos* in his own passible manhood.[35] When St. Paul speaks of the Lord of glory being crucified he means that the body of the Lord of glory was crucified, not that the Lord of glory was crucified in the flesh.[36]

Very intructive on the question of dividing the names between the two natures and uniting them, not in the *Logos,* but in the name Christ, which includes the *Logos,* is Theodoret's version of the formulary of reunion or Antiochene confession of faith. The linguistic variations between the confessions are doctrinally quite revealing. We will quote Theodoret's version[37] and insert in their proper places within parentheses and in capitals the longer text of John, and italicize the one phrase in Theodoret's creed missing from that of John:

> We confess one Lord Jesus Christ, (THE ONLY-BEGOTTEN SON OF GOD), perfect God and perfect man, of rational soul and body, before the ages begotten of the Father according to Godhead, but in the last days (THE SELF-SAME) for us and our salvation, of Mary the Virgin; *the self-same* consubstantial with the Father according to Godhead, and consubstantial with us according to Manhood.

For John it is the only-begotten Son of God who has a double birth and a double consubstantiality, whereas for Theodoret these can be predicated only

---

[33]Ibid., 148AB, 252CD, 231A.

[34]Ibid., 280BCD-281B.

[35]Ibid., 257CDE, 261BCD.

[36]Ibid., 280AB.

[37]*Ep. CLI,* PG 83:1420A.

of Christ, who includes the *Logos,* since only the single divine birth and consubstantiality can be predicated of the *Logos* himself. It seems highly doubtful
that Theodoret is the author of the formulary of reunion as is commonly
claimed.[38] On occasion he may profess agreement with John's confession, but
then he professed agreement with the Nicean Creed also. On the basis of this
crypto-Nestorianism, Theodoret could continue his attacks on Ephesus and
Cyril, and especially on the Twelve Chapters. It is very important to point out
that Theodoret's Christology is not that of John accepted by Cyril, nor that of
Leo's Tome and Chalcedon. Failure to realize this during the fifth century made
both Leo and Chalcedon guilty by association in the eyes of those who followed the lead of Dioscorus, in the same way that Dioscorus was made guilty
by association by his support of Eutyches.

Keeping in mind Theodoret's distinction between the titles Christ and
the only-begotten Son for the purpose of denying that the Nicean creed
speaks of the only-begotten Son himself as born, suffering, crucified, and
buried, it is instructive to turn to Leo's Tome. The bishop of Rome, in clear
contrast to Theodoret and Nestorius, writes:

> The Son of God is said to have been crucified and buried, although He
> suffered these things not in his Godhead itself, in virtue of which the Only-
> begotten is both co-eternal and consubstantial with the Father, but in the
> weakness of Human nature. And this is the reason why we all confess, too,
> in the Creed that "the Only-begotten Son of God was crucified and bur-
> ied" in accordance with that saying of the Apostle, "For had they known
> they would not have crucified the Lord of Majesty." (ch. 5)

If this is not *in toto* what Cyril is saying in the Twelfth Anathema of
his Chapters, it at least is certainly not what Nestorius or Theodoret were
saying. In the opinion of this writer, Theodoret's acceptance of Leo's Tome
in his need for help against personal disaster is no different from his acceptance of Cyril's Twelve Chapters at Chalcedon. He was a sorry sight
at the eighth session trying to publicly convince the assembly that he was
not now accepting all that was done, and anathematizing Nestorius because of any love of honor, rank, and wealth.[39]

---

[38]Also doubtful on the basis of his Christology is Theodoret's alleged authorship of what
seems to be a letter sent by Domnus to Flavian (PG 83:1297). See R. V. Sellers, *The Council of Chalcedon* (London: SPCK, 1953) 28 n. 5, in which it is confessed that all things
pertaining to Christ, although predicated of two natures, are attributed "to the One Only-
Begotten."

[39]Mansi, 7:188-92.

As long as Cyril and John were alive they were able to contain somewhat the extremists in their respective dioceses (*dioikeseis*). Even the
eruption of the controversy over the Christology of Diodore and Theodore
did not break up the union of 433. However, things changed for the worse
with the accession of Domnus (443) to the "Apostolic See" of Antioch,
and Dioscorus (444) to the "Evangelical See" (so they are called in the
minutes of the Councils) of Alexandria. Theodoret got the upper hand in
Antioch and pro-Nestorian activities increased seriously. Evidently at
Theodoret's instigation several Nestorians were ordained bishops, including the notorious Nestorian fanatic Count Irenaeus, the twice-married. Thus
the church was faced with a resurgence of a Nestorianism hiding behind
the formulary of reunion and Theodoretan Christological double-talk. Again
we must keep in mind that these people not only professed faith in the formulary of reunion, but also in the Nicene Creed, both of which they interpreted in their own way.

At the time Cyril accepted John's confession there were many who were
highly suspicious of the two-nature document, either feeling that Cyril had
compromised the decisions of Ephesus or believing that Cyril had been
tricked. They no doubt felt that now their suspicions had been justified. It
was now natural for them to feel and decide that the only way to uproot
this new Nestorianism was to insist on "One nature of God the *Logos* incarnate," "one nature after the union," and that Christ is "one from or
out of two natures." Only this would make it possible to insure the attribution of all the names and activities of Christ to the *Logos* incarnate. The
Theodoretan type experience had proven to them beyond all doubt that any
doctrine of two natures after the union could only mean two subjects and
centers of activity in Christ acting in a harmony of wills, the one or the
other performing its proper operations as the need arose. As we shall see,
he assailed even those who could accept "one nature of the *Logos* Incarnate," but who preferred to speak of "two *physeis*" which to them meant
two *ousiai*.

The opportunity for a decisive blow at two natures was presented by
the Endemousa Synod of Constantinople in 448, which was convened to
deal with the accusation of heresy filed against Eutyches by Eusebius of
Dorylaeum. The libel itself contains no specific heresy, but according to
the witness of those sent to invite Eutyches to attend the Council in order
to answer to unnamed charges, the aged Archimandrite denied that Christ
is consubstantial with us according to manhood.[40] The same denial was re-

---

[40]Ibid., 6:700-701, 741.

peated by Eutyches when he finally made a personal appearance at the synod. However, when told that this is a denial of the teaching of the Fathers (perhaps some patristic quotations were shown to him) he faltered and showed some willingness to accept this teaching. However, it is interesting to note that he was several times asked as one question what perhaps should have been asked as two separate questions—whether or not he confesses (1) that Christ is consubstantial with us, and (2) that after the Incarnation there are two natures in Christ.[41] There seem to be no indications from the minutes (except possibly in Leo's observation that no one reprimanded the monk when he spoke of "one nature after the union") that these two statements could have different meanings. That is it may be possible to speak of one nature of God the *Logos* incarnate or one nature after the union, and at the same time confess that Christ is consubstantial with us according to his manhood. Thus, although Eutyches could seriously entertain the possibility of accepting the teaching on consubstantiality, he could not for a moment think of anathematizing those who teach one nature after the union. Thus when the two questions were thrown at him as one he could only refuse to anathematize. It seems quite clear that for Eutyches (whose case seems to be one of simple ignorance), as well as for Eusebius and Flavian, *physis* was synonymous with *ousia*. Eutyches was excommunicated, but either during the Synod or later he appealed his case to the bishops of Rome, Alexandria, Jerusalem, and Thessalonica.

Although Eutyches was quite defendable in his refusal to anathematize those who teach one nature incarnate of the *Logos,* since, as he said, he could not anathematize the Fathers of the church, he could not be defended for his denial that Christ is consubstantial with us. Thus it was not after this synod that Dioscorus accepted Eutyches into communion. This could not be done until the question of Christ's consubstantiality was cleared up. This doctrinal deficiency was done away with on the basis of added testimony presented to the Review Conferences of April 449 (often called the *Latrocinium* or "Robber Synod"), convened to examine Eutyches' claim that the acts of the Endymousa Synod which condemned him were inaccurate and lacking.

Presbyter John, who, together with Deacon Andrew (with another deacon, Athanasius, happening along), was sent to invite Eutyches to the Endemousa Synod, and had then testified that Eutyches denied that Christ is consubstantial with us, now claimed that in private, while the other two were not listening, the Archimandrite expressed his belief that *Christ is*

---

[41]Ibid., 737, 808, 816.

consubstantial with his mother, although not with us.[42] When asked why this information was withheld in 448, Presbyter John answered that he had done this because the other two had not witnessed to this part of the conversation. The presbyter's testimony is peculiar since Eutyches did say that the mother of Christ was consubstantial with us.[43] If he believed that Christ was consubstantial with his mother, this would, as it seems, make him consubstantial with us also. It is interesting to note that Flavian himself uses the phrase that Christ is consubstantial with his mother in his confessions of faith.[44]

It is very important to realize that at this Review Conference it was established, truthfully or falsely, that Eutyches was excommunicated for refusing to anathematize those who say "one nature after the union" and for refusing to accept two natures after the union. Constantine the Deacon, one of Eutyches' advocates at the hearing, accused Flavian of doing just this.[45] The Patrician Florentius vigorously challenged the truthfulness of the acts which pictured him as attempting to get Eutyches to accept two natures after the union as though this only were Orthodox dogma.[46] There is also evidence indicating that on the basis of Cyril's "one nature of God the *Logos* incarnate" it was felt that Eutyches must agree with the bishops assembled.[47] This evidently meant that they felt Eutyches should accept a second nature in Christ since this is what to them *incarnate* meant. Of course, this would be true if *physis* meant *ousia,* but this is not how Cyril used the term in this phrase. He could not and never does speak of "one *ousia* of God the *Logos* Incarnate." This paralleling of Cyril's "one *physis*" with "Incarnate" in order to prove that Cyril speaks of "two *physeis*" in Christ was and is a mistake repeated by all Chalcedonians until today. The approach was and is a bad one since it could only lead to two *hypostases* and *prosopa.* Nevertheless, Eutyches was not restored to communion as a result of this Review Conference, either because Presbyter John's testimony was not accepted, or because Eutyches refused to accept two natures after the union.

---

[42]Ibid., 785.

[43]Ibid., 5:1233; 6:741.

[44]Sellers, *Chalcedon,* 130-31.

[45]Mansi, 6:808, 816.

[46]Ibid., 808-809.

[47]Ibid., 813.

What is of great significance from the foregoing is the fact that the re-view-conference meeting of the Council of Ephesus in 449 was not heretical since Eutyches' exoneration was obviously based on his confession that Christ is consubstantial with his mother. This explains why Anatolius of Constantinople at the Fourth Ecumenical Council could in plenary session claim that Dioscorus was not deposed for heresy.[48] The Ephesian Council review conference of 449 was rejected at Chalcedon because of the injustice done to Flavian and Eusebius, and the exoneration of Eutyches. On the other hand Theodoret and Ibas, who were also deposed at Ephesus in 449, were restored at Chalcedon as late as sessions eight, nine, and ten, and then only after they accepted all that had thus far been done at the Council and anathematized Nestorius. Even though Leo's legates considered Theodoret as a participant from the very beginning,[49] the assembly vigorously protested.[50] The result of the protest can be seen in that the imperial representatives informed the protesting Dioscorus that the bishop of Cyrus was admitted to the Council in the capacity of accuser only.[51] We recounted his restoration elsewhere.[52] It should be noted that Atticos, the bishop of Nikopolis in Old Epirus, who made the motion which brought about the careful comparison of Leo's Tome with Cyril's Twelve Chapters, was present at Theodoret's restoration and the Epirot's acceptance of it is another testimony to the Bishop of Cyrus' submission to Cyril.[53]

Another objection, and perhaps the most serious, which Chalcedonian Orthodox have with the Ephesian Council of 449 is its rejection of Cyril's allowance for two natures after the union and its one-sided exclusiveness in this regard. This comes out clearly in the fact that at the Flavian Synod of 448 the minutes of Ephesus were read and accepted,[54] and also by the fact that both Flavian and Eusebius accepted ''one nature of God the *Logos* incarnate'' so long as Christ's consubstantiality with us is clearly professed.[55] However, Dioscorus simply rejected all talk of two natures after

---

[48]Ibid., 7:104.

[49]Ibid., 5:589.

[50]Ibid., 592.

[51]Ibid., 644-45.

[52]Ibid., 7:188-92.

[53]Ibid., 188.

[54]Ibid., 6:665.

[55]Ibid., 637, 676-77.

the union. When the imperial representatives asked why Flavian was deposed since he did accept "one nature of the *Logos* incarnate," Eustathius of Berytus admitted making a mistake.[56] Dioscorus, however, claimed that Flavian contradicted himself by accepting two natures after the union.[57] The strange thing is that both were correct, since for Flavian *physis* meant *ousia*, whereas for Dioscorus it meant *hypostasis*. Nevertheless, knowingly or not, Dioscorus was bent on erasing what Cyril had done in 433.

In confronting Eutyches' denial that Christ is consubstantial with us, Flavian and Eusebius were clearly speaking of two *physeis* as equivalent to two *ousiai*. For them, double consubstantiality meant two natures. For Eutyches *physis* and and *ousia* were also synonymous and he evidently at first believed that Cyril's "one nature" meant one ousia, hence his hesitation to accept them as names for Christ's humanity. Cyril does use *ousia* and *physis* as synonymous when speaking of the Holy Trinity.[58] There is no question of course about his use of *physis* as equivalent to *hypostasis*. Yet he never speaks of there being one *ousia* in Christ, and clearly speaks of the flesh of Christ as beng consubstantial with ours.[59] In Christology he uses *physis, hypostasis,* and *prosopon* as synonymous, yet he never, as far as I know, speaks of "two *prosopa* before the union and one after," as he does with the other two terms. Equivalent to his "one nature of God the *Logos* Incarnate" is his "one *hypostasis* of God the *Logos* incarnate" of his Third Letter to Nestorius[60] and his *Defense of the Twelve Chapters.*[61] In the light of all this and all which was said at Chalcedon, the anathema pronounced in the definition on those who say "two natures before the union and one after the union" was intended for anyone with Eutyches who denied that Christ is consubstantial with us. There is no doubt that the definition should have contained the phrase "or *ousia*" as one finds after the phrase "one *physis*" in the eighth and ninth anathemas of the Fifth Ecumenical Council. This would have avoided much misunderstanding. Perhaps it was not done at the Fourth because Cyril's "one nature of God the *Logos*" was taken as equivalent to "one *ousia*," and the word "incarnate" as equivalent to a second *ousia* or *physis*. That this was possible is

---

[56]Ibid., 677.

[57]Ibid., 681.

[58]E.g., *Ad Monachos,* PG 77:17.

[59]Mansi, 6:677.

[60]PG 77:116.

[61]*Apologia Cap.* II, PG 76:401A.

borne out clearly by the Flavian Synod of 448, as well as the explanations given by both Eusebius and Flavian at Ephesus in 449, as we have already indicated.

It should be noted that "one *hypostasis* of God the *Logos* incarnate" and not "one *physis* of God the *Logos* incarnate" is to be found in Cyril's *Third Letter to Nestorius* approved by Ephesus and Chalcedon. These terms are, of course, absolutely synonymous for Cyril. Yet it seems very obvious that at the Flavian Synod of 448 and at Chalcedon, the true Cyrillian meaning or usage of "one nature" was overlooked simply because the phrase "one nature after the union" was not contained in the synodical letters of Cyril, which alone were familiar to all participants of both Councils.

At the Endemousa Synod of Constantinople in 448,[62] and in his confession of faith of 449, Flavian says that Christ is "out of or from two natures."[63] Yet he spoke in the same breath of "two natures after the union". At the Council of Chalcedon, Dioscorus vigorously rejected any talk of a "union of two natures" (as found in the formulary of reunion approved by Cyril) and insisted exclusively on "union out of or from two natures." For Dioscorus this meant that after the union there could be only one nature. Had this term had the same function for Flavian as it did for Dioscorus, the bishop of New Rome would have found himself believing with Eutyches in "one *ousia* after the union," since for him *physis* meant *ousia*. Nevertheless, the imperial representatives were so impressed by the fuss Dioscorus made over this question, that they used this as an example to convince the bishops of the need for drafting a statement of faith. It is at this point that Anatolius intervened to remind the assembly that Dioscorus was not deposed for heresy, but because he excommunicated Leo.[64]

In their interlocution at the fifth session the imperial representatives said that Leo says "union of two natures," whereas Dioscorus says "union out of two natures." "Whom do you follow?" they asked. The Reverend Bishops cried, "As Leo, thus we believe. Those who gainsay are Eutychianists."[65] In the light of what happened in sessions two and four with Leo's Tome, one wonders if a deliberate attempt was made with the minutes to make Leo look a little better at Chalcedon in order to offset the ob-

---

[62]Mansi, 6:680.

[63]Sellers, *Chalcedon*, 131.

[64]Mansi, 7:104.

[65]Ibid., 105.

vious humiliation he underwent. Keeping in mind the Council's subordination of Leo to Cyril, one must take seriously the fact that in the letters of Cyril which served as the basis of the Council's deliberations the terms "from two natures" or "from two one" occur several times. It is understandable that Dioscorus made this a big issue, and it so became subsequently. One can understand the imperial representatives trying to make the question look like a big victory for Leo. Attila had to be met by the force of an empire united in everything, and especially helpful was the bishop of Rome who must not now be humiliated. But even when "in two natures" is accepted as the original reading of the Chalcedonian definition (although "from two natures" is what the manuscripts contain) it should be taken as an anti-Eutychianist statement meaning "in two *ousiai*," since this is what had been denied. Thus the Fifth Ecumenical Council rejects as heretical "from two natures" only when its proponents mean to teach "one *ousia*" in Christ. It stands to reason that had anyone proposed "in two natures" in the sense of rejecting Cyril's "from two natures" he would have certainly been challenged. Anatolius's reply to the imperial representatives is indicative of the fact that the leaders of the Council were not in any mood to see in these phrases any contradiction, and in fact there were none. Would non-Chalcedonians say that Christ is "out of two *ousiai*" in the same way they say "out of two *physeis*"? If not, then they can't expect Chalcedonians to do what they won't. What is then left is to speak of Christ as "of two *ousiai*" or "in two *ousiai*." This is all Chalcedonian means by "of two natures" or "in two natures." It seems that bickering over such terms was the result of a heresy-hunting temper which lumped Leo and Theodoret into one theological camp because of the alliance between them.

Also one may point out that "hypostatic union" or "natural union" was accepted at Chalcedon by virtue of the fact that all done at Ephesus in 431, the most important part of which are Cyril's letters wherein are contained all his key terms and ideas on Christology, was incorporated with Cyril's letter to John and the Tome of Leo into the definition itself. It seems obvious enough that the Chalcedonian theologians of the fifth and sixth centuries should be taken very seriously when they point out that Chalcedon was not convened in order to condemn Nestorius, except by way of repeating what had been done so well at Ephesus in 431, but rather in order to deal with the Eutychianist heresy.

The Theodoretan crypto-Nestorianism, whose danger loomed so large in Alexandrian circles, was not at all grasped by Leo. In a similar fashion the danger of Eutychianism was not handled properly by Dioscorus. We must always keep in mind the serious imbalance of attitudes toward issues on each side. While the Chalcedonians concentrated on the *confusors of the ousiai* in Christ, the Alexandrians were still fighting the *separators of natures or hypostases*. In the light of this it would be wise to make allowances in terminology while none whatsoever in faith. I would suggest that serious consideration be given to the Fifth Ecumenical Council, not as one which modified Chalcedon, but as one which interprets it correctly. If we agree on the meaning of Cyril's Christology, we should also be as pliable as he on terms. In this regard the non-Chalcedonians should accept all of Cyril, including 433, and the Chalcedonians must stop overemphasizing the Cyril of 433.

Ecclesiological Issues Concerning the Relation of Eastern Orthodox and Oriental Orthodox Churches

Paulos Mar Gregorios

In a perceptive paper presented at the Bristol Conversations in July 1967, Professor Gerasimos Konidaris drew attention to the position of the Orthodox Churches in communion with Constantinople on "The Inner Continuity and Coherence of Trinitarian and Christological Dogma in the Seven Ecumenical Councils."

What was most interesting in his treatment was the division of the seven Councils into two parts. Nicea (325) and Constantinople (381) belong to the first part—the latter especially was a positive achievement of the "Greek-Christian" spirit in clarifying the trinitarian and Christological dogmas. The symbol of the faith is now finalized; no further changes are to be effected.

The five later councils—including Ephesus (431), Chalcedon (451), and the three subsequent ones—belong to a different class. They regard the symbol of the first two Councils as unchangeable. Their task is to further elucidate it, not to reformulate the symbol as was finalized in the perfect Greek of St. Gregory of Nyssa in 381.

This insight of Professor Konidaris is of central significance for the relation between our two churches. We can all agree that the formulations of Nicea and Constantinople have a unique and final quality which it is safest not to tamper with.

These documents were prepared by Fathers who are common to our churches. They were not all necessarily Greeks by ethnic origin or nationality. It is important to point this out. Most of these Fathers came from the churches of Africa and Asia, from what later became the patriarchates of Alexandria and Antioch. The chief among the Fathers of the three councils, Athanasius and Cyril of Alexandria and the Cappodocians, came from

Egypt or Asia Minor. There is no reason to claim that only the Greek church understood them and their terminology. The literate peoples of Asia and Africa were at least as capable of using Greek terminology as Indians and Americans are capable of using English terminology today.

But the more important point is the inviolable character of the formulation of faith of the first two ecumenical synods. Once this point is adequately grasped by the two sides, some of our ecclesiological differences become capable of resolution.

Historically speaking the question then is, what did the Third Ecumenical Council, Ephesus (431), do, and what did the Council of Chalcedon (451) do, in relation to the first two Councils?

In the case of the Third Council, there was a clear heresy against which the council proclaimed itself—that attributed to Nestorius, Archbishop of Constantinople. The Alexandrian church led the attack against this heresy as in the case of the Arian heresy more than a century earlier.

They condemned Nestorius and the heresy ascribed to him that in Christ there are two distinct *prosopa*, two distinct persons—one human and one divine. Whether Nestorius taught this or not, it is a heresy, and the church still condemns this teaching. In this sense the decision of the Third Council is of high doctrinal value, and clarifies the creed of Nicea-Constantinople.

The case of the Fourth Council seems to be different in several ways. In the first place, the heresy for which the Council of Chalcedon was held in order to combat is still unknown. If it was to condemn the doctrine of Eutyches, we neither know what Eutyches taught nor who followed him in his teaching. On the assumption, however, that there was a heretical teaching which held that the human nature of Christ was not consubstantial with ours, or that it was absorbed by his divine nature, those who accept Chalcedon and those who reject that Council agree that Christ is consubstantial with us in his humanity and that the human nature with all its properties and faculties remains distinct and unabsorbed in Christ. We also agree in condemning Eutyches on the assumption that he denied the double consubstantiality. It is clear that on the non-Chalcedonian side we do not do this on the authority of the Council of Chalcedon.

It is because our own tradition is authentic and true that we affirm the double consubstantiality and the united divine-human nature of Christ. We are happy that both those Orthodox churches in communion with Constantinople and even our Roman Catholic friends accept this double consubstantiality. In this respect all of us adhere to the one authentic tradition, even when some of us do not accept the Council of Chalcedon. This means that for us Chalcedon is not an essential element of the authentic tradition, and as far as we are concerned, other churches can also reject Chalcedon and still be in the authentic tradition.

This is not so with the Third Council. The church of the East rejects the Third Council of Ephesus (431). As a result, Nestorius as well as Theodore and Diodore, whose teachings have been condemned by the authentic tradition, continue to be operative in the church of the East. If the churches of our non-Chalcedonian family were now to seek communion with the church of the East, the acceptance of the Third Council, or at least the major teachings of that Council, would be a necessary condition. The *Theotokos* formula and the one *prosopon* formula would also have to be insisted upon. If these doctrines are accepted, we may not insist on their acceptance of the Third Council, but would find our unity on the basis of the *kerygma* of Nicea and Constantinople supplemented by a formal repudiation of the two-*prosopa* doctrine and by the affirmation of the *Theotokos* formula as well as a Christology of the hypostatic union.

This basic difference between the nature of Ephesus (431) and Chalcedon (451) needs to be further discussed among our churches. The reason why we have not included the church of the East—the only oriental church to be so kept out of our conversations—in these meetings is simply that there are real Christological differences between both, while among ourselves we find basic agreement about our Christological positions. It is not inconceivable that extended theological conversations with the church of the East will reveal that they too affirm the hypostatic union of the two natures in Christ, and thereby do in fact affirm the single *prosopon,* and that Mary was truly the bearer of the God-man.

If this were to be the case, then the Third Council as such need not be an obstacle, though condemnation of those heresies condemned by Ephesus may still be necessary to restore communion between us.

It is because some of us have now become convinced that in affirming the two natures of Christ, the Chalcedonian Orthodox Churches also affirm the hypostatic union and *all* the "four adverbs," that we are no longer afraid of pursuing further the possibility of restoring communion between our two families of churches. Professor Tsonievsky of the Bulgarian Church was basically right in referring to "the non-Chalcedonian fear" . . . that the Orthodox (i.e. Chalcedonian) Church has departed somewhat from the decisions of the Third Ecumenical Council against Nestorius and that it has introduced certain Nestorian elements into the faith."[1] This fear *was* actually there, and is only now being dispelled; just as is the fear also on the

---

[1]"Bristol Report," *Greek Orthodox Theological Review* 13:12 (Fall 1968).

Chalcedonian side that we who stand firmly on the three Ecumenical Councils, in rejecting the Council of Chalcedon, were affirming something less than the full human nature in Christ.

It is now possible for us to do what Professor Tsonievsky asked us to do, namely that we "must stop accusing the Council of Chalcedon of Nestorianism," especially if we take Chalcedon as corrected by the Fifth Council and its interpretation of Chalcedon.

We can also agree that even the Chalcedonian churches should not separate the Fourth Council from the Fifth. We are not able to say, however, that the Sixth and Seventh Councils of the Chalcedonians are organically or integrally related either to the Fourth and Fifth or to the first three. It was the Fifth Council that could dispel our doubts about the Fourth. For in first refusing to condemn the teachings of Theodore, Theodoret, and Ibas, the Roman church at least among the Chalcedonians gave ground to our suspicion that Chalcedon actually did have some Nestorian implications. It took quite a bit of time for Pope Vigilius to accept the Fifth council. If the Decretal Epistle of Vigilius[2] is genuine, the Pope admits he was wrong in defending the Three Chapters. It is this kind of defense of the Three Chapters and of teachers like Theodore, Theodoret, and Ibas by a large section of those supporting Chalcedon, that made Chalcedon itself suspect. It is also a historical fact that despite the retractions of Pope Vigilius (554/555) and the confirmation by his successor Pelagius I of the Acts of the Fifth Council, that council was bitterly opposed in the whole of Northern Italy, in England, France, and Spain, and also in parts of Africa and Asia. Milan was in schism until 571, when the Henoticon was published. In Istria the schism continued for a century and a half.[3] Even today opinions crop up in western theological manuals which give rise to fears that Nestorianism is still not quite dead among the western Chalcedonians.

The Third Council of Constantinople, called the Sixth Ecumenical (680-681), enumerated in its decree and "piously gave its full assent to the five holy and Ecumenical Synods." This decree also specifies the particular heresy or heretic against which each Council is convened: Chalcedon was against "Eutyches and Dioscurus, hated of God," while the Fifth Council was against "Theodore of Mopsuestia, Origen, Didymus, Evagrius, and the writings of Theodoret against the Twelve Chapters of the celebrated Cyril, and the Epistile . . . by Ibas."

---

[2]J. P. Migne, ed. *Patrologia Latina* (= PL), 221 vols. (1844-1864) 69: 133ff.

[3]See note in Philip Schaff and Henry Wace, eds., *A Select Library of the Nicene and Post-Nicene Fathers*, 2nd series, 14 vols. (New York: C. Scribners' Sons, 1890-1900) 14:323.

We were not there, the non-Chalcedonians. If we had been, we would probably have liked to find out what was the heresy of "Dioscurus, hated of God." Until we find out, there can be no question of our accepting the Sixth Council as being in any sense in the right tradition. The condemnation of Didymus and Evagrius must be for their Origenism. That is a question which we need to examine further. A whole series of people are condemned by the Sixth Council for their supposedly Monothelite views—Theodorus of Pharan, Sergius, Pyrrhus, Paul, Peter, Pope Honorius, Cyrus of Alexandria, Macarius of Antioch, and Stephen. They are accused of affirming "one will and operation in the two natures of Christ our true God." I am not sure which is the true heresy to which these men adhered—that of "two natures" or of "one will and operation." Their heresy is regarded as being "similar to the mad and wicked doctrine of the impious Apollinaris, Severus, and Themistius." Putting Apollinaris and Severus in the same bracket shows how little their thought was understood by the Sixth Synod. Themistius of Alexandria, on the other hand, so strongly affirmed the humanity of Christ as to attribute ignorance of certain matters to the human soul of Christ.

If acceptance of the Sixth Council thus means our agreeing to condemn Dioscurus and Severus, who are true teachers of the authentic tradition, then we must choose the two Fathers mentioned in preference to the Sixth Council, which appears to us badly muddled, not to say in grievous error.

Its *horos* or dogmatic definition we find interesting. The first part of this *horos* reads:

> Our Lord Jesus Christ must be confessed to be very God and very man, one of the holy and consubstantial and life-giving Trinity, perfect in Deity and perfect in humanity, very God and very man, of a reasonable soul and human body subsisting; consubstantial with the Father as touching his Godhead and consubstantial with us as touching his manhood; in all things like unto us, sin only excepted; begotten of his Father before all ages according to his Godhead, but in these last days for us men and for our salvation made man of the Holy Ghost and of the Virgin Mary, strictly and properly the Mother of God according to the flesh; one and the same Christ our Lord, the only-begotten Son, of two natures unconfusedly, unchangeably, inseparably, indivisibly to be recognized, the peculiarities of neither nature being lost by the union but rather the proprieties of each nature being preserved, concurring in one Person and in one subsistence, not parted or divided into two persons but one and the same only-begotten Son of God, the Word, our Lord Jesus Christ, according as the Prophets of old have taught us and as our Lord Jesus Christ himself hath instructed and the creed of the holy Fathers hath delivered to us.

This we find basically acceptable, though not as a formula of confession like or instead of the Niceno-Constantinopolitan *pistis*.

The second part is of a different kind, and needs separate examination:

> We likewise declare that in him are two natural wills and two natural operations, indivisibly, inconvertibly, inseparably, inconfusedly, according to the teaching of the holy Fathers. And these two natural wills are not contrary the one to the other (God forbid!) as the impious heretics assert, but his human will follows and that not as resisting and reluctant, but rather as subject to his divine and omnipotent will. For it was right that the flesh should be moved but subject to the divine will, according to the most wise Athanasius. For as his flesh is called and is the proper will of God the Word, as he himself says: "I came down from heaven, not that I might do mine own will but the will of the Father which sent me!" where he calls his own will the will of his flesh, inasmuch as his flesh was also his own. For as his most holy and immaculate animated flesh was not destroyed because it was deified but continued in its own state and nature, so also his human will, although deified, was not suppressed, but was rather preserved according to the saying of Gregory Theologus: "His will (i.e. the Savior's) is not contrary to God but altogether deified."

> We glorify two natural operations indivisibly, immutably, inconfusedly, inseparably in the same our Lord Jesus Christ our true God, that is to say a divine operation and a human operation, according to the divine preacher Leo, who most distinctly asserts as follows: "For each form does in communion with the other what pertains properly to it, the Word, namely, doing that which pertains to the Word, and the flesh that which pertains to the flesh."

> For we will not admit one natural operation in God and in the creature as we will not exalt into the divine essence what is created, nor will we bring down the glory of the divine nature to the place suited to the creature.

Here, as earlier in the decree, the Tome of Leo is expressly affirmed. The decree actually calls the Tome "the pillar of the right faith." You can perhaps understand that all this is rather difficult for us to accept. For us Leo is still a heretic. It may be possible for us to refrain from condemning him by name, in the interests of restoring communion between us. But we cannot in good conscience accept the Tome of Leo as "the pillar of the right faith" or accept a Council which made such a declaration. The Council approves explicitly what I clearly regard as heresy in the Tome of Leo— "Each form does in communion with the other what pertains properly to it, the Word, namely doing that which pertains to the Word, and the flesh that which pertains to the flesh.''[4] If one rightly understands the hypostatic union, it is not possible to say that the flesh does something on its own, even if it is said to be in union with the Word. The flesh does not have its own *hypostasis*. It is the *hypostasis* of the Word which acts through the flesh. It is the same *hypostasis* of the Word which does the actions of the Word and of his own flesh.

The argument in the *horos* of this Sixth Council is basically unacceptable to us. The reason it gives for not admitting one natural operation in Christ which is both divine and human, proceeding from the divine and human natures of the same *hypostasis,* is that they would ''not exalt into the divine essence what is created, nor . . . bring down the glory of the divine nature to the place suited to the creature.''

One can understand the first part of this objection, though not the conclusion drawn from it. The creature is not to participate in the divine *ousia,* but only in the uncreated *energeia* of the divine essence. But in Jesus Christ, man the creature *is* united to the divine person or *hypostasis.* If we deny that, we are not Christians. The operation of the incarnate *Logos* is a divine-human *energeia* and we cannot say that it was only the flesh or the human nature that was crucified. *"They crucified the Lord of Glory."* What is the point of saying, ''We will not bring down the glory of the divine nature to the place suited to the creature''—unless the Sixth Council wanted to deny the Incarnation itself?

It seems to us that the Sixth Council was much more based on the Tome of Leo than on the writings of St. Cyril. Where it is based on Cyrilline teaching, it is acceptable, as for example, where it says both the miracles and the sufferings were performed by one entity, Christ our true God who became man. We are unable to say what this council says when it affirms ''two wills and two operations concurring most fitly in him.'' We are not sure that ''each nature wills and does the things proper to it,'' for we believe that it is the *hypostasis* of Christ who wills and operates through his divine-human nature. The natures have no subsistence of their own apart from the *hypostasis* who operates in both natures. We would thus prefer to speak of the one incarnate nature of the *Logos,* both divine and human natures united in the one *hypostasis* of the *Logos,* with a divine-human will and operation.

* * *

---

[4]''Agit enim utraque forma cum alterius communione quod proprium est; Verbo scilicet operante quod Verbi est, et carne exequente quod carnis est.''

To summarize: acceptance of the Sixth Council is much more difficult for us than the acceptance of Chalcedon. The following are the chief reasons:

(a) Quite apart from the fact that our own fathers were not present at this Council, we observe that the Council explicitly and unjustifiedly condemns our fathers Dioscurus and Severus, calling the former "hated of God" and the doctrine of the latter "mad and wicked."[5]

(b) We are unable to accept the dithelete formula, attributing will and energy to the natures rather than to the *hypostasis*. We can only affirm the one united and unconfused divine-human nature, will, and energy of Christ the incarnate Lord.

(c) We find that the Sixth Council exalts as its standard mainly the teaching of Leo and Agatho, popes of Rome, paying only lip-service to the teachings of the blessed Cyril. We regard Leo as a heretic for his teaching that the will and operation of Christ is to be attributed to the two natures of Christ rather than to the one *hypostasis*. The human nature is as "natural" to Christ the incarnate Word as is the divine. It is one *hypostasis* who now is both divine and human, and all the activities come fron the one *hypostasis*. We therefore insist on the one theandric nature, will, and energy of Christ the incarnate Lord, and condemn the teachings of Leo. We cannot therefore accept the *horos* of the Sixth Council based on the teachings of Leo. This subject of course deserves further and more detailed study.

Conclusion

This paper has been written subject to correction by my learned brethren on the Chalcedonian and non-Chalcedonian sides. Its implications are quite serious. If the restoration of communion between our two families of churches were to be dependent on our acceptance of the four Councils now rejected by the non-Chalcedonian family, then we have little reason at present to hope that this condition can be fulfilled. If this is the *conditio sine qua non* in the minds of theologians on the Chalcedonian side, we would like to be told so, in order that we may communicate this to the holy synods of our churches and await further instruction from them as to whether we continue our bilateral conversations. My own view would be that we should so continue, because despite our basic disagreement on this point of the four Councils, we do still have so much in common, and we have a significant contribution to make together as Eastern Orthodox Churches to the worldwide ecumenical discussion.

---

[5]Severus is also called "God-hated" in the letter of the Sixth Council to Pope Agatho.

On the other hand, if we take seriously the valuable insight of Professor Konidaris, that the formulations of the First and Second Councils are of a decisive character, and later councils are to be seen only as exegetical to the meaning of the faith of Nicea and Constantinople, then it is possible for us to recommend to our parent churches to begin formal conversations with a view to restoring communion between our two families. The following is proffered as a basis or starting point for such conversations:

1. In a substantially common statement, to be formally declared by the holy episcopal synods of all the autocephalous churches with any necessary changes to suit the condition of each church, we should state clearly that we share, between our two families, substantially the same authentic tradition of the undivided Christian church in relation to our understanding of and teaching on the blessed Holy Trinity, the Incarnation of our Lord Jesus Christ, the procession and activity of the Holy Spirit, the nature of the church and the place of the blessed Virgin Mary, the saints and all the faithful departed in it, the nature of the ministry and sacraments in the church, and our expectation of the world to come with the advent in glory of our Lord and the resurrection of the dead.

2. This common statement would also include a page on our common Christology, emphasizing mainly those things which we have in common, but also speaking of our different formulations in regard to nature, will, and energy in our Lord Jesus Christ. It would be stated that variety in forms of worship, language, and culture, and in formulations of faith, can within certain prescribed limits serve to enrich rather than impoverish the common tradition of the church.

3. The statement would also make clear that while it is not possible for the Chalcedonian churches to repudiate or reject any of the Seven Councils, it is equally difficult for the non-Chalcedonians now to formally accept the Fourth, Fifth, Sixth and Seventh councils recognized by the Chalcedonian family. It could be made clear that the non-Chalcedonians would refrain from formally condemning either the Council of Chalcedon or Pope Leo. The statement will also make clear that the Chalcedonian churches would refrain from condemning Dioscurus and Severus as heretics. It could also be made clear that our two families agree in condemning the teachings of both Nestorius and Eutyches as heretical.

4. The statement would also say that at least for the time being, the jurisdictions would remain distinct on the basis of the different liturgical traditions—the two patriarchates of Antioch and Alexandria, as well as of Constantinople, could continue with their different jurisdictions. The hope should be expressed in the statement that as mutual confidence

grows between the various liturgical traditions a reorganization of the jurisdictions would become possible. Clear assurances can be given to certain churches that entering into communion with another church will not violate their administrative or jurisdictional integrity.

The next immediate step is the appointment of a joint commission by the two families, who will meet officially and work out the statement along the suggested lines. The standing committee of the Oriental Orthodox Churches has already been so authorized to act on behalf of the Oriental Orthodox Churches. As soon as similar action is announced by the churches of the Chalcedonian family, we could proceed to the convening of a joint meeting of the two commissions. One of our jobs here at the present meeting would be to prepare an agenda for the joint meeting, and to nominate a small group of people who will be prepared to assist in the organization of the joint meeting.

The Christological Dogma
and Its Terminology

Georges Florovsky

In Scripture we are faced with the mystery of Jesus Christ presented as an historical personality born of the blessed Virgin Mary, being human in the full sense, taken by many for an ordinary man who eventually suffered and died on the cross. The common picture of our Lord is of one fully human, displaying a glory which is a mystery. The true image of our Lord can only be depicted in a suprahistorical vision in an act of faith.

From the beginning there has been certain confusion about him. He has always been seen as something greater than his merely human appearance.

The mystery is described in the New Testament as a history of *kenosis* (which is also a Cyrilline term). It is the mystery of humiliation. In the early church the main concern was with the full and true humanity of our Lord. This is stated in the Epistles of St. John, who combines his emphasis as to the superhuman character of Christ in the beginning of his Gospel, that is the divine Logos becoming flesh, with his challenge in the First Epistle to those who would not believe that the Logos became flesh.

Distinction should be made between the *kerygma* of the church and the philosophical terminology in terms of which it is apprehended. The concern of the *kerygma* is with the message of salvation to be announced, with the saving person of Christ. The terminology of theology is for clarifying the conceptual grasp of the message and person of the Savior. The Christological problem is thus integral to the message of salvation, and should always be considered in that context.

The Christological dispute in the early church was concerned mainly with the message of salvation. When we turn to early Christological conceptions we always find them in a soteriological perspective. There are two different concepts of salvation linked with two different anthropological dispositions.

Anthropological minimalism: This is found in the preaching of Apollinaris, who went so far as to suggest that of the whole human fabric the *"nous"* could not be saved. Only fragments of Apollinaris' teaching remain, however. The *nous* in man is so perverse that it could not be human. *Nous* for Apollinaris is related to his pessimistic conception of the human being, and this affected his Christological conceptions. For him, Christ was the *logos* clothed only in the externals of human nature. The emphasis again is purely soteriological. In Apollinaris there is a very low evaluation of the human condition and of the predicament which could result from it. Anthropological minimalism leads to maximalism of the divine element in Christ.

Anthropological maximalism: This concept is effected by exterior conditions. This, as well as opposition to it, is found in the so-called Antiochene school which also opposed Apollinaris. The Nestorian Christ was seen to be a suitable redeemer for the Pelagian man. Nestorianism and Pelagianism are examples of anthropological maximalism. Man has not been destroyed by sin; he is only lost and needs a guide who may be only human. This human being can be the maximum human being evident in the Old Testament as the Messiah. In anthropological maximalism no high Christology is necessary.

This useful scheme of anthropological minimalism-maximalism can be taken as the core of terminological differences in the Christological debate. Christ has been regarded by some modern authors as a redeemer, and the Incarnation at the same time regarded simply as an act only of redemption. But this thinking in the early centuries of the Church was only really clarified in the Christological writing of Maximus the Confessor, where the Incarnation is said to have been the original purpose of the divine venture of creation. The later problem was whether redemption could be said to be the only reason for the Incarnation. Maximus developed a comprehensive scheme giving a reason for creation, that reason being in the Incarnation, and the Christology of the Eastern churches was affected by this thinking. In the period preceding Maximus, soteriological maximalism and minimalism were always rooted in the concept of man. This soteriology could be absolute or relative. When we discuss events, there can be misunderstandings and conflict about this, and terms must always be clarified.

Archbishop William Temple once wrote that "Chalcedon marked the bankruptcy of Greek mataphysics." But the glory of Chalcedon represents a fundamental intuition. Chalcedon states that Christ is one being, perfectly divine and perfectly human.

This is an expression of a certain intuition and vision of our Lord, and the conviction of a soteriological issue which is apparent at Chalcedon. Any lesser conviction would destroy the apostolic *kerygma* about our salvation.

It has been suggested that Cyril was interested neither in exact terminology nor in scholastic definitions. There are examples in which the term *physis* and adjectives related to it are used in a non-exact sense, and objections have been presented at this level. It is suggested that *physis* is used to emphasize that Christ was truly man. Cyril was not concerned with terminology but with truth, and more attention should be given to his soteriological intuition.

Ancient Greek was an unfamiliar language to many of the early theologians and patristic texts were often read then as now, unfortunately, merely as texts—and one can always be negligent about terms in texts. Dissertations have been written about single words such as *hypostasis*. Terminological clarity must only arise out of necessity when dealing with Christology. People have always tended to be rather indifferent to terminological exactitude in the understanding of texts.

The Chalcedonian definition provides no reason for embarrassment in emphasizing that Christ is fully human and fully divine. This was addressed against the language of the Antiochenes who endeavored to describe the unity of Christ in a minimalized anthropological form.

We are still imprisoned in the terminology of monophysitism and duophysitism. One must be clear what is implied in duophysitism, for there are two types, the symmetric type and the asymmetric type. The problem of terminology remains as long as ancient idioms are still used. The Christological dispute was extended to errors and areas where the Greek language was not the main language. We must look at the languages of the non-Chalcedonian churches much more closely. We must look at the psychological significance of the term "person," as it is used in different languages both ancient and modern. It must always be remembered that words do not of themselves express the ideas that are intended to be expressed.

What is important is to turn to the basic vision and conclusion of the early church. If we look at documents through Nestorian eyes they can be Nestorian in content, and so on. Divergence initially came and still comes in the sphere of spiritual vision and not in language. This is why western theologians find it difficult to understand eastern theologians—because they have a different vision.

In conclusion, we should not omit to discuss the metaphysical side and pay attention to spirituality. Anyone who insists in avoiding nature reduces man. The separation from the beginning will cease to be of importance when we cease to look at terminology and look at the life of the churches instead.

Problems of Consensus in Christology:
The Function of Councils

Tiran Nersoyan

A Christian, placing himself within the church and taking his stand as a believer, feels it to be his duty to profess the right faith and to act on that faith guided by his conscience, which in turn is guided by the church and is prompted by the Holy Spirit. The function of a Council is to point the way to the truth of the kingdom, by speaking to the church of the elements of the faith in the form of verbal propositions, when the question is doctrinal or dogmatic. Such propositions are necessarily dated inasmuch as they are couched in the language of a given point in time. A council speaks to the believers in order to corroborate their faith, relating its teaching to the tradition of the church.

A Christian's loyalty is not to a Council as such, but to the Church as a whole, which itself is the highest Council, and which is the keeper of the deposit of the faith. A Council is judged by the faith of the tradition and not vice versa. That is why some Councils have been rejected by the church in the course of time long or short, although they were convened and had done their work in proper form. Others have been accepted universally or partially and their pronouncements have been held as being orthodox. Consequently, there is a hierarchy of Councils, both with respect to the importance ascribed to them and with respect to the extension of their reception. It is an historical fact that councils have often been accepted after their statements have been the subject of further dialogue within the church.

The highest point in this hierarchy is the Council of Nicea. This is so not because of the formal canonicity of this Council, but because of the paramount importance attached to it by the church on account of the work it achieved, and because of the truly universal acceptance which it commanded in all places and in all subsequent centuries. Not only does it stand at the pinnacle of the hierarchy of Councils, but also its definitions have been generally held to be normative for all subsequent Councils.

The criteria by which Councils have been judged generally acceptable have not been constant or uniform. When should a general council be called? Who should call it? How representative should it be? What subjects should it deal with? How free should it be from external pressures? How far and how long should its decisions be considered binding? These questions have been usually answered post factum and often fortuitously in the course of the vicissitudes of history. Often the fortune of a Council has been dependent on the power of its sponsors. Nevertheless, Councils are expected to give expression to the mind of the church, whenever this is called for. They are expected to be the guardian and the manifestation of the unity of the church. They are expected to be moved by the Holy Spirit (Acts 15:28). Because of the vital necessity of these functions, conciliarity is of the essence of the structure of the church on all levels. And yet because of our human infirmities it is not always possible to determine with reasonable certainty the claim of an individual Council to authenticity. Therefore we should not be tempted to think that councils are some kind of supernatural intrusions into the life of the church, having an authority over and above their normal historical role within the context of the events surrounding them.

Divergence of opinions within a Council has often mirrored disagreements on matters of doctrinal interpretation within the church as a whole. But whereas the resolution of differences of views within a council can be brought about expeditiously by counting votes, or sometimes by other means, the same cannot be said about resolving differences in the church scattered throughout the world. Consequently, impatient majorities have often resorted to the easy way of branding the minority as heretics, claiming and reserving the Holy Spirit to themselves and consigning the minority to the devil by the logician's rule of the excluded middle. And then they have called upon the secular authorities to exorcise the devil by other methods of persuasion. These methods, which can hardly be squared with the belief in the operation of the Holy Spirit in the church, have mostly been counterproductive. Writes Nerses IV, the Armenian Catholicos in the latter part of the twelfth century, addressing himself to the Emperor of Constantinople:

> The cause of our running away from you is that you have been pulling down our churches, destroying our altars, smashing the signs of Christ, harassing our clergy, spreading slanders in a way even the enemies of Christ would not do, even though we live close to them. Such behavior will not only fail to unify the divided, but it will divide those who are united. For

human nature loves contrariness. And men are drawn to the execution of commands not so much by violence as by humility and love.[1]

Pegging down orthodoxy to the authority of Councils and to the fixity of theological propositions issued by them, and judging orthodoxy or otherwise of a section of the church on the basis of its acceptance or rejection, as the case may be, has failed to produce unity in the church, and most probably will continue to do so. This is because the fixity of the stance of a Council in history, and its image formed in the context of events surrounding it, make agreement on its evaluation extremely difficult. On the other hand, when we take a Council dealing with doctrinal matters as a teaching organ rather than a legislative organ of the church, and focus our attention on the insights contained in its expositions, then the desired consensus will be possible to produce, inasmuch as the teaching of the Council will be amenable to new understandings and interpretations. In other words, when we seek broad agreements on the affirmations of our faith and consider the councils as corroborative authorities rather than originative and determinative, then our goal of unity will be better served. For example, our church is in broad agreement with the decisions of the Second Council of Nicea of 787 against iconoclasts, in spite of the fact that iconoclasts have been strong in Armenia. Yet the Council itself has not been formally accepted as such. The same could be said of the Second Council of Constantinople in 553. The Vatican has shown to the world in our time that the effective way is to approach the problems in tolerance, understanding, humility, and prayerful reflection with a view to healing the wounds of division in God's good time, full of confidence in the power of the Holy Spirit.

The consideration of the nature and the status of general Councils is important, because the end purpose of our discussion of the Christological problem could hardly be served unless our attitudes with regard to the Councils are clarified and understood.

Locus of Unity—Liturgy and Sacraments

The bond "which knits the whole Body of Christ, with all its joints and ligaments and thus makes it grow according to God's design" (Col. 2:19) is the Christian life centered and manifested in the holy Eucharist. The function or role of ecumenical and other councils is to safeguard this unity when it is seen to be in danger. And the unity of the faith is only part of the larger unity of the life, in the sense in which Christ used the word when he said, "I am the way, the truth, and the life." Heresies are repudiated

---

[1]Nerses IV, "Encyclical" (Jerusalem: Jerusalem Patriarchate Press, 1871) 115.

and condemned because they threaten to break up the bond between the Body and the head, Christ, and among the members of the body. Now, when we examine the sacraments of our churches and specially the eucharist, there we find no cause or occasion for division. Our Christology professed directly and indirectly in our liturgical and generally sacramental life has not given rise to any controversy of significance. In fact it is used as they have always been by the Uniate Catholics who are in the Roman jurisdiction. Minor problems such as commixture or participation in both kinds and similar differences have cropped up now and then, but now such things are not even matters of discussion any more.

Gregory IV, the Armenian Catholicos, wrote in 1179, when negotiating for intercommunion with the Greeks:

> When two people walk along the same road, is it possible that one should be astray and the other aright? Of course not. It is proper that we should be considered fellow travellers on the road of the Scriptures and having the Holy Fathers as our leaders.[2]

The liturgical and sacramental life of a church is the authentic expression of the faith, of the mind, and of the spiritual experience of her clergy and people. On the other hand the liturgy stamps its imprint on the consciousness of the worshiping community, as a channel of grace. All dogmas are ultimately tested in the life of the church against the basic tradition on the one hand, and against the experience of the age on the other.

The question then arises: If problems of monophysitism or duophysitism do not arise in our sacramental and liturgical practice, why should certain propositions framed by a Council or Councils be allowed to disturb the real, existential unity of the church in the most vital area of its life? Our faith in Christ and in his gospel, our loyalty to the basic tradition of the church, our common liturgy and sacraments, have their own inherent power and grace supplied by the Holy Spirit that will lead us to unity if we do not block the road by seeking conformity in things that are not of the essence of the faith. As truth will lead us to freedom, so also freedom in the Holy Spirit will lead us to unity in the truth of Christ. When we recite the Nicene Creed in our worship we thereby implicitly pay homage to the Fathers who framed it by coming together in a Council. When we see our churches adorned with sacred icons and a multitude of other things which in the words of one of our liturgical prayers "hold God up for us" (*theodochos*) for our spiritual edification, we implicitly approve of the action of those who defended their usage. When we sing the praises of the Mother of God the

---

[2]Ibid., 320.

Theotokos and seek her intercession, we thereby agree with those who upheld the unity of the person of the God-man who was born of the Virgin. When we place equal emphasis in our liturgical prayers and sacraments on the divinity and the humanity of Christ without confusion or division and see in him a man like us save for sin and at the same time the Second Person of the Holy Trinity, we thereby express our assent to the teachings of those who repudiated the errors of Nestorianism and Eutychianism alike. Confession in this way is more real than subscription to certain formal propositions. Iconography, Christian art, liturgical practice, hymnology—all these and similar flowerings of grace in the church are expressions of the faith. And it is amazing that through the infinite variety of forms and styles through the centuries the original deposit of the faith, the fundamental tradition, has remained practically unimpaired in its unity.

The point is that if we have no cause for division in our Eucharistic and sacramental life, and if we are really in communion with the saints who have gone to their reward, then we should look for the causes of our divisions, or rather our social estrangement, elsewhere, and not in the formal acceptance or rejection of the Council of Chalcedon or any other subsequent Council.

In considering the teaching function of the church in the present age, we find that the fundamental problem is still Christology. That is always the central concern. Faith in Christ is the axis of the Christian teaching. And the New Testament is the original foundation of that teaching. Christ is the revelation of truth made to the church and through the church to mankind. That revelation is God's love responding to the perpetual cry of SOS by mankind. That cry receives its answer in Christ who is the Savior. No worldly miracles or scientific ingenuity will ever be able to silence that cry of the human soul for salvation. The appeal of Christ, in one form or another, in the church or out of the church, among the youth as well as the mature, is always strong. The only miracle by which man will be saved from being thrown on to the junk heap of universal decay and perdition is the miracle of Jonah, the miracle of change from old Adam and death to Christ the new Adam and life, the miracle of the rise of man from the temporal to the eternal. The function of the church is, therefore, to be an instrument of this change, this *metanoia,* by preaching Christ the Son of God, through the power of the Holy Spirit.

If so, then Christology is prior to theology so far as Christians are concerned. We begin by being Christologians, and our theology flows from our Christology. God is the Father of our Lord Jesus Christ and not the God of natural theology. There is no God but in and through Christ. "I am the door," said Christ. He is the door to salvation and to eternal life, wherein man will be woven into the divine scheme, into the mystery of the ultimate order of things, and will be united with God. Christ is the only proof of the existence of God, of the God beyond God, in the words of Paul Tillich, and there can be no other proof. For without him we could not know the Father. "Without me you can do nothing," he said. And if we can do nothing, then we can know nothing. He also said: "No one comes unto the Father but by me." Thus, we should not be surprised that when the Christ of the *kerygma* of the church, the risen Christ, the Son of God, and himself God, the Christ of the Christologians of the fourth and fifth centuries, when this Christ is made to be no more than a prophet like others in all ages and places, when he is made to be no more than a normal man of his time in history, then men lose their way to God, they lose the way to Christ. And as a result God is proclaimed, quite understandably, as being dead, as indeed he would be if men think of him independently of Christ.

Christ said: "I and the Father are one." Christians have to take this statement quite seriously, as did the church through the centuries, because the Father is not conceivable without the *Logos* incarnate. It is inconceivable in the sense that it will remain an unspecified, vague affirmation without real substance. Historically the trinitarian doctrine of God is the outcome of the Christological teaching of the church. Only sound Christology can surmount the pitfall of subject-object relationship between God and man, and ultimately the pitfall of atheism.[3] For in the oneness of Christ are found both God and man. That is why the church believes that he is consubstantial with the Father and consubstantial with men. For if Christ is not man like other men in every way except sin, then again the gospel will not be credible, its historical setting will not be real, salvation history will be a fiction, and once more God will be dead so far as man is concerned. In Christ, the eternal and the temporal blend (*synkrasis*), in him truth becomes existential and concrete, and not a pattern of objective relationships merely perceived by a subject. Christ bridges the gap between what man is and what he ought to be. He binds finitude and infinity together, the beginning and the end. In him one is present in the other. In Christ, Creator and creature coincide ontologically. Without belief in Christ, there is no reason for belief in God (John 17:21).

Christology seen in this light will welcome biblical criticism, exegesis in any form or method. Any kind of historical inquiry into the time and life of Jesus will be enlightening, because such inquiry will deepen and widen the description of the manhood of Christ, and the credal affirmation that

---

[3]Cf. Paul Tillich, *The Courage to Be* (New Haven: Yale University Press, 1953) 185.

the *Logos* became man will be laid on a stronger basis, inasmuch as the concrete historical setting of the life of Christ will be predicated to his manhood.

With the thought of these things, the work of the great Christologians of the fourth and fifth centuries comes alive. Their fierce struggles, their doubts and uncertainties, their insights and their affirmations take a new meaning. The present is seen in the womb of the past. The deification of human nature in Christ acquires a new significance.

Yet when we recall the tools and the methods which were employed in those early centuries we see the inadequacy of the results of their work for our time. But now it is necessary to make a distinction between the tools and the work. In and after the fourth century the church became the state church. Matters of faith and religious discipline became the concern of the state. Church leaders became statesmen. Church Councils became state organs and their dogmatic formulations acquired the force of legal enactments. Disagreement with these formulations became equivalent to insubordination against the authority of the state and consequently a punishable offense. When Nestorius insisted that *Christotokos* was a better term than *Theotokos* to be applied to the Holy Virgin, he was exiled to the Egyptian desert where he died of ill treatment. In this kind of environment, theological discussion and doctrinal development took turns which could not be said always to have been due to the working of the Spirit of truth and freedom, and which were sometimes tragic for the church. And the consequences of those events are still with us. It is of course an entirely idle speculation to seek answers to the questions: What would have happened if the emperors had not manipulated the general church Councils? What if the theologians had been allowed to work in a free and unfettered atmosphere? Nevertheless, it is important to keep in mind the way in which the dogmatic determinations of the Councils were brought about, and compliance with those determinations was sought and obtained.

Old Terms in Christology

We accept the fact that the results of the Christological controversies of the fifth and subsequent centuries have been woven into the tradition of the church and the churches. But that tradition has to be constantly reevaluated and newly understood in terms of the language with which our age is familiar and within the universe of discourse in which we have our movement. Consequently, the churches will have to recognize that there are certain elements in their dogmatic heritage which need reconsideration for the purpose of reordering their priorities, so to speak. One of these elements is the group of words over which the conflicts arose and continued without end. After reading Professor Grillmeier's masterful and highly erudite book, *Christ in Christian Tradition,* I feel that I have neither the competence, nor the need, nor indeed the desire, to discuss them. Yet I would like to be allowed to make a few remarks on the circumstances of their use as they appear to me from where I stand.

These words—*ousia, hypostasis, physis,* and *prosopon*—have behind them a field of philosophical, anthropological, and psychological speculation which at present has only an historical interest for us. They have almost become philosophical fossils and they should be taken as such. Even some of the bishops of the classical era of Christian dogmatics were not entirely unjustified in being wary of the injection of somewhat unclear philosophical terms into the statements of Christian beliefs, which had already taken a fairly stable form up to and during the fourth century in the *kerygma* of the church and in the popular mind. Three persons and one Godhead, one person of one or two natures in Christ, God and man at the same time, are paradoxical expressions of what is given in the gospel. While man's mind cannot and must not be prevented from analyzing and rationalizing his beliefs, as all teachers and preachers do, and while the attempt to define the terms used in credal statements is sometimes helpful and always creditable, yet it is at least unnecessary and often inadvisable to make subscription to those attempted rationalizations the test of the salvation or the damnation of the believer. Because it is one thing to say "this I believe" or "the church believes," it is another to say "this is what is *meant* by what the church believes."

The one is the constant, while the other is the variable. The fact that the variables are in flux, in keeping with social, cultural, and scientific evolution, must not be considered as endangering what is constant. However difficult, we have to accept the principle that while signs change, the signified remain. By way of accommodation we may have to consider a hierarchy of signs. A sign may be the signified with respect to the sign on a lower level, and conversely a thing signified may be the sign of something signified on a higher level. This may appear to be like the emanationism of Gnostics and Neoplatonists. Yet while emanationism may not be true or orthodox ontologically, it is nevertheless useful as a way of discerning the boundary between what is given in the gospel of Christ and the original *kerygma* of the church on the one hand, and what may be the subject matter of explanations and contemplation by the free exercise of the human mind on the other. So we can perhaps say the lowest level of the signified and the highest level of the signs coincide in the Gospels and in what is generally agreed to be the deposit of the faith. These we hold fast, and for the rest we leave the mind of the Christian free with a freedom that may be guided but not imposed upon. And the fact that the truths of the faith can be stated by a variety of ways is an indication of its durability. Vatican II has put the matter quite admirably: "The deposit of the faith or revealed truths is one thing, the manner in which they are formulated without violence to their meaning and significance is another."[4] These are words of consequence for our times. The purpose of formulating the elements of the deposit of the faith in seemingly rational propositions is to keep the believers in the way of Christ together in one body. Yet if these variable propositions are made *de fide,* so to speak, then the enterprise will be counterproductive and will defeat its purpose inasmuch as one variable will be picked up against another, and there will be dissension among Christians of the same period of time, or generation gaps between Christians of sequent periods of time.

Christological Minimalism

When you have said, One Lord Christ, true and perfect God and true and perfect man, *Logos* incarnate, you have described the Jesus of the Gospels and the Christ of the Faith. The notion of the integration of the two is embedded in the phrase itself, even though it is fatally paradoxical, as the apostle says. ". . . to Jews a stumbling block, to gentiles foolishness."

The theologoumena concerning the person of Christ, which was the subject debated by the Christologians of the fifth century, trying a kind of "reconciliation of science and religion" in their time, could hardly be said to have contributed to the strengthening of the faith. Yet the whole world was practically divided into opposing camps, even though "the difference between their positions could be recognized only with difficulty and not at all accurately. Formula was put against formula and these were judged by the opposing side in the light of its own presuppositions."[5] And if this was true for the situation *before* Chalcedon, it was certainly true also *after* Chalcedon.

In an Armenian *Collection of Citations,* St. Ephrem is quoted as saying:

> You have heard the truth revealed, do not slide into the secrets. Take refuge in silence O thou weak one, and glorify the Father, the Son and the Holy Spirit. Let us not get too close, for then we shall go too far; and let us not go too far, for then we shall be lost. It is a vast ocean, if you go out investigating, the overflow of the waves will engulf you; one wave can take

---

[4]Vatican II, "The Church in the Modern World," no. 62.

[5]Aloys Grillmeier, *Christ in Christian Tradition: From the Apostolic Age to Chalcedon (451),* trans. J. S. Bowden (New York: Sheed and Ward, 1965) 366.

you and dash you against the rock. It is sufficient for you, weak as you
are, to gain thy soul within the ship.[6]

Many theologians agree that in Chalcedon the bishops set out to settle
a problem and they failed. This was because the terminological instruments by which the attempt at a solution was made, even prior to the Council, were inadequate, indeed perhaps sometimes useless. They tried to seek
ontic unity in Christ, in order to save the doctrine of salvation. Apparently
their philosophical tools were not equal to the task. And if the doctrine of
salvation has stood firm all along, the credit does not go to the Council,
but to the deposit of the faith embedded in the *kerygma* of the church from
the beginning. Nor were the ecclesiastical structure, the political machin-
ery of the Empire, and the definition of authority in the church conducive
to consensus on the issues raised during the controversy. It does not seem
to have occurred to people in authority at the time that the Holy Spirit would
make good use of the freedom of the believer's mind and soul, enlightened
by the message of the gospel and the *kerygma* of the church, to build up
the unity of the Body of Christ during his pleasure. After all, the church
had survived the first three centuries in one piece, generally speaking. Now
that secular potentates are not imposing their unity on the church, the Holy
Spirit is still working for the unity of the church, not the less for the fact
that some of the established institutional structures are showing cracks.

St. Gregory of Nazianzus was not entirely wrong when he wrote,
somewhat facetiously, that he never saw any church Council come to any
good end, nor turn out to be a solution of evils. "On the contrary," he
wrote, "it usually increases them. You always find there the love of contention and the love of power, which beggars description."[7]

Similarly, Hilary of Poitiers, who made an important contribution to the
development of Christology in the West (see Grillmeier, 306-13), wrote:

> Believers have always found their satisfaction in that divine utterance,
> which our ears have heard recited from the Gospel at the moment when
> that power, which is its attestation, was bestowed upon us: "Go now and
> teach all nations, baptizing them in the name of the Father and of the Son
> and of the Holy Ghost, teaching them to observe all things whatsoever I
> command to you; and lo, I am with you always even unto the end of the
> world." What element in the mystery of man's salvation is not included

---

[6]*Knik havatoy,* 5.7.

[7]*Patrologia Graeca* (PG) 37:225a, in *Documents Illustrative of the History of the Church,*
trans. B. J. Kidd (New York: Macmillan, 1938) 2:85.

in those words? What is forgotten, what left in darkness? All is full as from the divine fullness, perfect as from the divine perfection. . . .

But the errors of heretics and blasphemers force us to deal with unlawful matters, to scale perilous heights, to speak unutterable words, to trespass on forbidden ground. Faith ought in silence to fulfil the commandments, worshiping the Father, reverencing with him the Son, abounding in the Holy Ghost. But we must strain the poor resources of our language to express thoughts too great for words. The error of others compels us to err in daring to embody in human terms truths which ought to be hidden in the silent veneration of the heart.[8]

The Concern behind the Dispute

The reasons for which the conflict over Christology was carried on endlessly and often violently from the fifth century down to modern times is well known. Monophysites were afraid that the doctrine of salvation and thereby the divine purpose of the Incarnation would be vitiated and jeopardized by the "two natures" formula if this was raised to credal status. It would impair the reality and the authenticity of the oneness of the personality of the Lord Christ. Duophysites on the other hand were afraid that the "one nature" formula would endanger the reality of the manhood of Christ, his true and complete manhood, and consequently the reality of the Incarnation itself. Both fears bespeak of the anxiety of the protagonists to remain faithful to the core of the message of gospel and to the Christ of the faith. There is no doubt that it was necessary to lay equal emphasis both on the divinity and the humanity of Christ. This is necessary also today.

It has been the task of the church, and still is after so many centuries of debate and strife, to describe, as rationally and as clearly as possible, the relationship of divinity and humanity in the unity of the person of Christ. The Fathers of the fifth and later centuries undertook this task by calling to their aid, quite legitimately, the philosophy and science of their own age and using the intellectual instruments available to them, however inadequate. By employing these instruments they tried to explain and to rationalize the unity of God and man in Christ. For it goes without saying that the message of the gospel, the *kerygma* of the Christian community, has to be scrutinized, elucidated and harmonized as far as possible with the thought patterns of a given age and its intellectual environment. Otherwise, preaching would be impossible or it would fly wide of its mark. The-

---

[8]*De Trinitate*, 2.1,2, J. S. McArther, trans., *Chalcedon* (London: SPCK, XXXX) 10; and see *The Nicene and Post-Nicene Fathers*, 2nd series, 9:52a.

ology will aways need the services of its handmaiden, philosophy. Her services have been indispensable in the past, they are indispensable now, and they will always be so. But this does not mean that it was legitimate for theologians and churchmen to fight over the handmaiden herself, using violent means against their rivals, through the coercive power of secular authorities, as was done here and there from the time of Constantine down to the end of the period of the Inquisition. Nor does it mean that the church or churches should use their canonical punitive powers to impose uniformity in theology, as distinct from what can be designated as the constant of the deposit of the faith.

History has shown that while the debates over Christology have been instructive, they have not produced the consensus which was their purpose. Yet the fears of either side have been proven to be without foundation. For the Christ worshiped in monophysite churches is not different from the Christ worshiped in duophysite churches. For both sides Christ has been the same, the one Son of God, Lord and Savior, God and man, perfect in both respects. This shows that in reality the opponents themselves were not as far apart in their Christology as it appeared on the surface. They struggled with terms which were ambiguous. Even the battle cry of monophysites may be explained in a manner different from the one in which it is usually understood. It may be taken to mean, for example, "One nature of the Word of God, which nature became incarnate," the implication being that while the *Logos* had his one nature, by being incarnate the one *Logos* became the Christ in two natures.[9]

Simply stated, monophysites were against the concept of Christ operating, as it were, under dual control, his divinity and his humanity acting separately or in turn. This would endanger the doctrine of salvation. All they tried to do was to avoid this danger. Yet it was recognized on all sides that Christ left a double-sided impression on his contemporaries and on the reader of the Gospels. He was *contemplated* in two natures. But in order to contemplate (*theorein*) him in two, he had to be one in the underlying reality of his person, his *hypostasis*. Gregory of Nyssa said: "The contemplation (*theoria*) of the respective properties of the flesh and of the Godhead remains without confusion so long as each of these is contemplated by itself (*ep' eauton*)."[10]

---

[9]Cf. *The Disputation of Nerses IV and Theorian*, PG 133:119ff. See also Grillmeier, *Christ*, 489, and J. Lebon, *Le monophysisme sévérien* (Louvain: J. van Linthout, 1909) 308.

[10]*Against Eunomius* 5.5, as in Robert Victor Sellers, *Two Ancient Christologies* (London: SPCK, 1940, 1954) 77; and see *The Nicene and Post-Nicene Fathers*, 2nd series, 5:180b.

It is readily seen, however, that the notion of split personality was entertained by nobody, not even by Nestorians. As to Pope Leo's teaching, if it is taken simply as an unsophisticated effort to demonstrate or uphold that Christ was both God, true and perfect, and man, true and perfect, then there would not be much difficulty in agreeing with him, as did the eastern bishops in Chalcedon. In fact, there are instances where monophysite writers use similar language, taking a middle road, so to speak. For example, Catholicos Nerses IV, whom I have already mentioned, and who always was on good terms with the Syrians theologically speaking, and who was a monophysite, writes:

> Sometimes as God he performs the acts that are proper to God and sometimes as man the acts that are proper to man. And we believe that it is the same as to the energy, where the divine and the human are in unity.[11]
> . . . Not one dead and one living, according to those who divide, but that the one and the same person (personality) and the one Christ suffered and died in the mortal body, that was from us, and was alive and immortal and life-giving in his Godhead, that was from the Father.[12]

It appears, therefore, that monophysites and duophysites alike skirted each other's central position on which they could not disagree and carried on their fight in the periphery. In other words, while both agreed on the substance of the teaching of the church, on the kerygmatic data, yet they violently disagreed on the way in which that teaching could be rationalized through philosophical propositions. What Vatican II states in this respect is noteworthy. It speaks of the legitimacy of the variety and differences in theological expressions of doctrine, of different methods and approaches in the investigations of revealed truth, and in understanding and proclaiming divine things; it acknowledges the complementariness of various theological formulations.[13] This is not different from what the Armenian Catholicos Nerses IV had said in the seventies of the twelfth century.

No one with an historical perspective could underrate or underestimate the vital importance of the problem with which the church and her leaders grappled for more than two hundred years from the Council of Nicea to the Fifth Council of 553. At stake was the doctrine of the divinity and humanity of Christ, and consequently the doctrine of Christian salvation, the very core of the deposit of the faith. But the tragedy was that the weapons cho-

---

[11]Nerses IV, "Encyclical," 127.

[12]Ibid., 92.

[13]Vatican II, "Decree on Ecumenism," no. 17.

sen and the methods used were not compatible with the ends that were sought. Words and phrases were endlessly tortured by innumerable writers and debaters, great and small, and more often than not they were used as shibboleths to ferret out adversaries and strike them down.

If the violent controversies over the nature problem had not been tied up with serious social and political conflicts, if the problem had been left to ride and take its course, if emperors and secular potentates had not made the faith a matter of legislation, the disputes would have exhausted their momentum with the passing of the protagonists from the scene and they would have been settled in time, as was the case with a multitude of other speculative excursions into the philosophical implications of Christian beliefs.

Dialogue in New Language

The intellectual frame of reference of our age has undergone a radical change. We cannot but make the effort to understand and to communicate the original *kerygma* of the church read in the gospel with reference to our own patterns of thought. On the other hand we have to take as our point of departure the fundamental dogmatic propositions that underpin the deposit of the faith. It is of course not easy to draw a boundary line between dogma and theologoumena. Yet such a boundary can always tentatively be drawn, as I have already remarked, even though it will have to be a shifting one from age to age, and even from place to place. It is the work of the Holy Spirit to show us where we should draw the line.

Because of the established notion that belief could and should be a matter for legislation by established authorities, formal propositions declaring credal statements acquired undue importance during the Byzantine period and even later, beginning with the council of Nicea. Overlooked was the fact that propositions that are fashioned as vessels for the truths of the faith are not equal to the function assigned to them. They are only compromises between the Holy Spirit and the spirit of this world (1 Cor. 2:1-5, 12) or the elements of this world (Col. 2:20). Truth is never imprisoned in static verbal forms. Furthermore, propositions are liable to abuse, because people are tempted to use them as ideological tools. The original significance of a credal proposition is subject to change with the change of patterns of thought and speech. "They shall wax old as doth a garment . . . and they shall be changed" (Heb. 1:12), so they will have to be constantly renewed. The church should welcome this renewal, because Christ and the Holy Spirit are alive and are with the church always. Formulations of beliefs constitute in reality responses to the world in an ongoing debate. The "Spirit of truth" lives in the whole church which sometimes cannot be telescoped into bishops or councils. This is not an advocacy of relativism or Protestant liberalism; we assume and take for granted the fundamental agreement between the churches to which we belong. So long as our ecclesiology is firm and sound it will be a strong bulwark, and the recognition of the limitation of the formulation of Christian truths will not jeopardize the mission of the church.

The church and churches have already long ceased to be obsessed with such philosophical terms as *ousia, physis, hypostasis,* and *prosopon* and other similar terms and ideas in her efforts to communicate the truth of Christ to the world. These terms have done their work and have now gone to their rest. They belonged to a world where the flat earth was the center of the universe, with a fluid dome above it, where everything was composed of earth, fire, water, and air, and everything was either in rest or in movement in relation to a stationary world. Soul was a substance that was extracted from the body at the time of death. Ancient Christologians in discussing the person of Christ analyzed his personality by reducing it into its component elements and found "the Logos assuming a reality with no intrinsic [*ontic*] relation to the person assuming it."[14] Against this, Karl Rahner's concept of the Incarnation is highly instructive:

> The Incarnation is rightly envisaged only if Christ's humanity is not only, ultimately speaking, a merely extrinsic instrument by which a God who remains invisible makes himself known, but is rather precisely what God Himself becomes (though remaining God) when he exteriorizes Himself into the dimension of what is other than Himself, of the non-divine. Even if it is obvious that God could create the world without the incarnation, it is nevertheless compatible with that statement that the possibility of creation has its ground in the radical possibility of God's self-exteriorization. In that case, however, the ultimate definition of man is that he is other than Himself; man is the potential brother of Christ.[15]

If Cyril of Alexandria were living today and teaching in some university, he would not have written differently, I believe. Because "the dead end of the Christological argument is whether matter or created things constitute an eternal absolute, coexistent with God, or whether they are a creation, a *doing* of God, bringing the world into existence out of himself and descending, entering and working in the realm of forms."[16]

---

[14]Karl Rahner, ed., *Sacramentum mundi,* 6 vols. (New York: Herder and Herder, 1968) 3:370.

[15]Ibid.

[16]Tiran Nersoyan, *The Christological Position of the Armenian Church* (Jerusalem: Jerusalem Patriarchate Press, 1957) 10.

It must be recognized that the form of the message of the gospel is determined by its content, which is constant in its appeal and power. Linguistic forms to communicate the content to succeeding generations constitute the point of contact between the faith and the world. Consequently with the changing of the world the point at which the power of the faith touches the world also has to change. "The message of the Gospel which was given in the past must be made accessible to the various 'universes of discourse' in terms of the world image available to their various languages."[17] The terms and concepts employed by the ancients to explain and formulate the mystery of the Incarnation had relevance and belonged to the thought patterns of their own times. The zeal shown by them in fighting their battles is understandable, no doubt, and sometimes elicits our admiration. But our ways of thinking are different. The old terms have lost their relevance to our times. We need new ways of understanding the mystery of the Incarnation. In the matter of Christology we have to have a new approach to the problem. We have to abandon the inquiry into the mode of juxtaposition of natures in Christ. Christ is the representation of the invisible God, of the eternal Almighty. He is the man in the first century and in all centuries. The core of Christology was stated by Christ himself: "I and the Father are one." He who saw me saw the Father."

Not that agreeing on new fixed formulations and definitions would solve the problem, but that we should agree to come together for an ongoing dialogue, on the basis of theological pluralism, using an expression of Karl Rahner. It is not likely that our dialogue will engender the kind of contention and division which we have inherited from the past. So the exigency of our time appears to be to leave the Councils and their definitions where they are, stop making them shibboleths for the determination of the orthodoxy or otherwise of one side or the other, and try to arrive at a new consensus on problems that the world is thrusting at us.

---

[17]Franz Mayr, in *Sacramentum mundi*, 3:274.

The Understanding
of the Christological Definitions of Both
(Oriental Orthodox and Roman Catholic)
Traditions in the Light
of the Post-Chalcedonian Theology
(Analysis of Terminologies
in a Conceptual Framework)

Aloys Grillmeier

In the times immediately after the Council of Chalcedon the question to be discussed here was not of particular urgency for the majority of oriental and occidental bishops. This is significant for the interpretation of the terms "concept" and "formula" not only in 451 at the Council proper but also in the early post-Chalcedonian period as well as in our own times. Whenever "Chalcedon" is mentioned today the theologian immediately thinks of the "one *hypostasis* in two natures." For him Chalcedon has become a "formula," a "concept." At the time of Chalcedon itself and in the early phases of the Chalcedonian discussion the Christological *kerygma* was clearly in the foreground. It was only because of the ensuing debate that the "concept," the "word," and the "formula" were given such a prominent place. This process, however, must not be regarded as intrinsically unconnected. Each conciliary pronouncement requires reflection, a reverting to the concept and its theological scientific implications. In the end, however, this theological reflection is to lead back to, and serve, the *kerygma* and the living faith of the church.

Therefore, no distinction is to be made here between *kerygma* and reflection. We shall first of all discuss the kerygmatic view and importance of Chalcedon, then go on to theological reflection and its significance for the Christological *kerygma*.

Chalcedon from the Kerygmatic Point of View

Codex Encyclius

We start out from an interesting document, or rather a collection of documents dealing with the Council of Chalcedon and going back to the years 457-459. This collection, the so-called *Codex Encyclius* or *ta Enkyklia,* was compiled under the auspices of the emperor Leo I on the occasion of the church revolt in Alexandria in the spring of 457.[1] After the emperor Marcian's death, Timothy Aelurus seized the see of Alexandria to replace Proterius, who was brutally murdered. A delegation of the new patriarch then went to the imperial court at Constantinople in order to obtain from the emperor Leo I (457-474) the recognition of Timothy and the convocation of an anticouncil to repudiate the synod of Chalcedon.

In order to come to a decision on these two questions—the legitimacy of Timothy's succession and the revision of the Council of Chalcedon— the emperor Leo sent a *sacra* to the metropolitans and some of the foremost monks in the East as well as to Pope Leo I (440-461) in Rome.[2] The metropolitans were to convene their suffragans with all haste and to let Constantinople have their concerted opinion on the subject. Altogether 34 answers signed by about 280 bishops and monks, respectively, are extant. According to Photius (Bibliotheca cod. 229 [Ephraem of Antiochia]), 470 bishops and monks are said to have signed the document.[3] This would be in line with the concluding remark made by the translator of the *Codex Encyclius* (CE): "Expliciunt Epistulae Encycliades id est totius Orbis Episcoporum Numero Quingentorum Feliciter."[4] According to the patriarch

---

[1]See Evagrius, *Hist. Eccl.* 2.9; Evagrius Scholasticus, *Ecclesiastical History,* J. Bidez and L. Parmentier, eds. (Amsterdam: Adolf M. Hakkert, 1964) 59, 25. The letters of the Codex Encyclius are extant—though unfortunately not in their entirety—in a Latin translation in the *Collectio Sangermanensis,* E. Schwartz, ed., in *Acta Conciliorum Oecumenicorum* (= ACO) 2/5:9-98, nr. V-XLVII. See Th. Schnitzler, *Im Kampfe um Chalcedon. Geschichte und inhalt des Codex Encyclius von 458, Annal. Greg. 16,* Rome, 1938).

[2]See the title in CE nr. 6: Exemplar epistulae Leonis Imp. ad Anatolium epm. Constantinopolitanum hoc modo scriptum est et aliis metropolitanis episcopis. Greek text in Evagrius, *Hist. Eccl.* 2.9; Bidez-Parmentier, 59, 26-29.

[3]Photius, Biblioth. cod. 229: *Patrologia Graeca* (= PG) 103:988D-989A; René Henry, ed., *Photius,* Bibliothèque T. 4 (Paris: Société de edition les Belleslettres, 1965) 142. In both editions some misunderstandings are to be found.

[4]ACO 2/5:98. The estimate of approximately "500" is fairly close to the figure given by Photius in cod. 299. Mention of this is made here to show that in the CE a great number of Oriental bishops are covered. In addition there is the answer of Pope Leo, who represents the West (ep. 165).

Eulogius of Alexandria (580-607) the number of undersigned bishops was an even 1,600.[5] "Among them were the great Symeon who as a stylite set a forceful example of the angelic, otherworldly life, as well as Baradatos and others who aspired to the same heights of perfection."[6]

Our question now is: What does this CE tell us about the Christological perception of the bishops, about their understanding of the definition of Chalcedon? To what extent were they able to realize what Chalcedon was to mean in the history of the Christological dogma? How did they see the main "formula" of the one *hypostasis* in two natures? Bishop Euippos (CE 40) very aptly illustrates the two possible approaches to a document of the faith—"following the fishermen or following Aristotle."[7] This is to say that Chalcedon may be considered either from the purely kerygmatic point of view or from the perspective of philosophically schooled reflection. By far the larger part of the letters of the CE remain on the *kerygmatic* level in the assessment of the Council and either want to bring the dogmatic document of 451 down to this level or confess to their own alienation from this text and classify it accordingly. Only a few bishops are able to go beyond the kerygmatic evaluation of the dogmatic formula and to grasp the meaning of the *terminological* and *theological-historical* innovation accomplished by Chalcedon. This basically kerygmatic attitude of the bishops of the CE is highly commendable. It is not "concepts" (*hypostasis, physis*) which come first but the baptismal symbol and baptismal catechesis—in short, the baptismal creed. This attitude is so pronounced that several bishops refuse to accept Chalcedon as a basis for baptismal catechesis, although they recognize the doctrinal substance of the Council.

The baptismal symbol they have in mind is the symbol of Nicea (325). This Nicean symbol is the universal yardstick:

> We adhere to and uphold the faith to which we were not only born and with which we pray to come before the awe-inspiring presence of God, but in which we were also baptized and with which we, who were called to the episcopate through no merit of our own, fill those upon whom the grace of faith is bestowed.[8]

---

[5]See Photius, Bibl. cod. 230; PG 103:1077C; Henry, *Photius*, 5.55.

[6]Ibid. These three monks are already mentioned in Photius, *Bibl.* cod. 228; compare Henry, *Photius*, 123, who gives a completely misleading commentary.

[7]CE 40; ACO 2/5:84.2-3: "haec ergo breviter piscatorie et non Aristotelice suggessimus."

[8]CE 45; ibid., 90.24-27.

This baptismal creed is founded on the teachings of the evangelists and the apostles, but was formulated in Nicea. It was there that the bishops gave a complete definition of the apostolic religion in keeping with the apostolic spirit, thus preserving the faith of the church. The other synods, including Chalcedon, had to be convened to *ward off* the newly (after Nicea) developing heresies, and they decreed only one thing: that this (Nicene) creed be preserved in its entirety.[9] The bishops of Paphlagonia underline their own solidarity with the "believers" on the basis of this evangelical-apostolic-Nicene creed,[10] which is upheld by subsequent councils. In fact, whoever does not recognize these councils and especially Chalcedon, himself destroys the basis of the traditional faith. However, because baptismal catechesis and liturgy are so inseparably bound up with the symbolum (Nicaenum) the formula of Chalcedon cannot—as we have already seen—be used in the *baptismal catechesis* itself.[11] Only the "bishops" are to concern themselves with it and then above all in the fight against heretics. Such a definite pastoral attitude is interesting. It pervades more or less the entire CE. This clearly contradicts the common generalization that Chalcedon had caused the church to surrender to hellenistic formulas and an abstract theology.

It is interesting to note how the relationship between Chalcedon and Nicea is more closely defined in this connection. A group of bishops regards Chalcedon as "*interpretatio*" of Nicea.[12] The Council is the "*revelatio*" of the intention of the Nicean Council, as is pointed out by CE 25, not without a specific reference to the preservative function of Chalcedon.[13] The very verbosity of this Council, so offensive to some bishops, has the sole purpose of offering a "broader interpretation" of the symbol of Nicea, an opinion also held by the renowned bishop Basil of Seleucia.[14] As seen from the modern point of view the word "interpretatio" (*hermêneia*!) already indicates the problem of, and even points the way to, the definition of the mutual relationship of different doctrinal formulas. In

---

[9]Ibid., 90.27-39.

[10]CE 42:86.28-36.

[11]See CE 31, 36.

[12]CE 14: ACO 2/5:27.4-9; CE 13 and in particular CE 33:65.9-16.

[13]CE 25; ACO 2/5:43.24-26, 31-33.

[14]CE 27; ACO 2/5:47.36-37; CE 47:96.11-14: "et licet plurimis sermonibus extendatur expositio fidei catholicae Calchedone celebrata, tamen ad illas respicit quarum in praecedentibus probatur fecisse memoriam et ueluti paucarum illiarum est interpretatio syllabarum. naturam docentes eundemque de part."

conformity with Basil the Council wants to guarantee a proper *understanding* of the symbol of Nicea. Therefore it became necessary to adapt the old symbol of the fourth century to the situation of the fifth century. However, Basil does not venture to go into the problem of the new terminology used in the definition of the Incarnation, nor does he attempt to interpret the contribution of Chalcedon to Christology in terms of the new dogmatic formula. Thus his *"interpretatio latior"* promises more than it actually keeps.

A perusal of the letters of the CE, moreover, shows that there is as yet little awareness of the "newness" of the terminology used in the definition of Chalcedon. In the entire CE only four or five letters hint at this definition. Basil, the metropolitan of Antiochia, together with the bishops of the *prima Syria,* gives a rather detailed quotation of the text, probably in mind of the Antiochene part in the formulary of union of 433 (see Cyril's Laetentur letter) and in the Chalcedonian definition—a part which, however, would bear closer investigation.[15] But even Basil says little about the two-nature formula so popular with the Antiocheans. The bishops give a paraphrase of the definition containing such important phrases from the original as *unus idemque* and the double *consubstantialis.* They use the word *"natura"* without, however, mentioning the literal version *in duabus naturis.* Similarly, they fail to speak of the "one *hypostasis"* or the "one *prosopon,"* just as they leave out the "perfect in Godhead" and "perfect in Manhood." They do not feel compelled to justify or interpret, for instance, the two-nature formula as opposed to the one-nature formula: for them there is no "terminological" problem. They are satisfied with emphasizing the kerygmatic aspect of "truths," and in doing so refer back to Nicea and to Constantinople 381. In the opinion of these Fathers the main statements of these Councils concern the consubstantiality and equality (*homoousion*) of the Son with the Father and the true Incarnation. Chalcedon reaffirms these cardinal tenets of the Nicene creed: to those who wrongly attribute to the divine nature of the Only-Begotten the ability to suffer, the Chalcedonian fathers reply that the divine substance is incon-

---

[15]CE 20; ACO 2/5:33.37, 34, 7: " . . . unum eundemque filium et secundum diuinam et secundum humanam naturam docentes eundemque de patre secundum diuinitatem, eundem de matre secundum humanitatem, tamquam deum, impassibilem, tamquam hominem passibilem, eundem secundem quod sumptum est de nobis, consubstantialem nobis, eundem secundum natiutatem de patre, consbustantialem genitori et hoc quod fuit ante saecula, natura manifestantem et quod in se adsumpsit, nouissimis diebus ueritate seruantem, non alium et alium per haec denuntiantes, sed eundem filium dominum et deum et quaecumque de eo dicuntur, conpetenter glorificantes."

vertible and unchangeable; to those who refuse to accept the true humanity of the Only-Begotten they answer in terms of the same symbol by interpreting the text: "As far as the Incarnation and the assumption of humanity are concerned it (the *symbolum* of Nicea) means to stress no less than the acceptance and union of our nature (with the only-begotten Son of the Father)."[16]

The relation of the formula of Chalcedon to the *kerygma* and the *symbolum* as a basis of baptismal catechesis is best expressed in the letter of the bishop Epiphanius of Perge:

> The unity of the two natures or substances in the one Christ is explained by many holy and famous fathers who have lived among us . . . (however, because the average believer takes exception to the two-nature formula, Pope Leo should declare that his letter to Flavian and the Chalcedonian definition were no "*symbolum*" but rather a repudiation of the heretics), as is the phrase of the "two natures" which was coined by these same fathers but might for him (the average believer) be difficult to understand (a source of doubt) since it was put forward by the father (Pope Leo) on account of those who deny the true Incarnation of God the Word; this should be expressed more clearly in this letter, though without prejudice to the holy synod. Instead of speaking of the "inconfused unity of two natures" we might just as well say "in two natures." But even when we talk of the "one nature of the Word," adding the word "Incarnate," we mean the same thing though putting it more elegantly. For we find that holy fathers in the realm of your piety have frequently pointed out what this means.[17]

The ecumenical significance of this text is obvious. It is the first post-Chalcedonian text of its kind for which the way had been paved by Cyril of Alexandria, Flavian of Constantinople, and Basil of Seleucia. Epiphanius thus takes up the Chalcedonian two-nature doctrine and accepts it as the legitimate interpretation of the tradition of the *oikonomia Christi,* though with certain reservations as to its valutation. He sees the function of this

---

[16]CE 20; ACO 2/5:33.35-37.

[17]CE 31; ACO 2/5:59.7-24: "duarum namque naturarum siue substantiarum unitatem in uno Christo declaratam inuenimus a plurimis apud nos consistentibus sanctis et gloriosissimis partibus . . . simul et illud quod ab eis est dictum in duabus naturis, quod forte eis dubium esse dinoscitur, dum a parte prolatum sit propter eos qui ueram dei uerbi incarnationem negant, his scilicet semonibus apertius indicatum, ita tamen ut in nullo sanctae synodi fiat iniuria, nihil enim differet siue duarum naturarum unitas inconfusa dicatur siue ex duabus eodem modo referatur. sed neque si una dicatur uerbi natura, inferatur autem incarnata, aliud quod significate, sed idem honestiori sermone declarat; nam et inuenimus saepius hoc dixisse sanctos patres apud uestrae pietatis imperium quod significat."

formula vis-à-vis Eutyches' denial of the true humanity of Christ. He points out, however, that the phrases "inconfused unity of two natures" or "in two natures" really mean the same; he considers the *mia-physis* formula orthodox. Nevertheless the structure and terminology of the Chalcedonian definition are not "analyzed"—the bishops remain on the kerygmatic level. There is hardly any awareness of the terminological "novitas" of Chalcedon.

Positive Contributions

And yet this kerygmatic view of Christology, which is based on the Nicene symbol and is, or may be, found in the Chalcedonian definition as well, does contribute to the understanding of the Chalcedonian concepts of *hypostasis* and *physis*. We should like to discuss this contribution before going into the development of post-Chalcedonian reflection.

The contribution of the Chalcedonian definition towards the better understanding of its new terminology consists in "intuition" and in a number of "paraphrasing" expressions which lay no claim to philosophical eminence.

Theological intuition. The strong emphasis on, or the stipulation of the agreement of the Council of Chalcedon with Nicea, is very often combined with a reference to the basic Nicean doctrine of the Incarnation—in arguments against both Nestorius and Eutyches. It is claimed that the refutation of Nestorianism as well as Eutychianism is contained in this doctrine, which says: the fact of the Incarnation or assumption of humanity by the one and true Son of the Father is asserted, the Son begotten from the Father, only-begotten that is, from the substance of the Father, God from God, light from light, true God from true God, begotten not made, of one substance with the Father (*homoousion*). In the symbol of Nicea the fathers therefore find expressed the unity of the subject in Christ as well as the truth of Godhead and manhood in the one Christ.

It is this very "intuition" of the one Son of God in true Godhead and true manhood which also guides the Council of Chalcedon. After all, the creed of Nicea comes first among the conciliar documents. The Council thus emerges as intending nothing else but an "*interpretatio*" of this symbol, though with a clarity that leaves no room for a denial of the manhood of Christ. By then asserting the *mia hypostasis* and the *hen prosopon* in Christ while maintaining the duality of the natures, Chalcedon in a conceptual language expresses what before the Nicenum had represented as the outline of a descending Christology.

Paraphrasing expressions. To a certain extent the meaning of "one *hypostasis* in two natures" is made unmistakably clear in a well-balanced formula which stands at the beginning of the actual Chalcedonian definition:

eundem perfectum in deitate, eundem perfectum in humanitate,
Deum vere et hominem vere eundem ex anima rationali et corpore,
consubstantialem Patri secundum deitatem
et consubstantialem nobis eundem secundum humanitatem. . . .[18]

(The Same perfect in Godhead, the Same perfect in Manhood,
Truly God and truly man,
   the Same consisting of a rational soul and body;
homoousios with the Father as to his Godhead,
and the Same homoousios with us as to his manhood. . . .)

The significance of the first two lines is made clear only by a reference to
the Symbolum Unionis of 433 and Flavian of Constantinople's "*professio
fidei*" of 12 November 448. Flavian had taken over the following formula
from Cyril's Laetentur letter:

Dominus noster Iesus Christus, filius dei unigenitus,
Deus perfectus et homo perfectus ex anima rationali et corpore.

The "Antiochene tendency" of this formulation was later offset by
Flavian in a symbol written in the spring of 449 on the order of the emperor. In it he says: We announce Christ

Deum perfectum et eundem hominem perfectum in assumptione
animae rationalis et corporis.[19]

It is quite obvious that in the second formula Flavian gives much clearer
expression to the unity of the subject in Christ than in the first. In fact, there
is a difference between the *coordinating* "perfect God and perfect Man
consisting of a rational soul and a body" (as found in the formulary of union
of 433) and the emphasis on the unity in Christ at the very beginning "*one
and the same* perfect in Godhead and perfect in Manhood"; an emphasis
so skillfully achieved by Cyril himself when he gave an interpretation of
the "*symbolum unionis*" in his Laetentur letter.[20] The Council of Chalcedon in taking up the text of the "*symbolum unionis*" of 433 follows this
version of Cyril's. In this context there is no need to conceal the fact that
it was Cyril's main concern in his arguments against Nestorius to stress the

---

[18]*Conciliorum Oecumenicorum Decreta* (= DOC) (Bologna: Instituto per le scienze re-
ligiose Bologna, 1973) 86.

[19]ACO 2/1.1.114:4-5; cf. Th. Săgi-Bunić, "*Deus Perfectus et Homo Perfectus*" a con-
cilio Ephesino (a.431) ad Chalcedonense (a.451) (Rome: Herder, 1965) 182.

[20]Text in DOC, 72; ACO 2/1.1.110:4-5.

unity in Christ, whereas the Council of Chalcedon in refuting Eutyches aimed above all at emphasizing the perfection in Godhead and manhood.

The Council furthermore underlines this double perfection of Christ in Godhead and manhood in an antithesis which has a history of its own:[21] Christ is *"consubstantialis Patri, consubstantialis matri!"* The reason for my mentioning this is that this formula, too, offers an "ecumenical possibility" of reconciling the Chalcedonian and the monophysitic-post-Chalcedonian understanding of Christ. None other than Timothy Aelurus used the special theological theme of Christ's double consubstantiality to combat the radical Eutychians. As far as I can see, it was he who compiled a florilegium of the fathers dealing specifically with this problem of Christ's double consubstantiality in his first letter to the city of Constantinople.[22] Apollinaris of Laodicea was the first to raise the question of the double *homoousion* in Christ in a Christological context. Although subsequently his terminology was retained, the Apollinarian content was eliminated. Therefore it is possible for Timothy to make frequent reference to the fourth century in his florilegium; however, slight text corrections are not unusual and use is made of the so-called Apollinarian forgeries as well as of other unauthentic texts. Timothy lays even greater emphasis on this double consubstantiality of Christ with man than does Leo I. If Pope Leo had known all this he would have rejoiced over the fact that Eutychianism was by no means rampant in Alexandria. Timothy's letters bear ample witness to his determined struggle against the radical Eutychians in Constantinople and Alexandria. In the end this double *homoousion* of Christ and the Chalcedonian two-nature formula mean exactly the same. Thus there was basically agreement as far as the content of these formulas was concerned, but terminology remained a divisive factor.

Let us now briefly summarize the conclusions to be drawn from this first part of the paper:

1. In the first decades after Chalcedon even its advocates were hardly aware of the fact that the Council had introduced a new terminology by distinguishing between *hypostasis* and *physis. The actual Chalcedonian "formula" was not the central issue.* What was intended was the clear

---

[21]On the history and meaning of the double "homoousios" cf. M. Wiles, "Homoousios Hemin" in *Journal of Theological Studies* 16 (1965) 454-65; and, above all, B. Studer, "Consubstantialis Patri. Consubstantialis Matri. Un Antithèse Christologique chez Léon le Grand," in *Rev. Et.* (18 August 1972): 87-115.

[22]Syrian and English in R. Y. Ebied and L. R. Wickham, "A Collection of Unpublished Syriac letters of Timothy Aelurus," in *Journal of Theological Studies,* n.s. 21 (1970): 321-69. Letter to the people of Constantinople, 351-57.

and unmistakable assertion of the reality of Godhead and manhood in the one Christ. That this had been achieved in the Council was common knowledge throughout the world. Therefore most of the bishops in the East and even more so in the West did not concern themselves with the actual "formula." *Physis* is nothing but reality—truth—as the emperor Marcian said after Chalcedon.[23]

2. Whoever did understand this Chalcedonian formula "Christ one *hypostasis* in two natures" could resort to the *paraphrasing* passages contained in the conciliar definition. In the phrase "One and the Same Son, the Same perfect in Godhead, the Same perfect in Manhood, consubstantial with God and consubstantial with us," the same idea comes to expression as in the abstract conceptual formula of the one *hypostasis* in two natures. Those who were able to understand the paraphrasing passages should conceivably have been ready to tolerate or accept the more abstract formula. Unfortunately, this similarity was as little recognized as was the fact that Timothy was engaged in a fierce struggle with the radical Eutychians.

3. The general concentration on the more limited and abstract Chalcedonian formula was a consequence of the arguments brought forth by Timothy in his writings against the Council of Chalcedon. The theologians became increasingly involved in conceptual analyses while running the risk of paying too little attention to the *kerygma* of Christ.

We shall now try to briefly sum up the important results of this struggle for concepts, and to find out how far the understanding of the *oikonomia* of the Incarnation of God in Christ has actually been furthered.

The Formula of Chalcedon ''Aristotelice''?

It is impossible in the scope of this short paper to follow all the meanderings of theological reflection in the course of the struggle over Chalcedon from the Henoticon of the emperor Zeno (474/5 and 476-491) to the emperor Justinian (527-565), to the controversy over one will or two wills in Christ in the seventh century, to the scholastic theology in the West and finally to the neoscholasticism of the twentieth century. Before discussing some of the results of this theological reflection we must point out that it

---

[23]Marcian, aug., ad Archimandr. et Monach, ACO 2/5:6.2-6 (cf. Pulcheria, ibid., 7-8): "proinde duas naturas audientes perturbatas vestras animas fuisse docuistis vluti quadam novitate auribus vestris inlata quapropter scitote quia vobis quidem harum rerum examinationmen facere non congruit, dum subtilitatem huius rei intellegere nequeatis, nos autem patrum suscipientes doctrinas naturam intellegimus veritatem."

must always serve the *kerygma* of the church and has to show above all how seriously we must take our Redeemer, Jesus Christ.

The Origin of the Reflection

From the formula of Chalcedon, "Jesus Christ one *hypostasis* in two natures," it may be seen that the Council was concerned with determining the levels of unity and distinctness in Christ. The differentiation between *hypostasis* and *physis* developed out of this problem. As a matter of fact it was not devised by the Council itself but was part of an already existing tradition. Proclus of Constantinople († 446) had already paved the way.[24] Whereas Cyril of Alexandria uses *hypostasis* and *physis* synonymously, the terms are now differentiated. What is the purpose of this distinction?

Perhaps the meaning of this differentiation is best understood on the basis of the work of Gregory of Nazianzus. The interpretation of the trinitarian formula of the "three *hypostases* in one nature" already required a definition of *hypostasis* as opposed to essence and nature (*ousia* and *physis*). *Hypostasis* and *physis* had to be so defined as to fit both the doctrine of the Trinity and the Christological dogma. Gregory of Nazianzus succeeds in making clear the purpose of this differentiation by simple linguistic means: in the one God Father-Son-Holy Spirit there is an *"allos kai allos kai allos"* rather than an *"allo kai allo kai allo."* "For the Three are one and the same in the Godhead" (*Patrologia Graeca* [= PG] 37:180AB). In other words, the distinction in the trinitarian God does not lie on the level of the "what" or the "nature" (neuter *"allo"*), but on the level of the "subject" or the "bearer" of the nature (masculine *"allos"* kai *allos*). Gregory applies this to Christ: according to him there is an *allo kai allo* in Christ but Christ is not *allos kai allos*. In Chalcedonian terms this would mean that there is "one *hypostasis*" in Christ, though in the double *allo* of the two *physeis*.

Thus the question for the *hypostasis* has become a question for the subject or the ultimate bearer of a nature, for the *"quis"*; the question for the *physis,* on the other hand, is the question for the *"quid"*, for the being what, the essence. Clear as the purpose of the Chalcedonian distinction seems to be, it was yet difficult to define it rationally in a logical conceptual or ontological analysis. The definition of "person" or *hypostasis* as opposed to "nature" took a long time to come forth. It did not succeed the very first time it was formulated. Since the days of Gregory of Nyssa this effort to achieve an ontological analysis of *hypostasis* and *physis* had to labor under

---

[24]See F. J. Leroy, "L'homiletique de Proclus de Constantinople. Tradition manuscrite, Inedites, Etudes Connexes" (Studi et Testi 247) (Città del Vaticano, 1967).

certain difficulties which were to be felt for a long time to come. Here again it was seen that an intuition based on the *kerygma* of the church and couched in simple language may often hardly be emulated in a process of rational reflection. Or, in other words: the use of the formula "one *hypostasis* in two natures" to give expression to the doctrine that the one Son of the Father has assumed a true and complete human nature requires sustained effort.

For the question is: What is the purpose of such a formula? What does it accomplish? Has not Chalcedon in the course of time acquired a new meaning through the close attention given to the concept? Were the fathers of 451 at all aware of the meaning of their concepts? Is not their opinion of the unity and distinctness in Christ better and more clearly expressed in their interpretations of the mystery of the Incarnation than in these philosophical-sounding concepts which are yet not defined in greater detail?

Important Steps toward a Solution

First definition of hypostasis. This definition is given by Gregory of Nyssa in the treatise wrongly attributed to St. Basil as letter 38 (PG 32:325-340). In the meantime, research has proved Gregory's authorship. Gregory tries to support the Christian creed of the one God as Father, Son, and Spirit by going into the philosophical and terminological aspects of *hypostasis* and *ousia*. Unlike Boethius later on, Gregory in doing so sets forth from the analysis of the *ens physicum concretum*. His arguments are ontological rather than logical. Since the results he obtained were to affect the Chalcedonian-post-Chalcedonian period (Nestorius, Leontius of Byzantium), we would like to give a brief outline.

First of all, *an ens physicum concretum* has "indefinite substance" (*ousia hyle*)—mere *hypokeimenon,* pure matter which has to be endowed with a determination. This *ousia hyle* is then imprinted with a "general character" (*koine poiotes,* "humanity") and finally concretized in the "individual character" (*idia poiotes*). The result is the "individual" or *hypostasis.* Hence the *hypostasis* becomes what it is through the addition of individual attributes to the "general substance."

Gregory makes use of this philosophical analysis in working out the distinction between Father, Son, and Holy Spirit within the one Godhead. The divine *hypostasis* is established through the individual attributes which differentiate the Father in God from the Son and the Spirit (PG 32:328C, 333B-336A). An example is the one sun and the many-colored rainbow. Gregory of Nyssa also applies his analysis of *hypostasis* and *ousia* to Christology. However, in doing so he already becomes aware of the shortcomings of his speculative proposition. In order to avoid having to accede a second *hypostasis* to Christ's manhood, Gregory contends that the humanity of Christ lacks any "individual human" attributes. According to Gregory such attributes are only due to the exalted Christ and are then divine:

> The first gift of the human nature, which the omnipotent Godhead has assumed . . . similar to a drop of vinegar in the boundless ocean, is contained in the Godhead, but not in its individual attributes. There would, after all, be two Sons if in the unspeakable Godhead of the Son there were a distinct nature characterized by its individual attributes so that *the one* (the human nature of Jesus) would be weak or small or corruptible or temporary, whereas *the other* (the divine nature of Jesus) would be powerful, great, incorruptible and eternal.[25]

Although, therefore, the human nature of Christ is not simply dissolved in the union with the Godhead, it does lack the human "attributes," which have given place to the specifically divine attributes (*idiomata*). Thus the humanity of Christ is characterized by exclusively divine attributes—wisdom, power, holiness, inability to suffer. And because only these divine attributes (*idiomata*) are present, it is impossible to speak of "two Sons" in Christ. Everything in the humanity of Christ is filled with, and pervaded by, the attributes of the Word! Hence there is only one *prosopon* in Christ—from which it follows that:

> The flesh . . . mixed with the Divine, no longer remains within its limits and attributes, but is raised to the Absolute and Supreme (of the divine nature). What remains unmixed is the contemplation of the attributes of the flesh and the attributes of the Godhead insofar as either of these is contemplated in itself.[26]

Thus Gregory might confess to the formula "one *hypostasis* in Christ, but two *ousia*." However, we can see that he worked out this formula under specific philosophical conditions which were inhibitive rather than helpful. We have to recognize that Gregory perceived the problem: the unconditional acceptance of the unity and trinity in God and its expression in the trinitarian formula makes it impossible to seek unity on the same level as distinctness. Therefore *hypostasis* must be defined differently from *ousia*, substance, nature (*physis*). Gregory, however, derives this distinction from the *ens physicum concretum*. This makes it extremely difficult for him to find even a remote analogy to the relation of *hypostasis* and *ousia*

---

[25]Gregory Nyssa, *Ad Theophil. adv. Apoll.*, in *Gregorii Nysseni Opera*, ed. Werner Jaeger et al., 8 vols. (Leiden: E. J. Brill, 1952–) 3:126-27.

[26]Gregory Nyssa, *C. Eunom.*, 5.5.63, in Jaeger, ibid., 2:130.

in God. He remains on the level of a qualitative definition of *physis* through individual attributes. He has not established a real contrast between *hypostasis* and *physis*.

Hypostasis at the Council of Chalcedon. We know only very little about what the fathers of Chalcedon understood by *hypostasis* as opposed to *physis*. However, the dispute between Andrew of Samosata and Cyril of Alexandria had already shown that contemporary thought had gone beyond the basic ideas offered by Gregory of Nyssa (see *Christ in Christian Tradition* I, 427-430). Cyril's work indicates quite clearly that the Chalcedonian fathers had to lay down one thing: the *henosis* in Christ must be based not only on the moral behavior of the "man Jesus" towards the Word, but has to be a *henosis kath' hypostasin,* a substantial, essential unity. To begin with, *mia hypostasis, hen prosopon* suggest a strictly substantial union of God and man (that is a union in being). How Chalcedon understood this union "in being" of God and man cannot directly be inferred from the concept of "hypostasis." The phrase "in two natures," however, is clearly and unequivocally defined. It has been shown convincingly that the formula "in two natures" was obtained from an exact interpretation of a phrase in Cyril's Laetentur letter (*perfectus existens in deitate et perfectus idem ipse in humanitate*). Obviously, Basil of Seleucia is responsible for this as is indicated in a "statement of faith" which was formulated by him at the synod against Eutyches in 448 and which was again read in the first "actio" at the Council of Chalcedon:

> We worship the one Jesus Christ, our Lord, manifest in two natures (*en dyo physesin gnorizomenon*). The one (nature) He had in Himself before all ages as the reflection of the glory of the Father; the other (nature) He, who was born from the mother because of us men, assumed from her, uniting it *kath' hypostasin;* and perfect God (*teleios theos*) and Son of God, He was also perfect man and called Son of Man; He wanted to save us all by assuming our likeness without sin.[27]

The above-quoted passage from Cyril's Laetentur letter was interpreted by Basil of Seleucia as if it read: "One and the Same existing in perfect Godhead and in perfect manhood." Proceeding from here Basil seems to reason as follows: the "*duo perfecta*" (*teleia*) are the Godhead and the manood of Christ. However, because according to a passage in Cyril's second letter to Nestorius "Godhead" and "manhood" are nothing else but the "distinct natures" which have become one without their

---

[27]Basilius Seleuc. prof. fidei, ACO 2/1:1,117,15-28, exp. 22-28. On the following cf. Săgi-Bunić, "*Deus Perfectus,*" 188-221.

distinctness having "dissolved" or "become lost," it is certainly possible to conclude that the one Christ is one *hypostasis* "manifest in two natures." This means that although there is essential unity in Christ (*henosis kath' hypostasin*) the distinctness of the natures remains evident. It is therefore that the definition of Chalcedon includes the words "inseparable and inconfused"!

It is now easier to determine what the post-Chalcedonian theologians could or could not take for granted on the basis of the Council:

(1) *Negative.* In the phrase "Christ one *hypostasis* in two natures" *hypostasis* is not yet used in the sense later on given to *hypostasis* (person): "distinct subject in intellectual nature" (*distinctum subsistens in natura intellectuali*).

(2) *Positive.* Here *hypostasis* still follows the definition of Gregory of Nyssa: an individual *reality*. Nevertheless, the meaning of the one *subject* in divine and human manifestation is already suggested by the paraphrasing passages: after all, Christ is "One and the Same, perfect in Godhead and the Same perfect in manhood." Moreover, Nicea regards the Incarnation as the birth from the virgin of the only Son of God who is the son even before his human birth. There is no new, no second Son. This is the interpretation adopted by Chalcedon. Eventually all deliberation sets forth from the *hypostasis* of the Son who is with the Father and remains with the Father, although he became true man and became united *kath' hypostasin*.

Clarifications and doubts after Chalcedon. It may be said that the concept of *hypostasis* as used at the Council of Chalcedon remains within the limits of the definition: *one individual concrete nature.* However, the formula of the "one *hypostasis* in two natures" necessitated a clearer definition of the term *hypostasis* in contrast to *physis*. For this purpose it was necessary to determine the meaning of *henosis kath' hypostasin.* The names Leontius of Byzantium, Leontius of Jerusalem, Boethius and Maximus the Confessor are of particular importance in this context. However, it is not yet sufficiently clear what they really mean for the development of the concept of *hypostasis* (*persona*). Only two aspects, which are discussed in particular by Leontius of Byzantium and Leontius of Jerusalem, are to be pointed out here.[28]

---

[28]See Stephan Otto, *Person und Subsistenz: Die Philosophische Anthropologie des Leontios von Byzanz. Ein Beitrag zur Spatantiken Geistesgeschichte* (Munich: W. Fink, 1968).

(1) Starting from the Cappadocian basis Leontius of Byzantium sees *hypostasia* primarily as the "bearer" of what he calls "*idiomata characteristics,*" which differentiates "person as definite being" from other definite beings.

> Hypostasis enim est natura, natura autem non iam est hypostasis. Natura enim rationem essentiae recipit. Hypostasis vero rationem per se essentiae [ton tou kath'heauton einai sc. logon], natura rationnem speciei continet; hypostasis declarat aliquem unum, natura rei universalis characterem [id est formam] declarat; hypostasis proprium a communi secernit. Et ut in summa dicam, unius naturae propria dicuntur consubstantialia, et quorum est ratio essentiae communis.[29]

Thus *hypostasis* is identified with the "individual." However, if this definition is applied to the mystery of Christ, it follows that the manhood of Christ would also have to be characterized as *hypostasis.* For Jesus of Nazareth is a concrete individual human being; he has his *notae characteristicae* which distinguish him as a human being from other human beings. If, therefore, *hypostasis* is used in the above-mentioned sense, one would have to assume two *hypostases* in Christ. Yet Chalcedon speaks of one *hypostasis* only. It seems that contrary to an "*opinio communis*" Leontius of Byzantium has not advanced much further.[30] It was believed that Leontius had found another meaning of *hypostasis* which went beyond the one given here: *hypostasis* signifies the absolute self-subsistence of an individual (*to kath'heauton einai*). In this context it is claimed that the concrete individual human nature of Christ has no *hypostasis* of its own, because its *hypostasis* rests in the Word, in the *hypostasis* of the Word. This according to a recent interpretation by Stephan Otto.

In a critical review of Otto's work David B. Evans writes:

> Happily, Leontius of Jerusalem is very much more what Otto would have him be than is Leontius of Byzantium . . . Leontius of Jerusalem does indeed believe . . . that the *hypostasis* of Jesus is the very *hypostasis* of

---

[29]PG 86/1:1279A-B. "*Hypostasis* is nature, nor again [is] nature *hypostasis,* because [nature] is not mutually predicable [with *hypostasis*] for *hypostasis* [is] indeed nature, but nature [is] not yet *hypostasis;* for nature admits of the definition of being, but *hypostasis* also [admits] the [definition] of [a being's] being in [or according to] itself. And the [former] looks to the definition of species, while the [latter] is significative of individuality. And the [former] indicates the character of a general [or universal] object, while the [latter] distinguishes what is peculiar [and proper] from what is common." (Trans. by David B. Evans.)

[30]Ibid.

the Word himself, and that the human nature of Christ finds its *hypostasis* only in him (ad St. Otto, p. 99 et passim) . . . He (Otto) grasps very well the essentials of Leontius's description of Jesus's human nature as a *"certain individual nature"* (see *Adv. Nest.* 1.20, PG 86:1485D et passim: *Physin idikèn tina*): "individual nature" is to be distinguished not only from *eidos*, but also from *hypostasis* (cf. *Adv. Nest* 2.7, PG 86:1552D). (See *Biblische Zeitschrift* 67 [1974]: 164.)

In *Adv. Nest* 2.7 (PG 86:1552-53) Leontius of Jerusalem gives the definition which may be considered *the "interpretatio"* of the Chalcedonian *mia hypostasis:* Simultaneously with the creation of Christ's human nature, with the institution of its physical existence, it becomes subsistent in the *hypostasis* of the Word. It exists only as the existence of the Word in the world, never as a separate existence of an independent human subject.

The human subject of Christ has all its human reality, its individuality. However, it is not founded in itself as an absolutely self-subsistent subject, but is rather the temporal and therefore limited existence of the preexistent Word. Therefore Leontius of Jerusalem in *Adv. Nest.* 2.10 (PG 86:1556A) feels justified in speaking of the humanity of Christ as not *"ahypostatic"* on the one hand nor *"idiohypostatic"* on the other. In *Adv. Nest.* 2.35 Leontius argues that only God's creative power could thus dispose of a temporal existence.[31]

(2) This induced theologians to go on asking what actually was the fact signified in that the *hypostasis* of the Word was also the ultimate "bearer" of the temporal existence of Christ. Is it significant for the existence of the human nature of Christ, which is the existence of the Word in the world, that it is thus hypostatically "borne" by the divine subject? Is being rooted in the divine subject detrimental to, or advantageous for, the human nature of Christ? Maximus the Confessor was aware of the problem and defended it against the monothelites: from the definition of Chalcedon he develops the idea that only through the *"asunchutos kai adiairetos,"* the presence "without confusion" and "without separation" of God and man in Christ, is humanity led to perfection and to self-realization. Maximus is sensitive to the basic precondition of true oneness and especially of the oneness of man with God (in Christ): "unity" can be regarded as perfect only when the elements to be unified do not disappear, but retain their natural character and yet become "one." "Obviously oneness can be achieved insofar

---

[31]Leont. Hier., *Adv. Nest.* 2.35:86,1593C: "Cum autem naturae et personae solus Deus sit auctor, quid eum prohibet unam naturam in alteram personam transferre, aut alienam personam in alteram naturam? Huic profecto omnia possibilia sunt. . . . "

as the physical distinctness of the elements is preserved."[32] This is important for Christological anthropology, and because the humanity of Christ involves the existence of the Word in the world, this is the culmination of humanity as such. A humanity sustained by the divine *hypostasis* is "perfect humanity" also from the natural point of view, because activity and freedom in Christ—remaining truly human—become activity of the Son before God. On the other hand, God's being "man with us" is made perfect only if he is truly man, that is, by the fact that the humanity of Christ is given the widest possible scope to develop.

The possibilities of theological reflection must not remain unused. If the mystery of the Incarnation is to mean anything in the modern world we must understand that in Jesus Christ we really encounter the one and consubstantial Son of God, though in his truly human existence which is sustained by his divine *hypostasis*. These dialectics are made possible by the Chalcedonian Christology: the more I recognize Christ as the Son of God, the more I may love him as the man consubstantial with us. The more Christ is God, the more he is also man.

---

[32]Maximus Conf., *Opusc. Theol.* pol. 8, PG 91:97A. The changes in the concept of person, the differences between the new and old concepts and the classification of both are excellently shown in the article "Person" by Karl Rahner and Herbert Vorgrimler, *Kleines Theologisches Worterbuch* (Freiburg: Herder, 1961).

The Christological Problem:
Some New Testament Aspects

M. V. George

It would hardly be useful for me to attempt here a conspectus of New Testament Christology. I am not competent to do so. And even if I were, it would hardly serve a very useful purpose in our deliberations here, since it could lead only to a debate among New Testament scholars which could very easily lead us astray from our main concern here.

I shall therefore limit myself to three fundamental points and then try to draw some conclusions. My first question is related to the methodology to be used for the interpretation of the biblical material on Christ. Second, I would like to say what is the core of the New Testament affirmation, which is also the affirmation of the church, about the person of Jesus Christ. Third, I would like to ask the question whether this fundamental affirmation about Jesus Christ is relevant in the world of today.

The Question of Methodology

If the question is asked within the tradition of the Orthodox Church, which is also the tradition of the undivided universal church, "Who is Jesus Christ?" our answer to that question would not be derived directly from the New Testament. The answer comes from the living tradition of the church. The New Testament bears witness to the apostolic authenticity of that affirmation. It is not that the church has recourse to the New Testament to find the answer. Quite a while before the New Testament began to be compiled, the church knew and proclaimed who Jesus Christ was. It is the same church which proclaims the same message today. The New Testament gives only some examples of this knowledge and proclamation based on the authority of the New Testament.

The church from that day to this day is one single organism. What the apostles testified within it in its earliest days is still what it bears witness to. If its proclamation at that time was not on the authority of the New Testament, then there is no reason why it should be so now. The tradition keeps alive the proclamation, and its original authority is that of the apostles, who were members of the church and not above it.

The tradition does not receive the proclamation from the New Testament. In fact the New Testament is an integral though unique part of that tradition, bearing witness to its early and apostolic form. The New Testament helps us to check the tradition's faithfulness to the apostolic teaching; but the tradition does not owe its knowledge of Christ to the Bible.

This does of course raise the question about *traditio,* or the form in which the tradition is kept alive from generation to generation; and about *traditum,* the content of the tradition. We can only say that tradition is the mind and memory of the church, and therefore the ways in which the church gains knowledge and stores it are as complex as or even more complex than the ways in which an individual mind gains and stores knowledge. The church being a divine-human organism has more than human resources at its disposal both for the gaining of knowledge and for its storing or for keeping it alive throughout the generations. The Holy Spirit both forms the tradition and keeps it alive and growing.

Therefore as a teacher within this tradition, I do not come empty-handed to the exegesis of the Bible. The tradition forms and informs my mind and trains me to understand the Bible in its proper sense.

Since this is the case, the so-called scientific methods developed in the West to interpret the Bible cannot be uncritically accepted by me or by my tradition. To us, many of the conclusions arrived at by "scientific" interpreters of the Bible appear both unscientific and contrary to the tradition of the Church. Let us take for example the contemporary form and redaction criticism. What are the assumptions behind this method?

(a) That the composition of the books of the New Testament are understandable on the same basis as the composition of other similar pieces of religious or non-religious literature.

(b) That the redactors used the same techniques of putting their materials together as would be used by a similar composer today.

(c) That the processes undergone by a "form" or "source" in the course of oral transmission and redaction into written form can be accurately and scientifically charted.

In addition to these conscious assumptions, all of which are severely questionable, there may be the further assumption that the critic who tries to disentangle the process of transmission and redaction does not inject his own theological, spiritual, and cultural predilections and prejudices into his work of criticism. To us this does not appear so obvious in the case of contemporary New Testament criticism. For example, it is unfashionable to believe in ordinary miracles today, but all the critics seem to believe in the extraordinary miracle of the incredible credulity of the narrators of the life of Jesus. That Jesus never performed any real act of healing or other miracle, many of these critics seem too ready to assume. On what grounds? Are these grounds not cultural and spiritual rather than properly scientific? How could you scientifically make the claim that the apostles and evangelists were telling tales when they recount the stories of Christ's healing, the feeding of the multitudes and ultimately his bodily resurrection? It requires a very unscientific cultural bias against all events which are not within our power to rule out these stories as fables or myths.

There is a cumulative weight of the New Testament evidence which lends support to the fundamental affirmation of the church from its earliest days, that the Messiah, the son of David, is also the Son of God. It is that affirmation that is the heart of our tradition and the foundation for our Christology. No amount of demythologization of the New Testament *kerygma*, nor the artificial separation between a historical Jesus and a kerygmatic Christ, nor even the results of form and redaction criticism, can undermine the massive witness of the New Testament to the central affirmation of the church that the Son of man is the Son of God.

If we examine the New Testament in the following section, it is not to prove from the New Testament that Jesus is the Christ or that the Son of Man is the Son of God.

This was the apostolic testimony in the church to which the church remains basically faithful. The New Testament testimony simply corroborates the faith of the church and bears witness to the apostolic testimony within it.

So let me make clear that I reject the *sola scriptura* principle which seems to be tacitly assumed by most modern hermeneutical writers. I do not get my Christology from the New Testament. I receive it from within the tradition. The New Testament is part of that tradition and bears witness to it.

The Christological Problem—Biblical Aspects

It is the God-man who presents himself to us in the person of Jesus Christ. There is no division between the Jesus of history and the Christ of faith. The apostles walked in the presence of Immanuel. It is their witness that Christ was not only human like any of us, but also sinless unlike all of us (Heb. 4: 15). As Ethelbert Stauffer points out, "Christianity has played down now the absolute meaning, now the relative appearance of the Christ-event—but the N[ew] T[estament] will give up neither, but holds on to both with the same radical determination."[1] The New Testament bears witness to the apostolic testimony to the *Mysterium Christi* (Eph. 3: 4). As in the case of the blessed Trinity, "Human speech labors in vain" while trying to exhaust the mystery of the Incarnation, its once-for-allness, humanity, divinity, and unity. Hence the Fathers who have spent all their lives to explain this mystery were not ashamed to confess that the mystery of Christ is "indescribable", "inconceivable," "completely inexpressible," "paradoxical," and a "magnificent mystery which surpasses understanding." "Christological formulae are so profuse in the N[ew] T[estament] that they by far outnumber all other credal formulae put together. . . . [It is] the coming of Christ that constitutes the central theme of primitive Christian thought."[2] We give below six outstanding aspects of New Testament Christianity.

The supreme paradox. Søren Kierkegaard has rightly called Jesus Christ the supreme paradox to reason, through fact to faith. Heim calls him "the concrete absolute." When Jesus calls himself by the title "Son of man" others invariably prefer the titles "Son of God," "Christ," "Lord." No wonder that when Chalcedon wanted to use four negatives to ward off various potential heresies, they could do no better than use two paradoxical negatives—"without division" and "without confusion," to indicate both the unity and the distinction of the one Person. We should be humble enough to confess that the *scandalon* of the gospel will remain until time and place will be replaced by eternity and infinity and we will then see him not as through a glass darkly, but "face to face." We can see that even St. Athanasius the Great was not able to see that full mystery of the ignorance of the incarnate *Logos* as he wrote in his third discourse *Against the Arians,* "not as ignorant, considered as Word, has said, 'I know not,' for He knows, but as showing His manhood, in that to be ignorant is proper to man."[3] Similarly, quoting a passage from Pope Leo, Professor Grillmeier observes, "Leo, like the Cappadocians, speaks here of a confusion of the two natures, and in this confusion as opposed to a mere indwelling of the Godhead in the manhood . . . he sees the unity of Christ. This is a very

---

[1] Ethelbert Stauffer, *New Testament Theology,* trans. John Marsh (London: SCM Press; New York: Macmillan, 1955) 159.

[2] Ibid., 244.

[3] Athanasius, *Orationes contra Arianos* 3.28.45 (cf. 3.28.45-46), in *The Nicene and Post-Nicene Fathers,* 2nd series, 4:418b.

incomplete and unclear idea of unity of person."[4] Where those theological giants have not succeeded to exhaust the incomprehensibility of the God-manhood of Christ, it would be wiser for us to be modest.

The Word became flesh. The four words of John 1: 14, *"Ho Logos sarx egeneto"* contain more Christology than any other four words in all the world. Karl Barth's profound discussion of each of these words in his famous *Church Dogmatics*[5] agrees with the Cyrillian Christology that the *hypostasis* of the incarnate *logos* was that of the *Logos*. To quote, "In the statement, the Word was made flesh, the word is the Subject. Nothing befalls Him, but in the becoming asserted of Him, He acts."[6] Again "the Word speaks, the Word acts, the Word prevails, the Word reveals, the Word reconciles. True enough, He is the incarnate Word; i.e. the Word not without Flesh, but the Word in the Flesh and through the Flesh, but nevertheless, the Word and not the Flesh."[7] We may compare with this St. Cyril's Christology summarized in the oft-quoted formula: "One nature of God the Word incarnate (*Mia physis tou Theou Logos sesarkomene.*)" To quote a brief passage from St. Cyril again, "He became man and did not change His properties, for He remained what He was; for it is assuredly understood that it is one thing which is dwelling in another, namely the divine nature in manhood."[8] There is complete agreement here with the Christology of Severus of Antioch, who also says.

When the fathers spoke of "one nature of God the Word," they made it clear by becoming incarnate the Word did not abandon His nature, but that He remained in His perfection without change and deviation; for He did not undergo any loss or diminution in His Hypostasis. When they said that He "became incarnate," they affirmed that the flesh was nothing but flesh, and that it did not come into being by itself apart from union with the Word. Therefore, it is just to say that the Word was simple, not composite, before the ages. When He willed to assume our likeness without sin, the flesh was brought into being but not separately. While signifying the lofty union, the words "became incarnate" refer to the assumption of

---

[4]Aloys Grillmeier, *Christ in Christian Tradition: From the Apostolic Age to Chalcedon (451)*, trans. J. S. Bowden (New York: Sheed and Ward; London: A. R. Mobray, 1965) 474.

[5]Karl Barth, *Church Dogmatics* (Edinburgh: T.&T. Clark, 1963) 1/2:131-71.

[6]Ibid., 134.

[7]Ibid., 136.

[8]Quoted by V. C. Samuel, Ph.D. diss., 115.

the flesh from the virgin, which was not separate by itself; so that from two natures, namely Godhead and manhood, one Christ came forth from Mary. The same is known to be at once God and Man, he is of the same Substance with the Father and the Godhead and He Himself is of the same substance with us in the manhood.[9]

I may also add that Martin Luther's Christology is also in agreement with the above interpretation. The major question is whether Christ was a synthesis of a divine person and a human person or whether his personality was that of the *Logos,* who assumed humanity in the Incarnation. While Nestorius taught that there was only a *synapheia* or *synthesis* of the Son of man and the Son of God in Jesus Christ with appropriate actions of human weakness and divine strength, St. Cyril taught that all the actions of weakness and strength were that of the one nature of God the Word incarnate. The personality was that of the *Logos.* Luther says:

> If he is natural and personal where he is, there too He must also be a Man, for there are not two detached persons, but a single person. . . . And where thou canst say, here is God! Thou must also say, Then Christ the Man is also there. . . . It was a person that became, who doth not sever humanity from Himself as Master John putteth off his coat and layeth it aside when he goeth to sleep.[10]

''Through God alone can God be known.''[11] When the Word became flesh, true God became true man. Otherwise revelation has not taken place yet. Human *nous* was not substituted by the divine *Logos* as Apollinarius taught, for then ''He could not redeem what he did not assume.'' There was hypostatic union of the divine and the human in such a depth that there was *communicatio idiomatum* in the *assumptio carnis.* The *Logos* who put on our human nature remained the Doer in the putting on and all that he did for our salvation. It was not a question of fusing together two personalities into one, but the creating and redeeming *Logos* assuming the universal *hypostasis* of humanity without its frailty of sinfulness. The individual personality is presupposed and embodied in the cosmic human nature that he assumed. So it is ''one nature after the union.'' Christ was not one person in two natures, but one person from two natures.

---

[9]Ibid., 351ff.; quoted from *Le Philalethes,* Robert Hespe, ed. (Louvain: Publications Universitaires, 1952).

[10]Luther's *Werke,* Weimar Ausgabe (1883–) 26:332.28, as quoted in Barth, *Dogmatics,* 1/2:166.

[11]Emil Brunner, *The Mediator* (Philadelphia: Westminster, 1947).

The mystery of "ekenosen." The *kenosis* passage of Philippians 2:5-11, 2 Corinthians 8:9, and so forth, has gained momentum in our century, and the so-called death-of-God theologians find in it the center of their theology.[12] No one can deny the importance of God's self-emptying. But what did he empty himself of? Did he empty himself of his divinity or only of his glory? The church has no gospel to preach if he emptied himself of his divinity, because it is a new form of Arianism. As St. Athanasius was fond of saying, no man or angel could save us. "For He alone, being Word of the Father and above all, was in consequence both able to recreate all, and worthy to suffer on behalf of all and to be an ambassador for all with the Father."[13] The kenotic passage, which is a Christ hymn of the early church adopted by St. Paul, is given in the context of the need of an ethical life of humility. What is the essence of divinity? If it is love, then the emptying was not an emptying of love or *agape.* The mistake of the Reformed Christology as represented by Brunner in his *The Mediator* and other works is that to him Christ was practically a man and "His Deity is the secret of his person, which as such does not enter into the sphere of history at all."[14] "God was in Christ reconciling the world into himself." God walked in history, though *incognito,* in the humiliated Jesus of Nazareth and vindicated his being in the resurrection, which truly happened as the central event between history and eternity, between B.C. and A.D. When St. Thomas uttered in ecstasy the epoch-making confession, "My Lord and my God" (John 20: 28), he was enriching the Petrine confession, "Thou art the Christ, the Son of the Living God" (Mark 8: 29; Luke 9: 20; Matt. 16: 16.) Though they saw the truth through their eyes of faith and as a result of the Father's revelation, they accepted the revelation as a historical event. The crucified and risen Christ, while revealing God in the incarnate and self-emptied state was the reflection of the glory of God and bore "the very stamp of his nature" (Heb. 1: 3).

Many regard some forms of western Christology today as pure Nestorianism of the old Antiochene school; if so it needs the corrective of the Alexandrian school which has always stressed the centrality of the divinity of Christ even in the incarnate and therefore fully human Jesus Christ.

------

[12]See Thomas J. J. Altizer, *The Gospel of Christian Atheism* (Philadelphia: Westminster, 1966) 62-29.

[13]St. Athanasius, *De Incarnatione Verbi* (London: Macmillan, 1946) §7; cf. *The Nicene and Post-Nicene Fathers,* 4:40a.

[14]Brunner, *The Mediator,* 343.

Propatheia of the incarnate Lord. The incarnate Lord had the potentiality of being tempted, yet he was without the actuality of sin (Heb. 4:15; 2:17-18). Mark 10:17-18, where Christ himself says that none is good except God, is regarded by D. M. Baillie as "the supreme instance of that peculiar kind of humility which Christianity brought into the world."[15] Paul Tillich takes it as the necessary self-negation of Incarnation which proves that Christ did not point to himself but only to the Father, and thus vindicated his deity instead of making any demonic claim. Yet, Tillich is prone to stress too much the humanity of the New Being and he finds fault with many of the traditional terms of theology.

> The conquest of estrangement [Tillich says] by the New Being in Jesus as the Christ should not be described in the term "the sinlessness of Jesus." This is a negative term and is used in the New Testament merely to show his victory over the messianic temptation (Letter to the Hebrews) to set forth the dignity of him who is the Christ in refusing to sacrifice himself by subjection to the destructive consequences of estrangement. . . . He rejects the term "good" as applicable to himself in isolation from God and puts the problem in the right place, namely, the uniqueness of his relation to God.[16]

The fact remains that no one could find any fault in Jesus during his earthly career, and he is pictured as the Lamb that takes away the sin of the world (John 1: 29). Yet St. Paul says that God sent his Son "in the likeness of sinful flesh and for sin," and "he condemned sin in the flesh" (Rom. 8: 3). The paradox here is that he was in himself sinless, yet he assumed our sinful nature by being born through the second Eve, the daughter of the fallen Eve. Anunciation was also purification of the blessed Virgin who needed grace which is always given to the undeserving. The *Logos* shared in the suffering and pathos of humanity in assuming flesh and also prevented the flesh from falling into temptation. This is the superiority of the second Adam (Rom. 5: 12-19; 1 Cor. 15: 21 f.) over the first Adam.

Professor Grillmeier praises the insight of an anonymous document, a commentary on the Psalms dated around the fourth century and discovered at Toura in 1941, concerning the psychology of Christ:

> The Psalm Commentary connects the *propatheia* and hence the possibility

---

[15]Donald M. Baillie, *God Was in Christ: An Essay on Incarnation and Atonement,* 2nd ed. (London: Faber and Faber, 1955) 126.

[16]Paul Tillich, *Systematic Theology,* 3 vols. (Chicago: University of Chicago Press, 1951-1963) 2:126-27.

of temptation and testing with this sinlessness of Christ. Only in this way can Christ's soul be said to remain truly human. Only in this way can there be any basis for merit there. This is a theological insight which stands with the best of the Christology of its time. Even modern interpretations have advanced little beyond it.[17]

Apollinarius was certainly wrong in asserting that Christ was incapable of sinning. Freedom of our Lord to rebel against the Father was in him, but actually he was in perpetual communion with his heavenly Father. *Propatheia* is a necessity of freedom and *pathéia* is an inability or weakness. Our Lord had the former, but not the latter. Sinning is not an ability, but an inability and so God does not sin. Temptation, however, is a necessity of human finitude that the *Logos* assumed; thus Christ was tempted. In this respect also the God-man was both like and unlike us.

Growth of our Savior. Another Christological problem is that of the perfection of the *Logos* and the growth of the incarnate *Logos*. Luke 2: 40, 52 are clear in asserting that the child grew and increased in wisdom and in stature and in favor with God and man. Moreover, we have the difficult verse in Mark 13: 32—"But of that day or that hour no one knows, not even the angels in heaven, nor the Son, but only the Father." The problem of an unfulfilled prediction of our Lord is shown by Mark 13: 30. It is not possible to explain these away as a "little apocalypse" or as later interpolations. The solution lies in emphasizing that Christ Jesus was not only *vere Deus* but also *vere homo*. Ignorance and growth are part and parcel of *vere homo,* unlike sin. The true humanity that the *Logos* became had certain inevitable limitations, to which the *Logos* submitted himself in the self-emptying of the Incarnation. As O. Cullmann points out:

> Hebrews says on the one hand that Jesus Christ is made perfect by the Father (2:10; 5:9; 7:28) and on the other hand that the High Priest Jesus Christ makes his brothers perfect (2:10ff.; 10:14). . . . We shall see that the author of Hebrews, as perhaps no other early Christian theologian, had the courage to speak of the man Jesus in shockingly human terms—although at the same time he emphasized perhaps more strongly than any other the deity of the Son.[18]

The lack of omniscience implied in Mark 13: 32 must not be taken in isolation, but in the light of other claims as in Matthew 11: 27: "All things

---

[17]Grillmeier, *Christ,* 274ff.

[18]Oscar Cullman, *Christology of the New Testament,* rev. ed., trans. Shirley Guthrie and Charles Hall (London: SCM Press; Philadephia: Westminster, 1963) 92ff.

have been delivered to me by my Father . . . and no one knows the Father except the Son . . . '' And ''Although he was a Son, he learned obedience through what he suffered'' (Heb. 5: 8). The identification of the preexistent Son with humanity in the incarnate state was complete in all points. As sin does not belong to the *esse* of humanity, lack of actual sin is not lack of identification. The *Logos* with no need for growth submitted himself to the normal growth of humanity. Omniscience, omnipresence and omnipotence, which are attributes of divine power, glory, and majesty were kept unused within himself as latent, using the essential attribute of love to the full while he emptied himself and took the form of a servant. Even while he grew from the normalcy of a boy to the normalcy of a man, ''in him dwelt the fullness of Godhead bodily'' (Col. 2: 9). ''The entire mystery of economy,'' said St. Cyril of Alexandria, ''consists in the self-emptying and abasement of the Son of God''[19] We have to hold on to the humanity and divinity of the Son and say with Sergius Bulgakov, ''Our Lord in his abasement never ceased to be the Second Person of the Holy Trinity.''

Vere Deus, vere homos. The New Testament has only one theme: Immanuel. In Christ our Lord, the true God became true man. There is no ambiguity in the New Testament in bearing witness to Christ's divinity, humanity, or unity. To quote Stauffer again:

> In the New Testament Jesus can be quite simply called ''God.'' [Cf. Heb. 1:8ff. application of Ps. 44:7ff.] . . . Paul goes a step further and in Rom. 9: 5 transfers a doxological formula which originally applied to God the Father to God the Son. [Cf. Rom. 1:25; 2 Cor. 11:31; Eph. 4:6.] . . . The pastoral epistles abound in solemn formulae which are applied now to God and now to Christ. [E.g., Tit. 2:13.] In the Johannine writings we find such *theos*-predicates as regular Christological titles. [E.g., John 1:1, 18; 20:28; 1 John 5:20.][20]

There is no adoptionism in Rom. 1: 3 f. or any other passage in the Bible. When we take the whole witness of the New Testament, passages like John 10: 29, 14, 28 have no subordination Christology, but are to be ascribed to the kenotic state of the economy. The preexistence of Christ is taken for granted in the kenotic (Phil. 2: 5-11) and cosmic Christologies (Col. 1: 15-20) of St. Paul and the prologue of the Fourth Gospel. There

---

[19]Quoted by Vladimir Losskey, *A Mystical Theology of the Eastern Church* (London: James Clark, 1957) 144.

[20]Stauffer, *Theology,* 114.

are a number of trinitarian passages (2 Cor. 13: 14; Eph. 4: 4 f.; 1 Pet. 1: 2; Mt. 29: 19) which are to be taken as the witness of a church which believed in the deity of the Father, Son, and Holy Spirit, and which later developed a trinitarian dogma, particularly through the great Cappadocian fathers. Jesus Christ of the New Testament is "true God and eternal life" (1 John 5: 20), "great God and Savior" (Tit. 2: 13), "Who for us men and our salvation, descended from heaven, and took flesh from the Holy Spirit and the Blessed Vigin Mary *Theotokos,* and became man."

Relevance of the New Testament Witness to Jesus Christ in the Modern World

I have tried simply to adumbrate in a few lines the core of the New Testament witness to Jesus Christ as my church understands it. Now I shall attempt to explain what relevance and significance this unique witness has in our period of history. Before that I venture to make a few remarks on the questions of "relevance" itself.

To start with, one must try to reexamine the very notion of "relevance" as it is understood today. In the cultural climate of our thoroughly pragmatic, urban-technological society, anything has "relevance" for us only when it helps promote our material advancement or resolve our ecological problems. We test the relevance of anything by raising our own self-fabricated questions which come out of our selfish desires. We come to a crisis when this kind of approach is applied to the question of the relevance of the New Testament message. To resolve the crisis we will have either to reject our methodology or to dispose of the New Testament affirmation as irrelevant. I accept the first alternative.

Secondly, in our desperate agony to win the misdirected battle of "relevance," we twist the Word of God to conform to our worldly demands. We precondition Christ the *Logos* within the limits of our language and logic and ask him for relevant answers, just as we treat a computer by feeding it with all the data necessary for our possible questions and then asking it for answers. But the poor secularized Christ deprived of all transcendent and translogical attributes finds our questions part of our disease, and not a way to seek the cure. Like the Christ imprisoned by the grand inquisitor in Dostoyevsky's *Brothers Karamazov,* he never answers a word to our questions, but comes forward, gently kisses us on our cheeks and passes by. Naturally we find him irrelevant to us. Then some bold spirits speak of the myth of Christ and start demythologizing him, thus disposing of the whole matter. Now we return to the position we started from, for we started without Christ, seeking him, and when he comes we reject him because he does not conform to our expectations. This is the vicious circle in which we are trapped.

Thirdly, we have not let the Word of God raise its own questions from within us and let the same word of God answer these questions. We, on our part, actively participate with the *Logos* in raising these questions and answering them. This process ensures the raising of the right questions and the receiving of the right answers. Again this process encompasses all the spheres of our existence and helps to avoid the danger of leaving out some aspects of our being and existence and giving undue importance to some others which now seem all important to our misguided minds. Finally, our scientific methodology combined with our analytical bent of mind and our academic emphasis on the minute details of hermeneutics have rendered us unable to perceive the total meaning and significance of the New Testament affirmation and its bearing on the life of the church. Any discussion of the question of relevance must be oriented towards a corrective to this defect of not being able to see the wood for the trees.

With these remarks, I would like to suggest the following points which, I think, are more important in the discussion on relevance.

1. When St. John the Evangelist summed up the core of the New Testament affirmation in his words *ho Logos sarx egeneto,* the underlying issue was not transcendence but the gnostic-docetic denial of the true humanity of Christ. Transcendence was not at stake. Today the issue has been reversed. The problem confronting the presentation of the New Testament message today is not the denial of humanity, but the disappearance of the sense of transcendence. But the New Testament message that the *Logos* became *sarx* holds equally good for both times. However, the problem of transcendence in our times cannot be resolved as easily as that of humanity in the apostolic period, since we tend to ask whether we can speak meaningfully of God beyond the limits of our language. No wonder we raise such questions in an age which has enthroned logical positivism and historicism, and in which there is no more talk *to* God, but only ''God-talk.'' Our exaltation of the realm of *sarx,* including both man and matter, has been devoid of any adequate basis in reality and without any ultimate reference. Consequently, we suffer from the loss of freedom and the tyranny of many oppressive forces set in motion by outselves. Matter acquires meaning and significance on the basis of the unique fact that it has been inseparably united to the *Logos* of God and exalted to the trinitarian status. This has been the New Testament affirmation and it is relevant for our age in the face of our spiritual malady.

2. The Word was not "relevant" to the poor Galilean fishermen, in our ordinary sense of the term. Instead Christ was totally irrelevant to their life situation. They had to undergo a radical and painful transformation before they could perceive his relevance and proclaim that he was God. This calls for a similar transformation on our part as a precondition to grasp the relevance of the New Testament message. We will have to reexamine our fundamental attitudes, values, and objectives. The process, of course, is painful. We run the risk of becoming unfashionable for the spirit of our world.

3. This demand for transformation cannot be squarely directed to the secular man. The church must be the continuing community of witness to the relevance of Jesus Christ, as it was in the New Testament period. Of course, Christ does not make himself relevant through any abstract or non-material medium, but through human flesh. The church, as the new humanity, must testify concretely its existence among the secular men, proclaiming the message of salvation by living it also.

4. In proclaiming the cosmic redemption, the church must take a deliberate step to dissociate the gospel of Christ from any national, racial, or cultural prejudices. We must regretfully admit that our presentation of the gospel in the past has been dominated by parochial elements alien to the spirit of Christ. Unless we sincerely repent for the injury we have done to our less fortunate brothers in the name of a Christian civilization, we can never hope to make Christ relevant to the modern world of poverty, hunger, and injustice.

5. *Christos aneste* was the dominant motif in the *kerygma* of the early church. The New Testament affirmation has its basis in the resurrection experience of the church. Participation in this basic experience of the church is particularly significant in our times when the question of the meaning of existence is raised even more crucially and agonizingly. Our hope in the risen Christ assures us of our true destiny over against the threat of fleeting time and decaying matter. It strengthens us inwardly, and enables us to live joyfully in a world of anguish, absurdity, despair or alienation, sharing in all these, but not crushed by them.

The ultimate word remains in the ancient cry "*Maranatha*"—Come, Lord Jesus, come.

The Relevance of Christology Today

Paulos Mar Gregorios

In a perceptive article in *The Christian Century*, Dr. Robert Kysar raised some questions about the contemporary Protestant Christological debate. Referring to the attempt of thinkers like William Hamilton (*Radical Theology and the Death of God*), John Vincent (*Secular Christ, A Contemporary Interpretation*) and Paul van Buren (*The Secular Meaning of the Gospel*) to make Christology independent of any transcendent theology, Kysar posed the question whether these writers were seeking to find a God-substitute in the Jesus of history, and thereby engaging in a special form of idolatry called Jesusolatry.

Dr. Kysar himself would propose a radical secular Christology which would not be guilty of Jesusolatry. Such a Christology would recognize and readily admit that the Christ figure is an ideal, a sort of ethical model which functions to incite Christian values in men. It is not simply historical in origin, nor is it docetic. It is the result of Christian thought about a historical figure which provoked the nurturing of human "existence as valuable and lovable."[1]

I found the Kysar approach refreshingly direct and uncomplicated. He had seen clearly the problem of the "historical Jesus," and rightly concluded that the "new quest" was not much more successful than the old one of the last century and the earlier part of our century. He accused the secular approach of not being radically secular, and of still trying to find some transcendent reference in the secular; van Buren's "experience of freedom," Vincent's "redemptive act of service" and Hamilton's "struggle for one's values" could be seen as mere aspects of human experience without dragging in any theological reference to "the hidden God" or to "unmasking the secular" to find Jesus. Accept the secular as secular, acknowledge the fact that one's allegiance to Christ is simply another "way

---

[1] Robert Kysar, "Christology without Jesusolatry," *Christian Century* 87:10 (2 September 1970): 1038.

of saying that he belongs to this culture, that the Judeo-Christian heritage is his.''

I was struck by the fact that Kysar, working toward an honest radicalism, had finally arrived at the traditional notion of tradition. After reading his article I went back to my notes on that amazing storehouse of historical Christological erudition—Fr. Aloysius Grillmeier's *Christ in Christian Tradition*. Again I was struck by the total dissimilarity of ethos, issues, and interests in the Christological debate then and now. They were in those days arguing and fighting about *ousia, hypostasis, prosopon, physis,* union, distinction, *logos, sarx, theos sarkophoros, anthropos theophoros* and all that kind of metaphysical gibberish which makes no sense to many moderns. A discussion on whether Christ is *en duo physesin* or *ek duo physeon* would not sound very relevant to many theologians today, not to speak of most laymen.

This raises the question, What is this Judeo-Christian tradition in which you and I stand? Why is there such a hiatus between one of the most earth-shaking discussions in Christian history and the mind of Judeo-Christians today, especially in the West?

I could not answer this question without dealing with three related questions.

(1) What was the crux of the Christological debate among the early Christians? Was it a purely metaphysical point unrelated to our existence on earth as human beings? What was really at stake? And what is at stake today in the Christological debate in the West? Is it important?

(2) What were the things taken for granted by the fathers of the fourth and fifth centuries? What philosophical and theological assumptions underlie that debate as well as that of the twentieth century?

(3) Is the dispute about the two natures or one nature of Christ still relevant today? If so, how?

In answering these questions, I may have helped to clarify to myself the difference between the two debates, and perhaps to psychoanalyze myself as regards my passionate interest in the fourth- and fifth-century Christological debate, whether it is anything more than mere archaism on my part, a sign of advanced decadence and degeneration.

The Crux of the Ancient Christological Debate

If one separates the trinitarian and Christological debates, one loses perspective. They are of one piece. The one implies the other. If you have no trinitarian presuppositions, if you are strictly unitarian, then Christology is no problem; you can settle down to reading the story, whether fictitious or historical, of an inspiring personality, and that is it.

But if you make that dreadful assumption which the early Christians dared to make, that the identity of Jesus is not exhausted by his humanity, that his humanity is a manifestation of deity, then you are in all forms of trouble. It was the scandalous statement of the gospel that God was in Christ reconciling the world to himself that is at the root of the trouble. If we can dismiss the cosmic Christology of Colossians and Ephesians as myth; if we can throw out the claims of Jesus as reported by the Fourth Evangelist (no matter whether it is an original source or the result of redactors); if we can ignore the repeated emphasis of the New Testament, the liturgy, and the Fathers, that the relationship between God and Jesus is one of identity of being, then we have no need to bother about the fourth-and fifth-century Christological debate, and we can settle down to deal with the functional Christology of a secular radicalism. But then on what presumptuous grounds do we still make that astounding claim to be standing in the Judeo-Christian tradition, when we reject the central affirmation of that tradition that Jesus is both God and man?

We must learn afresh to grapple with this fact—that the Christian church, the Christian gospel, and the Christian tradition are all squarely based on the affirmation that Jesus Christ is both God and man, and when one of these realities is denied what we have is no longer Christianity. Secular Christologies do not appear to have any legitimate ground for claiming that they are Christian Christologies.

It was because they recognized Jesus as God that the whole trinitarian and Christological debates were generated. The literature of the Christian church leaves us in no doubt that the two great mysteries, the mystery of the holy Trinity and the mystery of the Incarnation, are of the foundation of Christianity. There is no satisfactory, logical way of explaining either of these mysteries—that is why they are called mysteries. They relate to the very ultimate ground of our own human existence. The whole Christian tradition has grown up on these two roots. The tradition that denies the two mysteries can no longer properly be called Christian, though it may have obvious affinities with the Jewish tradition.

I wish therefore to submit that these two mysteries and our adherence to them in faith is the distinctive feature of a Christian tradition, and where these two are implicitly or explicitly denied or ignored, the discussion is no longer taking place in the Judeo-Christian tradition. Much of modern Christology should prove acceptable to many Jews, and they can adhere to it without ceasing to belong to the Old Covenant.

Christology and trinitarian doctrine are thus tests of the Christian gospel which help to distinguish it from Jewish or pagan religions. The gospel is "concerning his Son, who was born of the seed of David according to the flesh, who was declared Son of God in power according to the spirit of holiness, through resurrection from the dead" (Rom. 1: 3-4). Philippians 2 does not say merely that Jesus lived in the form of a servant on earth. He was one who "became" man and thereby assumed the form of a servant, without losing his identity as "Lord," as equal to God, "*isotheos*." It is this transcendent identity of the servant-Master that early Christian Christology was trying to grapple with, not just "the values of our culture," or "the form of a servant," or mere "personal freedom." The gospel is about the "one Lord Jesus Christ, through whom is the whole universe as well as our own selves existing through him," as St. Paul affirms in 1 Corinthians 8: 6. If this is mythology or metaphysics, then such mythology and metaphysics belong to the heart of the Christian tradition as history knows it, and we have to grapple with them if we are to remain Christian.

The issue in the Christological debate of the fourth and fifth centuries is precipitated by the conviction that Jesus is God. If this conviction is absent, if the person of Jesus were understood through the ordinary processes of human generation, existence and death alone, then there would have been no Christological debate of the kind there was. If that debate appears irrelevant to some of us today, it is not so much because our philosophical outlooks have changed since then as because our convictions about the person of Jesus have been fundamentally eroded.

The new quest of the historical Jesus and the current Christological debate belong to a different world, a different ethos, a way of thinking fundamentally alienated from the Judeo-Christian tradition, which tradition centers around Jesus Christ the unique Son of God become Son of man without ceasing to be what he was, who was born, who taught, suffered, died, rose again, and is to come again. If we are to engage in Christological debate with those who deny these basic realities, we shall do so only as in a dialogue with non-Christians.

What was at stake in the fourth and fifth century debate about Christ was the question of the origin and the destiny of man, the two transcendent poles of his existence in time (secular?) upon this earth. These Christians saw in Jesus both their origin and their destiny, and in that vision they were rescued from the restless drift towards nonbeing that characterizes human existence in time upon the earth. It was as momentous as that.

In the new secular Christologies, the two transcendent poles of origin and destiny are sought to be ignored, in order to find meaning and significance within the time-span of our terrestrial existence. Some images and phrases from the old transcendent metaphysics are imported into a secular Christology by Hamilton, van Buren, Vincent, and others, and Dr. Kysar is fully justified in questioning the *bona fides* of such an operation. But we need to ask Dr. Kysar: "Why do *you* still need to drag in the historical mythological Jesus Christ as an ideal or as a model? Why not Socrates, Gandhi, or Schweitzer? What is the difference?" I would like sometime to hear the answer to that question.

Dr. Kysar describes the dilemma of the modern Christian as "posed by developments within the theistic debate on the one hand and Jesusolatry on the other." Why is this a dilemma? What is at stake? The theistic debate has led to the clarification of the human situation that any God caught within its rational web would not be God and is therefore bound to die. This was always the human situation. Our fathers in Christ in the fourth century knew that it is impossible to conceive or articulate the existence of God. They did not, unlike many of us lesser men who came later, believe in a "God of the gaps" or a *deus ex machina*. There is no new impasse in theology for those who are acquainted with what the Christian tradition has held about God.

The question of Jesusolatry is not a new one. It was exactly the charge made by Emperor Julian the Apostate, in replying to which Diodore of Tarsus, his classmate, fell into the most dangerous Christological errors. Julian the neopagan accused the "Galileans" of Jesusolatry, of worshiping a common Jewish criminal who was hanged by the power of Imperial Rome, of adoring a "new Galilean God" whose death and burial refutes his claims to God-head. Diodore, whom Julian called "the Sorcerer of the Nazaraian," had to defend himself by saying that they did not worship the man Jesus, but only the *Logos* who could not be crucified or die. So there was no Jesusolatry, but only Logolatry, Diodore claimed, in Christianity. It is this issue which is still important today. The secular charge of Jesusolatry needs to be taken seriously.

Let me put it more bluntly: a secular Christology is not Christian Christology. The adjective "Christian" relates to a community with a gospel and a tradition which affirm that Jesus Christ is Son of God and Son of man. There is no way to secularize that gospel without denying it.

In fact the total secular approach is itself not Christian. It is an attempt to make the mind of man in his finitude normative for truth. It is a denial of the basic questions about the origin and destiny of man, neither of which can be answered for a Christian in a purely secular or temporal framework. Both at the beginning and at the end of human existence and of time-existence there are antinomies that invalidate the absolute claims of the secular to find meaning within finitude and by finite reason. Finitude-infinitude, and time-eternity involve logical difficulties which reveal the limits of logic and of the time-space existence of man. To reduce man to time-existence without attention to questions of origin and destiny is a repudiation of humanity itself, which is gifted with a reason capable of detecting the limits of finite existence and of finite reason.

My submission therefore is this. If the debate of the fourth and fifth centuries appears irrelevant to us, it is for two reasons. First, we have not paid enough attention to what it was all about. Second, for the Christians of that time the debate arose out of their conviction that Jesus is God. Today it is irrelevant to us, not because our philosophy cannot cope with terms like *ousia, hypostasis* or *physis,* but because we do not believe what the Christian gospel affirms—namely that Jesus is God and man. We have today become monophysites in reverse, believing that Christ has only one nature—the human.

But we misunderstand the early Christological debate if we evaluate it only as an intellectual or academic debate. The participants were passionately concerned, for the debate was about their salvation, about their ultimate destiny, and about the destiny of the world. To them, it was an existential problem which arose from their very awareness of finitude.

The intellectual discussion, however, had a context—the context of a transcendent community, a community of the Holy Spirit, a community which spanned heaven and earth, in which they experienced the mystery of existence at three interpenetrating levels. We cannot go into detail, but the most proximate level of experiencing the mystery existence was the eucharist, where the Word was proclaimed and union with Christ by the Holy Spirit was experienced. The word "sacrament" is open to dangerous misunderstandings, but for the sake of convenient shorthand, we will say that the early Christological debate should be seen in the context of the church's experience of the *sacramental mystery of the church.*

The experience of the Eucharist was a way of experiencing the second level of mystery—the Incarnation of Jesus Christ, the only begotten Son of God, inside the limits of finite human existence. It is in the community's being united to the crucified and risen Lord that its members are able to transcend the limits of finitude and to become established in the source and destiny (alpha and omega) of their existence. The Incarnation is not just a historical event, to be analyzed and understood by the finite categories of the historical method. It is a mystery in which the church participates now, not simply an event that happened then. By mystery I mean an event enabling participation in ultimate reality transcending the categories of finite existence.

The mystery of the church and the mystery of the Incarnation are ways of participation in a third level of mystery—the holy Trinity. This is ultimate reality in its ultimately transcendent aspect conceived, of course, in the language of finitude but enabling participation at a level far above the temporal and the historical. To speak more about the mystery of the Holy Trinity can be dangerous and I desist.

These three levels of reality and our participation in them alone can make us see the vitally important nature of the Christological debate then and its relevance today.

The crux of the Christological debate, then, is the affirmation that Jesus is God. If that affirmation is denied, then the whole discussion becomes flatly irrelevant. But my contention is that it can be denied only by non-Christians, for it seems to me that in the very process of that denial one ceases to be a Christian.

The Contemporary Christological Debate

That statement may make the rest of my paper irrelevant to some people. I need, however, to mention at least the contemporary Christological debate in its two aspects—the biblical-theological debate about the relation between the historical Jesus and the kerygmatic Christ, and the attempt to find a secular Christology acceptable to "modern man."

The biblical debate began with the *Leben-Jesu-Forschung* of Hermann Samuel Reimarus, the deist biblical critic of Wittenberg, whose *Wolfenbüttel Fragments* were published by Lessing in 1774—1778. The first stage of the process ended in the famous synopsis of Albert Schweitzer, *Von Reimarus zu Wrede*. The historical Jesus was now acknowledged to be totally lost to us, but known to be different from the picture provided by the New Testament sources.

The second stage of the modern Christological debate centers around two personalities again in Germany—Martin Kähler and Rudolf Bultmann. Kähler's untranslatable distinction between the *historische Jesus* (the bare uninterpreted facts about the man from Nazareth) and the *geschichtliche, biblische Christ* (the notion of Messiah as it became influential and decisive in subsequent history) became the basis for Bultmann's thought. For Kähler, the inaccessible *historische Jesus* was not as significant as the *geschichtliche Christ,* who as the *kerygmatic* Christ is the object of faith. By this distinction the existential Christology of our time received a subjective orientation.

The kerygmatic Christ, according to Kähler and Bultmann, is what we need and what we have. The only problem is that the church's kerygma clothes this Christ in archaic, mythological form, and language. The eschatological act of God in Christ should be demythologized and translated into contemporary form. Then it becomes relevant and powerful to evoke an existential faith. We are not interested in either the historical Jesus or his message, his *ipsissima verba,* for all that belongs within Judaism.

Christianity begins with the kerygmatic Christ as proclaimed by the church after Easter. Our faith is not in the Jewish teacher but in the Lord proclaimed by the church. Revelation takes place not in the dim past of 2,000 years ago but in the here and now, when the *kerygma* is proclaimed and men respond in faith. It is not the teaching of Jesus but the teaching about Jesus that matters. And to that we have full access in the Scriptures.

The third stage began with Ernst Käsemann's 1953 address at Marburg to Dr. Bultmann's former students. Käsemann reopened the historical Jesus problem, and suggested that to say that the kerygmatic Christ is totally unrelated to the Jesus of history would be a hoax. The gnawing suspicion in the minds of many that Bultmann's Christology was a kind of kerygmatic docetism now found open utterance when Fuchs, Bornkamm, Conzelmann, and others joined the fray. The historical Jesus was now necessary to interpret the *kerygma,* and many set out in quest of him. What the quest has so far found is stuff that reveals more of the prejudices of the scholars than the mind of Jesus. When Gerhard Ebeling says, for example, that the link between "Jesus as witness to faith" and "Jesus as object of faith" is the Easter event, I am not sure that I understand. If we know so little about the historical Jesus, how do we become so sure that the historical Jesus did not present himself both as witness to faith in God and as object of faith?

My mind fails to follow when Ebeling claims that the *kerygma* gives us access to the historical Jesus and his message, through the event of the resurrection. My friend Käsemann has now come around to say that the existential Christ is not sufficient, and that we have to go back to some historically rooted saving event in which the Jesus of history is central. We must burrow our way back to the pre-Hellenic Christ of Palestinian Jewish Christianity, through the special material in Matthew's gospel.

What is the "peeled person" who emerges after the form critics have done their paring of the biblical materials? Conzelmann arrives at a Jesus who proclaimed the reign of God as something coming, demanding decision, an answering response to the challenge of proclamation. Jesus' historical life is an advance proclamation of the coming kingdom, which is primarily ethical. His eating with sinners, publicans, and other social outcasts is already a kerygmatic act, demanding confrontation with the will of God and obedience to it, as Fuchs would say. His demand for faith is a demand to overcome *angst* by being at the receiving end of God's action. Jesus' own style of life was a declaration that he who is in complete submission to the will of God achieves perfect power and poise, gaining mastery of every situation. To be the Servant is to fulfill the will of God; and the historical Jesus, by his actions, declares this revealing truth.

I hope I have not badly caricatured the new Christology of my Protestant friends—Jesus as the man-for-others, as the servant who reveals the
will of God for all men, the one who submits perfectly to the will of God
and thereby manifests and declares what it is to be truly human (without
self-righteousness), justified by the grace of God but decisively committed
to obey the will of God and to serve one's fellow men.

Two things strike me in this picture. One is the refreshing moral ear-
nestness, this desire to obey—a characteristic which not all nationalities
enjoy equally. It is neither in my personal ethos nor in my national character. So I can appreciate that kind of obedience only from a distance.

The other is this Christology's utter monophysitism in reverse. There
is no suggestion here that the historical Jesus could have been anything more
than a mere man. And there the issue is squarely joined—in the most el-
ementary but most fundamental terms.

Is a Christology which seeks to make no use at all of the transcendent
aspects of Jesus' person, life, and teaching, *Christian?* It may, after some
more pruning *a la* Robert Kysar, become faithful to the modern supersti-
tion of secularism, which seeks to find security in ignorance, and release
from its intellectual restlessness by cutting out a manageable chunk of reality and by dealing with it in categories which are supposed to be in the control of man. But some of my secularist friends secretly retain a transcendent
reference within the "secular" world through vague expressions like "the
beyond in our midst," "experience of freedom," "unmasking of the face
of Jesus," and so on. A straightforward humanism without all this Christological garb will be more honest and therefore more understandable to
Christian and non-Christian alike.

It is also noteworthy that while the fourth and fifth century debate was
an attempt to deal with the person of Jesus in terms of his metaphysical
identity, the twentieth century debate is more concerned with his intellectual and ethical positions. The concern then was about the being of Jesus.
Today it is about his actual saying and doing.

There were certain assumptions about the acts and words of Jesus in
the fourth century—the chief one being that no basic controversy was necessary on the subject, since the tradition of the church as attested to by the
Scriptures, the liturgical prayers, the writings of the Fathers, and the memory of the original teachers, was essentially reliable, and that there was no
particular problem to debate.

Today we cannot make that assumption, according to many of my
friends. In our time many scholars feel that the canons of literary criticism
and *Formgeschichte* should be strictly applied to sift the truth from poetry
and legend in the materials. This literary orientation to history is a special

phenomenon of our time. ''Only that which is documented can be re-garded as having happened''—that seems to be the first assumption. ''Whatever has happened, we can know it by scientific analysis of the evidence left to history''—that seems to be a second assumption. ''Only that which is ascertained as scientifically true can be proclaimed as truth by the church''—is this a third assumption?

The problem behind these assumptions is the conclusion that they lead to—namely that the scientific method is the way to truth in all cases. But if something is proved as indubitable by scientific investigation, what then is the nature of the faith demanded in accepting these conclusions? Nothing more seems to be needed than faith in the method and faith in the integrity and inerrancy of the investigators. Would that still be the Christian faith? What is faith? Is it a decision about ourselves or a relation to a person? And why that person, if he is only a man? Until I hear some satisfactory answer to these questions, my interest in this new quest of the historical Jesus can be little more than marginal. You will forgive me if I thus regard the twentieth century Christological debate as being less relevant to me than that of the fourth and fifth centuries.

The Relevance of the Classical Debate

But in what sense is the classical debate still relevant? It is relevant to those Christians who still believe that ''the *Logos* became flesh and dwelt among us'' and that the apostles ''beheld his glory, glory as of the only Son from the Father'' (John 1: 14).

If the divine *Logos* became a member of humanity in Jesus of Nazareth, and our own ultimate destiny is dependent on that event, then I have a passionate interest in knowing who the divine *Logos* is and how he became a human being.

I affirm that the *Logos* is God. Then if I take into account the fact that he constantly spoke of God as his Father, I have a passionate interest in knowing how God the Son is related to God the Father, when there is only one God.

I have no confidence that I will be able to penetrate either of these mysteries—the mystery of the Godhead and the mystery of the Incarnation—at any time. My passion for knowledge is only to make sure that I do not go wrong in whatever I claim to know. It is a negative knowledge that I am after, a knowledge which can protect the mystery but never hope to be able to reveal it in its full depth.

In such a context, I have a third question. How does the event of the Incarnation become effective in our time for the salvation of the world? It is at this third level that the preaching of the Word, the sacramental mysteries, and the life and work of the church become effective. My Christological interest is integrally related to this third level, which has also its own elements of mystery.

But in what sense would a two-nature Christology or a one-nature Christology make any difference at the soteriological level? This is our question. Here I must begin first by making the statement that I am able to understand the Christological definition of Chalcedon itself in a nonheretical sense. By that I do not mean that I find the Chalcedonian formula an admirable statement of Christology. If it claims to "solve" the Christological issue, then I must protest. I believe that the nature of Christ cannot be reduced to concepts comprehensible to a finite mind, precisely because as God and as man, his being transcends the categories of finite reason or of time-space existence.

There are two dangers in affirming two natures. The first is most clearly exemplified by the Tome of Leo itself. This interesting document soberly sets forth the doctrine of Christ with great clarity, especially in contrast with the muddleheadedness of a Eutyches. "Each nature in union with the other performs the actions which are proper to it, the Word those which are proper to the Word, the flesh those which are proper to the flesh. The one is resplendent with miracles, the other succumbs to injuries" (ch. 4).

But this amazing clarity is deceptive. For Leo would normally affirm that it is the same One who is the subject of both actions; but he falls into error when he says that the Word does certain actions and the flesh certain others. This could imply two subjects—the essence of the Nestorian heresy. Leo's personal faith may have been orthodox, but the way he stated it is subject to misinterpretation. To certify such a teaching as accurate is for us one of the major mistakes of Chalcedon. We do not really believe that the two-nature Christology as interpreted by Leo is completely faithful to the authentic tradition.

Chalcedon also falls into the error of too symmetric a Christology when it puts the two natures side by side as if they were parallel to and equal to each other. Our tradition insists on basic asymmetry between the two natures—the center is the *hypostasis* of the *Logos,* the divine nature. The human nature is not uneasily linked to the *Logos* and his divine nature. It is the nature of the *Logos* incarnate to be human. Christ who now sits at the right hand of the Father is a human being—the Son of man. The two natures are not linked in such a way that the divine nature is the subject and the human nature the instrument. Nor are the two natures placed side by side in such a way that human beings can have contact only with the human nature of Christ. Our union is with God in Christ, and not merely with the human nature of Christ.

It is this element that is at stake in the ancient Christological debate being brought up to date. There is the primary question: Are we saved by an encounter of faith in Christ, or by union with him? Do we stand simply face-to-face with him at a distance, or do we become united with him in such a way that from one perspective we are Christ, and from another perspective Christ can be distinguished from us and prayed to? I think the latter view, which emphasizes both union and distinction, is more faithful to the original tradition.

It might at first appear that the two-nature Christology is better suited to uphold the ideas of both union and distinction. But it is obvious that the insistence on keeping the emphasis on the *distinction* at the level of the natures, and *unity* at the level of the person or acting subject, leads to more emphasis on the distinction between the divine and the human. For at the level of the person, where unity is affirmed, it is the divine *hypostasis* that stands alone. The human in the two-nature Christology exists only at the level of the nature, and at that level it is distinction that is emphasized by the two-nature formula. The four adverbs ("without confusion, conversion, division, or separation" [*asunchutos, atreptos, adiairetos, achoristos*] could be more accurately, though much more awkwardly, translated as "uncommixedly, unalteredly, undividedly, unseparatedly") belong to our common tradition, and are also used in the one united nature Christology.

It is the union of the divine and the human, without loss of the distinction between them, without one changing into the other in such a way that it loses its original identity, that is at the heart of our salvation. It is this union of the divine and human that the one-nature Christology emphasizes, without losing sight of the distinction. In Christ there is unity both at the level of *hypostasis* and at the level of nature.

Of course if the divine is denied in Christ, then the question is not relevant. It is even less relevant if our union with Christ itself is underemphasized, with overemphasis on the personal encounter. Then, too, the two natures *vs.* one-united-nature controversy can hardly be relevant.

If we affirm, as theologian Emile Mersch does in the *Total Christ,* that our union is only with the human nature, which since it is the human nature of the divine *Logos* has divine properties transmitted to it, then we are still emphasizing the distinction of the natures, and there may be implied here a fear to affirm that our human nature can be really united to the divine nature. But then is that not the point of the Incarnation? If Christ's human nature was united to his divine nature, our human nature can also be united with Christ's divine-human nature—not just with his human nature. This is fundamentally what the one united-nature Christology seeks to affirm. Our commitment to a *theosis* soteriology is at the base of our one-nature Christology, which does not deny the distinction between the divine and the human, but places the emphasis on their union rather than on their distinction.

Terminology

The categories used in the Christological formula are extremely problematic for Christians today. Archbishop William Temple of Canterbury was one of the first to question the very usefulness of these categories, quite apart from the opposition to dogma itself which was characteristic of German and American liberalism.

The main terms—*hypostasis, physis,* and *ousia*—have been ably analyzed by Father Grillmeier in his magnificent study on the history of Christology, and I need not repeat the material here. The problem, however, was recognized as early as the fourth century by the Cappadocian Fathers. Whoever may be the author of Epistle 38[2] attributed to St. Basil, the problem gets clearly stated there. I want only to draw out some conclusions here.

(a) Physis *or nature.* First of all, nature is not a thing, it is the name of a class. It belongs to a group of words which do not correspond to any particular thing but have a more general sense *(katholikoteran tina ten semasian echei)* such as *anthropos* or man. Human nature or humanity does not mean something which a man possesses as one owns a thing. It is rather a word to denote the fact that certain realities have certain common characteristics—which are the *koinotes tes physeos.* Every reality has some characteristics which are *idion* or *idia* or particular, and others that are *koinon* or *koina* (common). The *koina* belong to *physis* or nature and the *idia* to the *hypostasis* or person. Or, to put it differently, nature is what all members of a class have in common. But it is not a particular thing to be counted as one or two.

(b) Hypostasis *or person.* This is perhaps the most ambiguous term. The Stoics used it in a much wider sense. it is any particular visible object, animal, or person with its own *idiomata* or set of characteristics. All existing realities are *hypostases* with their own *physei* or natures. A *hypostasis* for the Stoics is thus similar to a *Dasein* for Heidegger.

Theodore of Mopsuestia, on the other hand, would insist that only man has *hypostasis.* He rejects even the more restricted view of *hypostasis* as any *autokineton*, any living being which is moved by its own *anima.* Theodore almost identifies the *hypostasis* (in Syriac, *qnŏma*) with the soul, which is capable of existence independent of the body.

---

[2]Epistle 38 was actually read at the Council of Chalcedon in 451 as an epistle of St. Basil. It seems to have been composed ca. 370 A.D. either by St. Basil or his brother, St. Gregory of Nyssa.

Basil's Epistle 38 follows a different line. If nature or *physis* refers to the common characteristics of a class, *hypostasis* refers to those identifying particulars which separate each particular member from other members of his class. Paul is a man, but when we speak about Paul we are referring to the individual person as he can be identified by certain specific characteristics. The common in a class refers to nature; the particular refers to *hypostasis*—this is the Cappadocian view, which is not so terribly metaphysical. "It *(hypostasis)* is the conception which, by means of the specific notes that it indicates, restricts and circumscribes in a particular thing what is general and uncircumscribed."[3]

Thus the man Jesus is the *hypostasis* of Jesus with the *physis* of man.[4]

(c) Ousia *or being*. In the Cappadocian fathers *ousia* is the term normally used for the *physis* of the Godhead, for that which is common to the three *hypostases* in the Trinity. The three *hypostases* in the Trinity are distinguished by their specific characteristics: *agennesia* or unbegottenness in the case of the Father, begottenness in the case of the Son, and procession from the Father in the case of the Holy Spirit.

Now the central affirmation of the Christian tradition with which Chalcedon also agrees is that the *hypostasis* of Jesus, who is a particular member of the class or *physis* of man, is none other than the *hypostasis* of the Second Person of the Trinity. These are not two *hypostases* united into one; but the one hypostasis of the eternal Son, without losing the *ousia* or *physis* of the Godhead, assumed or took on the *physis* of man. He is thus simultaneously a *hypostasis* in the Godhead and in humanity. On this point Chalcedonians and non-Chalcedonians agree.

In calling it hypostatic union, the Chalcedonians are not saying two *hypostases* were united to form one. But since it is the same *hypostasis* who has the nature of God and the nature of Man, the nature of the *hypostasis* of the Son is now after the Incarnation one single *physis,* which is formed by a union of the divine nature and the human nature in the one *hypostasis.*

---

[3] Ep. 38 in St. Basil, *The Letters,* trans. Roy J. Defarrari (Cambridge: Harvard University Press, 1950) 1:201.

[4] The affirmations sometimes made by Byzantine theologians to the effect that St. Cyril of Alexandria used *hypostasis* and *physis* interchangeably have not yet been sufficiently documented. There is near-identity between *physis* and *ousia,* especially in relation to the Trinity. This is so in the Cappadicians as well as in Cyril. But it is not yet clear that Professor Karmiris of Athens and Professor Tsonievsky of Sofia and others are justified in stating that when Cyril says one *nature* he means one *hypostasis.* The only evidence they bring is that he used both expressions, but that does not mean that *hypostasis* and *physis* are one. The meaning is rather that the one *hypostasis* has one united *physis.*

We insist on saying that that which is united is one after the union. This is why we reject the "in-two-natures" formula of Chalcedon and acknowledge the one *hypostasis* with the one united divine-human nature.

We do not claim that this settles the issue. We agree with St. Gregory of Nyssa, when he says:

> . . . as in the case of the union of soul and body, while we have reason to believe that the soul is something other than the body, because the flesh when isolated from the soul becomes dead and inactvie, we have yet no exact knowledge of the method of the union, so in that other enquiry of the union of the Deity with manhood, while we are quite aware that there is a distinction as regards degree of majesty between the Divine and the mortal perishable nature, we are not capable of detecting how the Divine and the human elements are mixed together. The miracles recorded permit us not to entertain a doubt that God was born in the nature of Man. But, how— this, as being a subject unapproachable by the processes of reasoning, we decline to investigate."[5]

One Nature vs. two Natures

The controversy between one united nature *vs.* two natures which has raged for fifteen centuries does not thus really cover a matter of great substance. What has caused the separation between the two sides appears now to have been primarily cultural, political, and terminological. The division has been sustained through the centuries by force of mutual suspicion, mutual caricaturing, and ecclesiastical inertia.

There are reasons for which my tradition still prefers the one-united-nature terminology today. We have a fear that the two-nature formula is sometimes misunderstood by some people as meaning two different persons—the preexistent *Logos* and the man Jesus somehow uneasily yoked together. We know that theologians on the Chalcedonian side do not teach this. But the distinction between the historical Jesus and the kerygmatic Christ in contemporary Christology worries us. We do not recognize a historical Jesus who is distinct from the incarnate Christ known and proclaimed by the church. The proclamation of the church is about the man Jesus whose *hypostasis* or identity is that of the Second Person of the Trinity. The Son of man *is* the Son of God. It is this total identity which we call *henosis physike,* though the two expressions are not parallel (*hypostasis* was always one; the natures have come together in the one *hypostasis*).

---

[5]*The Great Catechism,* ch. 11, in *The Nicene and Post-Nicene Fathers,* 2nd series, 5:486a.

Conclusions

1. The reason the Chalcedonian controversy appears irrelevant to some today is that they deny the reality of the Christian faith, which affirms that
   the Son of man is the Son of God, and thereby created the discussion
   about the relation between the two identities.

2. The contemporary Christological debate in Reformation circles is irrelevant to us, since it does not take the central affirmation of the gospel
   with sufficient seriousness.

3. The terminology of Chalcedon is not so obsolete as some people suggest. We have as yet no alternate philosophical terminology into which
   to translate the basic Christological affirmations in current language. This
   is primarily a defect of our philosophical language today and not of the
   affirmations of the faith.

4. The terminological differences need not separate us, if we really agree
   on the substance of the church's faith and tradition.

One Incarnate Nature of God the Word

V. C. Samuel

Introduction

The person of Jesus Christ transcends so much of our comprehension and linguistic expression that no formulation is adequate to describe him. At the same time, the church has adopted certain statements, thereby setting a limit beyond which we should not go in our theological reflection with reference to his person, although there is disagreement between the Chalcedonian and the non-Chalcedonian churches on the question of what these statements are.[1] Even here the crucial difference between the two traditions of churches may be said to lie in the attitude of each toward the phrase "one incarnate nature of God the Word." Thus on the whole the western churches are rather suspicious of this phrase. But in the East, while the Byzantine Orthodox Church is in favor of accepting it in a sort of partial way, the non-Chalcedonian Orthodox Church of the East regards it as a central linguistic tool to affirm the mystery of the Incarnation.

That the phrase came originally from Apollinarian forgeries ascribed to Athanasius of Alexandria is vigorously upheld by many modern scholars.[2] Even if this view is granted, it does not follow that therefore the phrase

---

[1]The non-Chalcedonian tradition accepts the "Nicene Creed," the Second Letter of Cyril to Nestorius, the Third Letter of Cyril to Nestorius and the Twelve Anathemas, and the Letter of Cyril to the Easterns, otherwise known as the Formulary of Reunion. It also accepts the theology of the Henotikon as orthodox. In the Chalcedonian tradition, many of the Western churches are rather halfhearted in their acceptance of Cyril's Third Letter to Nestorius with the Anathemas, and no church either in the East or in the West thinks much of the Henotikon. All the Chalcedonian churches accept the Tome of Leo and the Chalcedonian Formula of the Faith, both of which are rejected by the non-Chalcedonian body.

[2]For a summary treatment of this point see Robert Victor Sellers, *Two Ancient Christologies* (London: SPCK, 1940, 1954) 89, esp. n. 2. Panagiotes N. Trempla, *Dogmatike tes Orthodoxou Katholikes Ecclesias* (Athens, 1959) 2:98. The present writer has not had a chance to examine the basis on which this view has been put forward by modern scholars. So his acceptance of it is only provisional.

should be discarded. For the crucial phrase in the Nicene Creed, namely "of the same substance with the Father" (ὁμοούσιον τῷ πατρί), had not only a pagan origin,[3] but it had also been condemned by the Council of Antioch in 268, which excommunicated Paul of Samosata.[4] Therefore, the unorthodox origin of a term cannot be cited as an argument against its adoption by Orthodox theology, so long as the meaning assigned to it is orthodox and there is need for pressing that meaning. Cyril of Alexandria, the great bulwark of orthodoxy against the teaching of the Nestorian school in the fifth century,[5] saw in the phrase "one incarnate nature of God the Word" a most crucial linquistic tool to conserve the church's faith in the person of Jesus Christ.

However, like the Nicene phrase "of the same substance with the Father," which came to be misunderstood and misconstrued by various men for a long time, the phrase "one incarnate nature of God the Word" also was given different shades of erroneous meanings in olden times. Before taking up these heretical ideas for a brief discussion, it is necessary to look into the question of Eutyches.

The Teaching of Eutyches

The question as to what precisely were the ideas held by Eutyches is not easy to answer. Two sets of statements made by him at the Home Synod of Constantinople in 448 are certainly to be considered confused, if not heretical.[6] Thus in the first place, when he was asked whether he would affirm that our Lord was "of the same substance with us" (ὁμοούσιον ἡμῖν or *Shewa bousia lan*), he answered in this way: "Since I confess my God to be the Lord of heaven and earth, I have not till this day let myself enquire into His nature. That He is of the same substance with us, I have not affirmed till now, I confess." Again, "Till this day I have not said concerning the body of the Lord that it is of the same substance with us. But

---

[3]George Prestige has shown in his *God in Patristic Thought* (London: SPCK, 1952) 197, that Valentinians had used the phrase *homoousios*.

[4]In defending the Council of Nicea, both Athanasius and Hilary of Poitiers acknowledge this fact and proceed to answer the problem derived from it.

[5]The fact that there are a number of modern scholars who are critical of Cyril's theology should be noted here. But to the present writer they seem to misread his theology in their enthusiasm to defend the theology of the Antiochene school.

[6]All the statements of Eutyches referred to here are noted in J. D. Mansi, ed. *Sanctorum Conciliorum Nova et Amplissima Collectio* (= Mansi) 6:697-753, and in *Acta Conciliorum Oecumenicorum*, ed. Schwartz (= ACO) 2/1:122-47.

the Virgin is of the same substance with us, I confess." When, however, he was pressed as to how, if the mother was of the same substance with us, the Son could be otherwise, Eutyches said: "As you say now, I agree in every thing." It is clear from these statements that Eutyches was hesitant to affirm that our Lord was of the same substance with us.

Secondly, to the question of whether he would affirm that our Lord was two natures after the union, he answered: "I confess our Lord to be of two natures before the union, but after the union I confess one nature" (ὁμολογῶ ἐκ δύο φύσεων γεγενῆσθαι τὸν Κύριον ἡμῶν πρὸ τῆς ἑνώ σεως, μετὰ δὲ τὴν ἕνωσιν μία φύσις ὁμολογῶ).

Pushing these two statements to their logical conclusion, it is possible to read into Eutyches a position like this: Before God the Son became incarnate and Godhead and manhood were united in Jesus Christ, he was "of two natures."[7] When, however, the natures were united, he came to be "one nature." Since Eutyches was reluctant to affirm that Christ was of the same substance with us, the expression "one nature" may well have meant for him that the manhood was lost, as it were, subsequent to the union.

It is this meaning that the Tome of Leo, some Bishops at Chalcedon, and the Chalcedonian Formula of the Faith have seen in Eutyches. The Tome of Leo, for instance, has made out that "using deceptive words," Eutyches said that "the Word was made Flesh in such wise as to imply that Christ having been conceived in the Virgin's womb, possessed the form of a man without a real body taken from His mother."[8] At Chalcedon, Basil of Seleucia reported that for Eutyches a mere affirmation that God the Word became man by the assumption of flesh was enough to conserve the faith. (ὥστε εἰπεῖν αὐτὸν τὸν τρόπον τῆς σαρκώσεως καὶ ἐνανθρωπήσεως εἰ κατὰ πρόσληψιν σαρκὸς οἶδε τὸν Θεὸν Λόγον γενόμενον ἄνθρωπον.) The Chalcedonian Formula, referring in all probability to Eutyches, states that "others introduce a confusion and mixture, shamelessly imagining the Nature of the flesh and of the Godhead to be one, and absurdly maintaining that the Divine Nature of the Only-begotten is by this confusion passible"; and that the Council "anathematizes those who

---

[7]Unless we ascribe to Eutyches an Origenist Christology, this statement makes no sense. To read that into him is to make of him a thinker of eminence, which he certainly was not.

[8]See T. H. Bindley, *The Oecumenical Documents of the Faith* (London: Methuen, 1950) 224-31. For the Greek passage below see Mansi 6:633B and ACO 2/1.92:164-66.

imagine Two Natures of the Lord before the Union, but fashion anew One Nature after the Union.''[9]

But there are other statements of Eutyches in which he shows that this is not his position. So in an oral statement made by him at the Home Synod of Constantinople he said: "Concerning His coming in the flesh, I confess that it happened from the flesh of the Virgin, and that He became man perfectly (τελείως) for our salvation." By this statement Eutyches did affirm a real Incarnation. He made the same point still clearer in this confession of the faith.

> For He Himself, who is the Word of God, descended from heaven without flesh, was made flesh of the very flesh of the Virgin unchangeably and inconvertibly in a way which He Himself knew and willed. And He who is always perfect God before the ages, the Same also was made perfect man for us and for our salvation."[10]

This statement was certainly not unorthodox, insufficient though we may judge it to conserve the church's faith fully. So we have to say with J. N. D. Kelly, "The traditional picture of Eutyches, it is clear, has been formed by picking out certain of his statements and pressing them to their logical conclusion. . . . He was not a Docetist or Apollinarian, nothing could have been more explicit than his affirmation of the reality and completeness of the manhood. . . . ''[11]

In any case, from the point of view of initiating a discussion of the issue which separates the Chalcedonian church from the non-Chalcedonian church, the question of whether Eutyches himself had, in fact, held the view ascribed to him by the Tome of Leo and the Chalcedonian Formula is not important. What is important, on the other hand, is the question as to whether the non-Chalcedonian church has ever held the ideas thus ascribed to Eutyches. On this question the answer is quite clear. For Dioscorus of Alexandria did himself express this rejection of the ideas read into Eutyches at Chalcedon.[12] Following him, the non-Chalcedonian church has

---

[9]Bindley, *Documents,* 232, 235.

[10]For the confession of Eutyches, see Georg Hahn, *Bibliothek der Symbole und Glaubensregeln der alten Kirche* (Hildesheim: G. Olms, 1962) 319-20, and Mansi 5:1016C.

[11]J. N. D. Kelly, *Early Christian Doctrines* (London: Adam and Charles Black, 1958) 332-33.

[12]See Mansi 6:633C, and ACO 2/1.92:168.

throughout the centuries condemned these ideas[13] and even the person of Eutyches.

The Erroneous Ideas Assigned to the Phrase
"One Incarnate Nature of God the Word"

Broadly speaking, these ideas may be classified under three heads. We will mention them one by one.

A Tendency to Ignore the Manhood of Christ

This, as we have seen, is the position ascribed to Eutyches. Whether he himself held it or not, there were some in olden times, called "Eutychianists," who maintained this view. A certain John the Rhetorician of Alexandria is reported to have taught "Eutychianism" during the decade after the Council of Chalcedon.[14]

According to Zacharia, John the Rhetorician was a student of philosophy, who tried to combine some ideas derived from the Christian faith with his rational speculation. So he maintained that Jesus Christ was God the Word, who came into the world, being born of a virgin without conjugal relation. Being born in this way, he could not have been fully man. So he was "one nature" in the sense that he was God, but not also man.

A Teaching That Ignores Human Properties in Jesus Christ

A more subtle position than the foregoing one, this emphasis may be illustrated by referring to Sergius the Grammarian. A correspondent of Severus of Antioch in the sixth century, Sergius expressed it in this way: "Godhead and the flesh are two *ousias*. Eternality is the property of the former and corruptibility that of the latter." In becoming man, God the Son assumed flesh which "was born supernaturally," and the flesh "did not see corruption." But "by reason of the union the human property was passed over." Therefore, "it is better to say that there was one property" only in Christ.[15]

We find here an emphasis which takes Godhead and manhood as two different *ousias*, each possessing its own property. But they were united

---

[13]"Eutychianism" was opposed by the non-Chalcedonian body from the very beginning. Thus we have evidence that Theodosius of Jerusalem, who led the movement against Chalcedon in Palestine soon after the Council, and Timothy Aelurus of Alexandria condemned those who held it.

[14]See Zacharia Scholasticus (Rhetor), *Historia (Ecclesiastical History)*, trans. F. J. Hamilton and E. W. Brooks (London: Methuen, 1899) 1.163-64.

[15]See *Ad Nephalium*, Joseph Lebon, ed. (Louvain: J. van Linthout, 1949) 71-72.

in Christ in such a way that the human properties came to be lost in the union. Those who taught this idea took the phrase "one incarnate nature" as a convenient linguistic tool to conserve it.

It may be useful in this context to refer to the misunderstanding of the non-Chalcedonian position expressed by men of the Chalcedonian side in ancient times. John the Grammarian is referred to by Severus of Antioch to have criticized the non-Chalcedonian position as having maintained that "the Godhead and the flesh of Christ constituted one *ousia* and one nature."[16] The argument of the Grammarian may be put in this way: The non-Chalcedonian leaders were insisting that Christ was one incarnate nature, and that he was not two natures after the union. But the very emphasis that Christ was of the same substance with the Father as to Godhead and of the same substance with us as to manhood should be taken as an adequate basis for saying that he was in two natures. The non-Chalcedonian leaders were, however, opposed to the phrase "in two natures." This must be because in their view Christ was one *ousia*. In other words, the opponents of Chalcedon were considered unwilling to affirm the reality of Christ's manhood.

The answer of the non-Chalcedonian leaders to this criticism we shall see in a moment. What we should not in the present contest is the fact that their position was very much misunderstood and even misinterpreted by men of the Chalcedonian side in olden times.

A Teaching That Maintains
That the Manhood of Christ Was Incorruptible

This position was held by Julian of Halicarnassus. In fact, it had adherents in both the Chalcedonian and the non-Chalcedonian bodies in ancient times. Justinian himself adopted a form of it toward the end of his life, and Justinian was a persecutor of the non-Chalcedonians.

The teaching of Julian may be summarized in this way.[17] God created man in the beginning essentially immortal and incorruptible. But by the sin of Adam and the consequent fall, he lost this essential property. In order to save man from this fallen state, God the Son became incarnate by uniting to himself real and perfect manhood. But the manhood which he thus assumed was so sinless

---

[16]John the Grammarian was a critic of the non-Chalcedonian position, whose work in defense of Chalcedon was refuted by Severus in his *Liber contra impium grammaticum.* For this criticism, see ibid., 20.

[17]This discussion of Julian's teaching is based on a study of the writings of Severus of Antioch against Julian. For the early letters exchanged between them see Zacharia, *Historia,* 2.102:12. For other writings, see Severi, *Antiiulianistica,* ed. A. Sanday (Beirut, 1931) and British Museum MS no. 12158.

that it was the manhood of Adam before the fall, and so it was essentially impassible, immortal and incorruptible. Julian, however, maintained that Christ suffered passions and died on the cross voluntarily for us. At the same time, he insisted that the body of our Lord was from the moment of its formation in the womb of the Virgin incorruptible.

Of the many ideas which Julian emphasized, some are orthodox while others are heretical. The following orthodox ideas in the teaching of Julian may be noted:

(a) God the Son became incarnate by uniting to himself real and perfect manhood.
(b) As man, Christ was absolutely sinless.
(c) The suffering and death which Christ endured were indispensable for our salvation, and God the Son himself assumed them as his own.

But the following ideas of Julian seem heretical:

(a) When God the Son became incarnate, he united to himself the manhood of Adam before the fall. So it was essentially impassible and immortal.
(b) The body of our Lord was incorruptible, not merely after the resurrection, but from the moment of its conception in the womb of the Virgin.
(c) As man, Christ was of the same substance with us, not in the sense that his manhood was our manhood, but only in the sense that it was the essential manhood of Adam before the fall. In other words, according to Julian, the manhood was not only sinless, but it had no involvement in the fallen state of the human race.

The Non-Chalcedonian Orthodox Church in the Face of These Erroneous Emphases

These three positions were, in fact, not only rejected but even refuted by the leaders of the non-Chalcedonian Orthodox Church. As we have already noted, John the Rhetorician lived during the decade after the Council of Chalcedon. Theodosius of Jerusalem, who led the movement against Chalcedon in Palestine soon after the Council, opposed his teaching and even wrote a treatise refuting it.[18] It is reported that he took strong measures against other "Eutychianists" in Palestine also. Timothy Aelurus, the immediate successor of Dioscorus on the See of Alexandria, was equally opposed to "Eutychianism." During his exile in Gangra, Bishop Isaiah of Hermopolis and Presbyter Theophilus of Alexandria left Egypt and made their home in Constantinople, where they disseminated "Eutychianist"

---

[18]See Zacharia, *Historia,* 1.161-64.

ideas. On hearing this news, Timothy sent letters opposing them and in the end he excommunicated them.[19] Thus from the point of view of condemning "Eutychianists" and their ideas, there is no ground for doubt that the non-Chalcedonian church has done it with as much vigor as the Chalcedonian church. We can, in fact, say that the ancient Orthodox Church of the East which renounced the Council of Chalcedon has, from the beginning, excluded also the heresies which the Council has condemned.

The second and the third erroneous positions noted above came to be expressed during the days of Severus of Antioch. He refuted them, and, under his leadership, his section of the church also excluded them categorically.

As we have noted, it was Sergius the Grammarian who expressed the second position. Severus answered him by saying that the affirmation of a difference of properties was the teaching of the fathers. The natures which were united in the one Christ, they affirmed, were different. "For one is uncreated, and the other is created." But while "the difference in properties of the natures" continued to be real, "the natures of which the one Christ is, are united without confusion." In this way, "the Word of life is said to have become visible and tangible." When we think of the Emmanuel, we shall see that Godhead and manhood are different, and as we confess the union, "the difference signifying the natures of which the one Christ is" we do not ignore, "though by reason of the *hypostatic* union" we discard division.[20] In fact, it is on the ground of this admission that Severus works out his emphasis on the *communicatio idiomatum*. For he maintains that there is an exchange of properties in Christ, so that "the Word may be recognized in the properties of the flesh," and the human properties have "come to belong to the Word and the properties of the Word to the flesh."[21] A passage from the work of Severus against John the Grammarian may be quoted here to show how he maintains a recognition of the principle of difference in the one Christ.

> Those, therefore, who confess that the Lord Jesus Christ is one (made up) of Godhead and manhood, and that He is one *prosopon*, one *hypostasis*, and one nature of the Word incarnate, recognize and affirm also the difference, integrity, and otherness of the natures, of which the one Christ is ineffably formed. As they perceive this by subtle thought and contem-

---

[19]For this incident and the letters that Timothy Aelurus wrote in this connection, see ibid., 185-205, and 215-16. That Timothy Aelurus opposed "Eutychianists" is mentioned even by Evagrius. See *Patrologia Graeca* (= PG) 86:2603A.

[20]*Ad Nephalium*, 74-77.

[21]Ibid., 79.

plation of the mind, they do not take it as a ground for dividing the Emmanuel into two natures after the union.[22]

It may be shown that in maintaining this point of view Severus was not adopting a position discontinuous with the non-Chalcedonian leaders before him. As we know, the Formula of Chalcedon contains four adverbs with reference to the union of the natures in Christ: ἀσυγχύτως, ἀτρέπτως, ἀδιαιρέτως and ἀχωρίστως (without confusion, change, division, or separation). The Formula was adopted at Chalcedon 22 October 451. But on 8 October, fourteen days before this incident, Dioscorus stated at Chalcedon that in opposing the phrase "two natures after the union" or its cognate "*in* two natures," he was not speaking of confusion, division, change, or mixture (οὔτε σύγχυσιν λέγομεν, οὔτε τομήν. ἀνάθεμα τῷ λέγοντι ἢ σύγκρασιν ἢ τροπὴν ἢ ἀνάκρασιν).[23]

Another equally important statement of Dioscorus made at Chalcedon should also be noted here. On one occasion he signified that he was in agreement with the affirmation "*of* two natures after the union."[24] These evidences are sufficient to say that in protesting against the council of Chalcedon, Dioscorus was not showing any sympathy for a theological position which ignored the manhood of our Lord.

All the non-Chalcedonian leaders have affirmed that in his Incarnation God the Son united to himself manhood animated with a rational soul and of the same substance with us, that he endured in reality blameless passions of the body and the soul, and that there was no confusion or mixture of the natures in him. Taking these emphases seriously, if we evaluate their teaching, we shall certainly see that in opposing the Council of Chalcedon they were not led by any sympathy for "Eutychianism" or monophysitism of any kind. We shall also realize that they had not interpreted the phrase "one incarnate nature of God the Word" to mean absorption of the manhood or the human property.

Severus answered also the charge of John the Grammarian that the non-Chalcedonian body was arguing, on the basis of the phrase "one incarnate nature of God the Word," that in Christ Godhead and manhood formed one *ousia*. In fact, he challenged the critic to show at least a single bit of evidence to prove his charge and made it very clear that his section of the

---

[22]*Contra Grammaticum* 3.106, Joseph Lebon, ed. PUB INFO PLS

[23]Manis, 6:676D-677A; ACO 2/1,112:262-263.

[24]Manis, 6:692A; ACO 2/1,120:332.

church did not hold that view.[25] This means that for Severus and the church which he represented "one incarnate nature" did not mean "one *ousia*."

Julian of Halicarnassus was refuted by Severus. Relying on the work of R. Draguet, R. V. Sellers maintains that the difference between the teaching of Severus and that of Julian is largely one of terminology.[26] The present writer finds it difficult to agree with this reading of the difference between Severus and Julian.[27] Even granting that this reading is correct, would the Chalcedonian side maintain a position more adequate than the one held by Severus?

Severus on "One Incarnate Nature of God the Word"

Following Cyril of Alexandria, Severus accepts four phrases with reference to the Incarnation. They are: "of (ἐϰ) two natures," "hypostatic union," "one incarnate nature of God the Word," and "one composite nature." In his view all these phrases stand together. So in order to understand what the phrase "one incarnate nature of God the Word" means to him and to the church which he represents, the meaning of these phrases should be noted.

The crucial word in these phrases is "nature" (φύσις or *kyono*). As to its meaning, both Severus and the Chalcedonian writers of his time agree that it may be taken either in the sense of *ousia* or in that of *hypostasis*. Severus shows that *ousia* stands for him both as an equivalent of the *eidos* of Plato and as a generic term including all the members of a class. By *hypostasis* (ὑπόστασις or *qnumo*) Severus means a concrete particular in which the *ousia* (οὐσία or *ousio* [Syr.]) is individuated. In other words, for both sides "nature" means either the dynamic reality existing in the realm of ideas or the concrete object resulting from its individuation. But they disagree on the application of the word "nature" to the person of Christ. Whereas the Grammarian takes it in the sense of *ousia,* Severus sees in it the meaning of *hypostasis*.[28]

Coming now to the phrases themselves, Severus makes it clear that Christ was "*of* (ἐϰ) two natures.*"* But by this phrase he does not sanction

---

[25]For this discussion of Severus, see *Contra Grammaticum* 1.20-24.

[26]Robert Victor Sellers, *The Council of Chalcedon* (London: SPCK, 1953) 309-10, n. 6. Cf. R. Draguet, *Julien d'Halicarnasse et sa controverse avec Severe d'Antioche sur l'incorruptibilité du corps du Christ* (Louvain, 1924).

[27]For our reading of the difference between the two men, see above.

[28]Severus himself discusses the meaning of the crucial terms both in his *Contra Grammaticum* and in some of his doctrinal letters.

the expression "two natures before the union."[29] He says that "no one who has thought correctly has ever affirmed" this phrase "even in fancy."[30] For the "*Hypostasis* of God the Word existed . . . before all the ages and times, He being eternally with God the Father and the Holy Spirit"; but "the flesh possessing a rational soul did not exist before the union with him."[31] The phrase "of (ἐκ) two natures" means, for Severus, two ideas. On the one hand, it conserves the emphasis that in Christ there was a union of God the Son with an individual manhood, and on the other that Christ was unceasingly a continuation of that union. So Christ was always "of (ἐκ) two natures"; and thus he was at once perfect God and perfect man, being "of the same substance with God the Father" and "of the same substance with us."

The union of the natures was *hypostatic,* by which Severus means that:

> It was in union with the Word who is before the ages that the flesh was formed and came *to be,* and in concurrence it [namely the flesh] received with Him concreteness into the union. In this way, from two, namely Godhead and manhood, Christ is known indivisibly one Emmanuel.[32]

The phrase "hypostatic union," then, means for Severus that in Christ there was a coming together of everything that the Godhead of the Son implies and of everything that an individuated manhood connotes. The phrase means also the absolutely inward and personal character of the union.

In a long passage in his *Philalethes,* Severus discusses the phrase "one incarnate nature of God the Word." When the Fathers spoke of "one incarnate nature of God the Word," he writes, "they made it clear that the Word did not abandon His nature"; neither did he undergo any "loss or diminution in His *hypostasis.* When they affirmed that "He became incarnate" they made it clear that "the flesh was nothing but flesh, and that it did not come into being by itself apart from the union with the Word." Again the words "became incarnate" refer to the Word's assumption of the flesh from the Virgin, an assumption by which from two natures, namely Godhead and manhood, "one Christ came forth from Mary." He is at once God and man, being of the same substance with the Father as to Godhead and of the same substance with us as to manhood.[33]

---

[29]He opposes "two natures before the union" in several places in his writings.

[30]*Contra Grammaticum* 2.239.

[31]*Patrologia Orientalis,* 12:190-91.

[32]This is a passage taken from *Contra Grammaticum* 2.239-41.

[33]See *Philalethes,* 139, ed. Hespel (Louvain, 1952) (Syriac) 139.

There are three emphases made by the phrase "one incarnate nature."
(1) It was God the Son himself who became incarnate.
(2) In becoming incarnate, he individuated manhood in union with himself and made it his very own.
(3) The incarnate Word is one Person.

The "one" in the phrase "one incarnate nature" is not a *simple one,* so that the characterization "monophysite" cannot be considered applicable to the position of Severus. As "one incarnate nature," Jesus Christ is one *composite* nature. In the Incarnation, by a divine act of condescension, God the Son willed to be so united with manhood that the two of them came together, without either of them being lost or diminished. At the same time, their union was so real and perfect that Christ was "one composite nature."

In the face of the misunderstanding expressed by the Chalcedonian tradition that the non-Chalcedonian position has ignored the manhood of Christ, we shall put together the ideas emphasized by Severus on this point.

(1) Christ's manhood was an individuated manhood, fully like and continuous with our manhood, with the single exception that it was absolutely sinless.
(2) The manhood of Christ was individuated only in a hypostatic union with God the Son, and it continued to exist in perfection and reality in that union. Therefore, the manhood of Christ did not exist independent of its union with God the Son.
(3) The union did not lead to a confusion of the manhood with, or a loss in, the Godhead; and therefore in Christ Godhead and manhood with their respective properties were hypostatically united with each other. But the two should not be separated.
(4) The Union brought into being one Person, and this one Person is the Person of God the Son in his incarnate state. There is a distinction between the preincarnate Son and the incarnate Son, so that the *hypostasis* and *prosopon* of Jesus Christ are not simply the *hypostasis* and the *prosopon* of God the Son.
(5) The manhood of Christ was real, perfect, and dynamic in the union.

Having made all these emphases, why did Severus and the leaders of the non-Chalcedonian church refuse to accept the phrase "in two natures"? In fact, both in his letters to Nephalius and in his *Liber Contra Impium Grammaticum,* Severus admits that some earlier Fathers had said of Christ that he was two natures. These Fathers, insists Severus, meant by the expression only that Christ was at once God and man. However, the Nestorian school adopted the phrase to assert a doctrine of two persons. The phrase should not, therefore, be used any longer. Severus says also that

When we anathematize those who affirm of the Emmanuel two natures after the union and their operations as well as properties, it is not for speaking of natures or operations or properties that we place them under condemnation; but for saying two natures after the union and assigning the operations and properties to each of them, thereby dividing them between the natures.[34]

The passage is clear enough. Christ is "of two natures," the properties and operations of each of which are there in him in a state of indivisible and indissoluble union. To illustrate the point, people saw Christ hunger or thirst or suffer physical and mental agony. It is right on their part to say on the ground of what they saw that Christ's manhood was the subject of these experiences. So also they saw him heal the sick and raise the dead. It is correct again to say that the Godhead of Christ did these signs. But in Christ the hunger and all other physical disabilities were human, united with, and made his own by God the Son in his incarnate state. In the same way, the superhuman words and deeds were expressions of the Godhead of the Son in union with manhood. In other words, it was the one incarnate Person who was the subject of all the words and deeds of Christ. This one incarnate Person was the "one incarnate nature of God the Word" or the "one composite nature" of the incarnate Son. When we reflect on him, we can, in our contemplation, distinguish the two natures of Godhead and manhood and their respective properties and operations.

But the Tome of Leo went beyond this sound principle, and in declaring it a document of the faith the Council of Chalcedon also committed a great error. According to the Tome, "Each nature performs what is proper to the Word, and the flesh carrying out what is proper to the flesh." A teaching of this kind does not affirm Christ's personal unity, but regards the natures as two persons. The phrase "in two natures" defined by the Council of Chalcedon must have meant the same teaching as that of Bishop Leo. So it cannot be accepted.

The Real Difference between the Chalcedonian and the Non-Chalcedonian Positions

As we have noted, the Chalcedonian East accepts the orthodoxy of the phrase "one incarnate nature of God the Word." It believes that it is even necessary to maintain this phrase as a safeguard against Nestorianism. But it adds that since the phrase can be taken in a misleading sense, the expression "in two natures" should also be added to it. Thus by "in two na-

---

[34]*Ad Nephalium,* 80.

tures'' Eutychianism can be excluded, and by ''one incarnate nature'' Nestorianism may be kept out.

The non-Chalcedonian church, on the other hand, maintains that these two phrases contradict each other in meaning, and that in the light of the theology of the Tome of Leo ''in two natures'' cannot have meant for the Council of Chalcedon anything more than the teaching of Nestorius. As for excluding ''Eutychianism,'' it can be done by insisting on the phrase ''of two natures'' and by emphasizing that the ''one incarnate nature'' is ''one composite nature.'' The real terminological difference between the two traditions can thus be seen to lie in the two prepositions of ''in'' (ἐν) and ''of'' (ἐκ).

A Word in Conclusion

It is quite clear that neither Dioscorus of Alexandria nor the non-Chalcedonian Orthodox Church took the phrase ''one incarnate nature of God the Word'' in order to ignore, or minimize the importance of, Christ's manhood. But they considered it crucial because it was the phrase by which they affirmed the indivisible unity of the person of Christ. In fact, while opposing the Council of Chalcedon with reference to its positive affirmation of the faith which they believed was Nestorianism in disguise, they excluded the heresies which the Council had condemned.

II

Protestant Views

Lutheran Teaching
on Christology
and Its Implications
for Lutheran-Orthodox Relations

William G. Rusch

Within the last twenty years two remarkable series of ecumenical agreements on Christology have occurred. Between 1964 and 1971 a number of unofficial consultations took place between Eastern and Oriental Orthodox Churches. Supported by the Faith and Order Commission of the World Council of Churches, these consultations resulted in a convergence in Orthodox Christology. Participants in these meetings declared that after 1,500 years of schism over acceptance or rejection of the Council of Chalcedon in 451, they recognized in each other the one orthodox faith of the church and found full agreement on the essence of Christological dogma, although each side used different terminologies.[1] Formal acceptance of the Agreed Statements of Aarhus in 1964, Bristol in 1967, Geneva in 1970, and Addis Ababa in 1971 by the sponsoring churches has not yet occurred. When it does, it will mean that a major healing in the breach between the churches has been effected. During the 1970s a similar set of conversations, organized by the Foundation *Pro Oriente,* in Vienna, were held between theologians of the Oriental Orthodox and the Roman Catholic churches. These non-official consultations issued four communiqués in 1971, 1973, 1976, and 1978.[2] Once again a noteworthy convergence was claimed in Christology and in other areas of the church's faith and life.

---

[1]The full reports are found in *The Greek Orthodox Theological Review* 10:2 (1964-1965); 12:2 (1968); 16:1,2 (1971). Selected essays, discussions, and the Agreed Statements appeared in *Does Chalcedon Divide or Unite?: Towards Convergence in Orthodox Christology,* Paulos Gregorios, William H. Lazareth, and Nikos A. Nissiotis, eds. (Geneva: World Council of Churches, 1981).

[2]*Wort und Warheit,* suppl. issues nos. 1 (1972); 2 (1974); 3 (1976); and 4 (1978).

When the Oriental Orthodox Churches and the Roman Catholic Church officially accept the consultations' work, a painful cause of division between the eastern and western parts of the church will be removed.

The purpose of this essay is to explore how the convergences on christology described above relate to the Lutheran tradition within Christianity. Can Lutheranism enter into these convergences, and if so what difference should such participation make in the relationships between Lutheran churches and Eastern and Oriental Orthodox churches? These are the questions that will be explored here; the problem of Lutheran/Roman Catholic relations will only be addressed indirectly. While the author can only speak for himself as a Lutheran, it is hoped that he will have faithfully enough represented his tradition that some wider implications can be drawn from his work. In order to determine Lutheran reactions to these ecumenical convergences, it will be necessary for us to examine the teachings of Lutheranism on Christology. These teachings can be found both in the writings of Martin Luther and in the Lutheran Confessions.

At the outset the place and authority of Luther should be made clear. Contemporary Lutherans neither enshrine Luther nor ignore him. They see Luther as a religious genius, one of God's most useful and influential witnesses, but as a sinful human being with serious flaws. He was not a saint. Luther taught and wrote much. Not everything he wrote has equal authority. In fact only his writings that became "received" as part of the Lutheran Confessions have special authority in Lutheran churches, and these writings, as all Lutheran Confessions, stand under the authority of the Scriptures. Perhaps a helpful way to describe Martin Luther's role in contemporary Lutheranism is to compare him to one of the great Fathers of the early church—a major teacher of faith, but not one above the Scriptures and tradition of the church. He should not be regarded as the founder of a new church or as the leader of a school of church life. Luther and his fellow reformers always insisted that they were not establishing a new church. The Lutheran Reformation had one main focus : the *continuity* of the *one* church. The gospel had not been lost in the medieval Roman church, but the followers of Luther believed it had been obscured and must be uncovered and purified to shine forth once more. The reformers had an ecumenical emphasis in their stress on the continuity of the church and in their desire to present the true gospel.

Luther was a child of the sixteenth century. He was intensively involved in the affairs of his time. In addition, Luther was not a systematic theologian. He never wrote a treatise on Christology. Luther scholarship has often had a hard time summarizing his thought. Nevertheless, it is not difficult to sketch out his teaching about Christ.[3]

Luther considered his reform movement to be clearly grounded in the catholic substance of the trinitarian and Christological doctrines of the ancient church. In Luther's thinking God's Incarnation in Christ and Christ's two natures cannot be divided. "This is the first article of our faith that Jesus Christ is essential, natural, true and complete God and man in one person, undivided and inseparable."[4] He accepted the great ecumenical creeds. In 1538 he published expositions of the Nicene, Athanasian, and Apostles' Creeds. His work *On the Councils and the Church* of 1539 reveals that he studied almost all the available sources dealing with the christological controversies, and contains his views on the Council of Chalcedon.[5] He knew the differences between Greek and Latin theologians. Along with the tradition, Luther affirmed that Christ makes satisfaction not because of the ability of human beings but because God wanted to save humankind; Christ overcomes the powers of sin, death, and evil; he is present already in the "Word" here on earth, pointing to that end-time when sin, death, and evil will be no more. In Luther can be seen a union of Pauline and Johannine thought. The mystery of the Incarnation can finally be expressed only in paradoxical language. Although Luther did not develop a properly systematic Christology, he insisted that God's work in Christ is his proper work of salvation, as over against God's strange work of creation.

Luther follows the traditional way of establishing the true deity of Christ. The authority of Scripture guarantees this. He repeats thoughts that are reminiscent of the Greek Fathers: Christ could not be our Redeemer if he were not the true and eternal God. Here it is possible to observe Luther's great interest and stress on the saving work accomplished by Christ. Soteriology becomes the framework within which Luther will deal with questions of the divinity and humanity of Christ, and their union in his per-

---

[3]Fuller treatments of Luther's Christology are Ernst Wolf, *Die Christusverkindigung bei Luther* (Munich: Kaiser Verlag, 1954); P. W. Gennrich, *Die Christologie Luthers im Abendmahlsstreit* (Gottingen: Vandenhoeck & Ruprecht, 1929); J. K. Siggins, *Martin Luther's Doctrine of Christ* (New Haven: York University Press, 1970); and Marc Lienhard, *Luther: Witness to Jesus Christ* (Minneapolis: The Augsburg Publishing House, 1982) with complete bibliography.

[4]Martin Luther, *Confession Concerning Christ's Supper*, vol. 37 of *Luther's Works* (hereafter LW), Robert H. Fischer, ed. (Philadelphia: Muhlenberg Press, 1961) 214, 360-62.

[5]Martin Luther, *On the Councils and the Church,* vol. 41 of LW, Eric W. Gritsch, ed. (Philadelphia: Fortress Press) 9-178, esp. 106-21.

son. For Luther it is the work of Christ that provides the insight into the mystery of his person. But Luther is well aware that it is not enough to describe the work of Christ without speaking about the One who accomplished it. His thoughts about Christ are more kerygmatic than technical or speculative. Without elaborate systems or terminological precision, Luther affirms a number of things on the basis of the biblical witness. He did not believe that he was inventing anything in Christology. He shared with Rome the current Christological tradition.

Controversies over the Eucharist with Zwingli and his followers forced Luther to express himself more exactly about the union between the two natures of Christ. A fundamental reality of his faith was the union of the two natures. In the face of a medieval Christology that saw Christ as a model or an image to inspire, thus favoring the "human" Christ, Luther placed himself within the tradition of the dogmatic Christology of the early church. He used the Christological vocabulary of the early church. This use was never simply formal. He never considered the creeds obsolete, although he felt called to interpret them in the light of the doctrine of justification by faith through grace. His thought was permeated with the writings of Augustine, Athanasius, Chrysostom, Irenaeus, and Gregory of Nazianzus.

Certain aspects of post-Chalcedonian Christology and monophysite tendencies have been identified in Luther. Perhaps it is more accurate to say that Luther had gone beyond the Latin Middle Ages with its rather Nestorian tendency to an earlier eastern Christology. He stressed the unity between the two natures and developed a conception of the communication of attributes and even of the suffering of God. Luther cannot be judged a modalist, although some individual texts could suggest this. He did stress repeatedly that God cannot be found apart from the man Jesus. During his struggle with Zwingli in the Eucharistic controversy, Luther's strong stress on the divine nature of Christ was to the detriment of the human nature. Yet a complete survey of his writings discloses that Luther never ceased to insist on the reality of Christ's humanity.[6] In developing his interest in the union between the two natures of Christ, Luther's attention is focused on the concrete person of Christ, who saves the individual believer. Especially in his early works, Luther presents an eschatological view of Christology. The presence of the divine in the humanity needs to be revealed by the Word and this will only be grasped on the last day. There is an unprecedented tension in his thought of the two natures in which the divine power and human weakness coexist. Luther endeavored to address

---

[6]See references in n. 4 above.

this situation by the use of the concept of communication of attributes. In so doing Luther probably contradicted his eschatological view of Christology. Several commentators have seen a fracture at the heart of Luther's Christological thought. It may be better described as a paradox that he could not logically resolve.

But in this paradox there is a role for the humanity of Christ. It is not fair to Luther to suggest that for him this humanity has no other function than that of hiding the "naked" God and allowing God to realize his eternal being in time. Luther in Johannine terms teaches that the Son became incarnate to reveal the love of God to human beings who are subject to his wrath. Christ is delivered up to the wrath of God. The patristic image of combat is used. Christ becomes human to clear the way for the love of God. Luther's trinitarian thought is the context from which to see his insistence on the place and importance of Christ's humanity.

As mentioned previously, Luther's Christology was not systematic. Yet it goes beyond the gathering and popularizing of some Christological items which were more or less current. Luther was concerned with a Christology that was a coherent whole of themes concerning the action of God and man in Christ as well as the salvation brought to human beings. The matrix of Luther's thought may have become strange to twentieth-century persons, yet the motifs of faith are there: the hidden but real presence of God in his humanity and the reality of this humanity with ours; the true participation of God in the human condition; the constant call addressed to human faith, inviting human beings to turn away from themselves in order to rest entirely on Christ. In all of this, Luther wanted to make real to his contemporaries the biblical witness to Christ.

The newness in Luther's thought in all of this is his deep insight into the meaning and significance that Jesus Christ is true God. With his intense soteriological concern Luther pushes the question: What does God intend to do with us sinners? He finds the answer in Christ. In the person, activity, and history of Jesus Christ, God has opened his heart. Christ is the mirror of God's fatherly heart. Luther finds God the Father in the person of Christ.[7] Luther does stress the humanity of Christ, but he moves beyond it. It is through knowing Jesus as a man that we penetrate to the heart of God. The Incarnation discloses the depth of our salvation. God is for us.

Regarding objective knowledge of Christ, Luther includes everything that the ancient dogmas say about Christ's two natures. But he believes that it is

---

[7]See Martin Luther, *Sermons on the Gospel of St. John 14,* vol. 24 of LW, Jaroslav Pelikan, ed. (St. Louis: Concordia Publishing House, 1961) 24:60-61.

not the metaphysical unity of the two natures but rather the personal unity of the Son with the Father, of the man Jesus with the eternal God, that is ultimately decisive in the matter of salvation. But this is completely personal, practical, and existential—grasping Christ with the heart and whole person. Luther's basic Christological confession that the Father's heart and will are present in Christ will always be significant. His dogmatic efforts to describe Christ as true God and true man were never unified, and they displayed paradoxes if not contradictions. In struggles with other reformers Luther's followers sought to move beyond his inconsistencies.

Perhaps Luther's deep faith in Christ is nowhere so simply and clearly expressed than in his Small Catechism when he speaks of the second article of the Apostle's Creed:

> I believe that Jesus Christ, true God, begotten of the Father from eternity, and also true man, born of the virgin Mary, is my Lord, who has redeemed me from all sins, from death, and from the power of the devil, not with silver and gold but with his holy and precious blood and with his innocent sufferings and death, in order that I may be his, live under him in his kingdom, and serve him in everlasting righteousness, innocence, and blessedness, even as he is risen from the dead and lives and reigns to all eternity. This is most certainly true.[8]

In the course of the sixteenth-century Reformation not only Luther but other Lutheran reformers set forth their views in a number of writings. By 1580 several of these documents were collected into *The Book of Concord*.[9] The texts in this volume assessed a special importance for Lutherans and explained what the Lutheran Reformation taught.

The Book of Concord contains three documents that did not come from the disputes of the sixteenth century—the Apostles', the Nicene, and the Athanasian Creeds. The primary Reformation document is the unaltered Augsburg Confession of 1530. Written by Philip Melanchthon for the Diet at Augsburg, it represents the theological consensus of those who accepted the Lutheran Reformation. It became the most authoritative confession for the Lutherans. *The Book of Concord* also included the "Apology of the Augsburg Confession," written by Melanchthon to elucidate the headings of the Confession over against the misunderstandings of its opponents; the

---

[8]Martin Luther, Small Catechism II,2.

[9]The confessions of the Lutheran churches may be found in the original German or Latin in *Die Bekennisschriften der evangelisch-lutherischen Kirche* (Gottingen: Vandenhoeck & Ruprecht, 1959). The best English edition is *The Book of Concord*, Theodore G. Tappert, trans. and ed. (Philadelphia: Fortress Press, 1959).

"Smalcald Articles of 1537" from Luther that were intended for an anticipated general council; "The Treatise on the Power and Primacy of the Pope" by Melanchthon that completes themes raised in the Augsburg Confession; Luther's Large and Small Catechisms as summary presentations of Reformation doctrine for the laity; and the Formula of Concord of 1577, in short and long forms that resolved doctrinal disputes over the interpretation of the Augsburg confession.

All these documents were generally regarded as Confessions by the churches of the Lutheran Reformation. This means that these churches assumed a responsibility for them. They were no longer considered merely writings of individuals. Rather the claim was made not that Lutheran churches are speaking here but that the one, holy, catholic and apostolic church can find its teaching in these confessions. These documents are expounded by the church itself. As Confessions, they make the claim to be the obligatory model of all the church's preaching and teaching without limit of time and space. As Lutherans have tested these claims they have developed principles of interpretation. A prevailing view among many, for example the Lutheran Church in America, is that greater weight be given to the Augsburg Confession and Luther's Small Catechism than to the other documents. Some Lutheran churches have refused to recognize the Formula of Concord as a confession and see it as the beginning of the post-Reformation developments.

We will now briefly survey what these authoritative Lutheran documents teach about Christology. One important fact will emerge immediately: a basic consensus existed between the Lutheran reformers and the Roman Catholic Church of the sixteenth century. Controversy over christology occurred among Lutherans, Zwinglians, and Calvinists. This dispute was occasioned by different teachings about the Lord's Supper. These difficulties caused intra-Lutheran disagreements about the correct interpretation of the communication of attributes.

We will begin with the Augsburg Confession. Three articles deal directly or indirectly wth our topic. Article I, on God, teaches in agreement with Nicea and rejects all anti-trinitarian views, including those of the sixteenth century. Article III on the Son of God states:

> It is also taught among us that God the Son became man, from the virgin Mary, and that the two natures, divine and human, are so inseparably united in one person that there is one Christ, true God and true man, who was truly born, suffered, was crucified, died, and was buried in order to be a sacrifice not only for original sin but also for all other sins and to propitiate God's wrath. The same Christ also descended into hell, truly rose from the dead on the third day, ascended into heaven, and sits on the right

hand of God, that he may eternally rule and have dominion over all creatures, that through the Holy Spirit he may sanctify, purify, strengthen, and comfort all who believe in him, that he may bestow on them life and every grace and blessing, and that he may protect and defend them against the devil and against sin. The same Lord Christ will return openly to judge the living and the dead as stated in the Apostle's Creed.

Article XVII, on the return of Christ, declares that Jesus Christ will return on the last day for judgment. There will be eternal life and joy for believers; hell and eternal punishment for the ungodly and the devil. Certain Jewish opinions, millennial views, and Anabaptist teachings are rejected.

All three of these articles in the Apology of the Augsburg Confession are succinct, and reaffirm the statements of the Augsburg Confession. In each of these instances the Roman Confutation to the Augsburg Confession accepts the teaching of the Confession: on God, the Son of God, and the return of Christ. Here is clear evidence that Melanchthon repeated the ancient Christological confessions, and they found agreement with Lutherans and Roman Catholics.

In the Smalcald Articles Part I, Luther turned to the Creed. In this section he makes the following statements about Christ. The Father was begotten by no one, the Son was begotten by the Father, and the Holy Spirit proceeded from the Father and the Son. Only the Son became man, neither the Father nor the Holy Spirit. The Son was conceived by the Holy Spirit without the cooperation of man, and was born of the pure, holy Virgin Mary. He suffered, died, was buried, descended into hell, rose from the dead, ascended, sits at the right hand of the Father, and will come to judge the living and the dead according to the Apostle's Creed, the Athanasian Creed and the Catechism. Luther treats all these points briefly. He says that on these points there is no dispute or contention with the Roman Catholic Church.

In the first part of Part II of the Smalcald Articles, Luther discusses "Christ and Faith." A number of Scripture quotations from Romans and the Gospel of John are used. Luther declares that this work of Christ must be believed. It cannot be obtained or apprehended by any work, law, or merit. Faith alone justifies. Thus nothing in this article can be given up or compromised. Luther says that on this article rests all that we teach and practice against the pope, the devil, and the world. Luther's teaching on Christ in the Small Catechism has been described above in his statements on the second article of the Creed. These thoughts are basically repeated in his Large Catechism. As is typical in Luther, there is the strong stress on the work of Christ for the individual believer, "he paid all that I owed, all this in order to become my Lord."

If the Lutheran reformers and Roman Catholics could agree on christology, this was not to be the case with Lutherans and the followers of
Zwingli and Calvin. Against Zwingli and his followers Luther would repeatedly insist that Christ was really present in the Lord's Supper. It is also
the context of the Lord's Supper and the real presence that became the
principal dogmatic difference to set apart Lutheranism from Calvinism.
Luther, we have seen, taught the communication of attributes to safeguard
the real presence against the objection that the real presence was precluded
by the ascension of the humanity of Christ to the right hand of God. Lutherans charged the Reformed with being Nestorians; Reformed saw Lutherans as Eutychians. Lutherans protested that they were only teaching
the real union and the communication of natures which was Chalcedonian
theology. Reformed theologians appealed to the Tome of Leo, the Council
of Ephesus of 431, and John of Damascus. Criticism of Lutherans saw their
teaching as a threat to Christ's human nature. Lutherans insisted that they
were echoing the Greek Fathers who spoke of the deified human nature of
Christ. This controversy over the real presence was responsible for the most
detailed western church preoccupation with the intricacies of Christology
since the early church. Despite some of the debates, the essential content
of the Chalcedonian dogma stood firm in Lutheranism. The underlying issue was the proper recognition of the relation between the divine and human in the person of Christ, not as speculative theory but as a necessary
basis for the doctrine of the work of Christ. Christ was what he was in order to do what he did.

This dispute even influenced the unity of the Lutheran party. Some Lutherans—the followers of Melanchthon, called the Philippists—tended to
see the assertions of the communication of attributes as figures of speech
in order to preserve the independent realities of each nature, a position defended by Calvin. Other Lutherans, the Gnesio-Lutherans, stressed the real
interpenetration of Christ's human and divine natures, a position Luther
had defended against Zwingli.

Two Lutheran theologians, John Brenz and Martin Chemnitz, sought
to preserve Lutheran unity during these debates. The work contributed to
the last of the Lutheran Confessions, the Formula of Concord of 1580. This
Lutheran confession and later Lutheran systematic theology adopted
Chemnitz's summary about the communication of attitudes by speaking of
(1) *genus idionaticum* —to ascribe to the entire person what is the property
of one nature; (2) *genus majestaticum* —the person does not act in, with,
through, or according to one nature only but in, according to, with, and
through both natures; and (3) *genus apotelesmaticum* —for the exercise of
Christ's office, the human nature in Christ is employed after its own fash-

ion along with the other. It has its power and efficacy not only from and according to its natural and essential properties, or only as far as their capacity extends, but primarily from and according to the majesty, glory, power, and might which the human nature has received through the personal union, glorification, and exaltation.

This doctrine of the communication of attributes in three *genera* united many Gnesio-Lutherans and Philippists. It did not create unity with the Reformed wing of the Reformation. Zwinglians, Calvinists, and "Crypto-Calvinists" could not affirm the *genus majestaticum*. The Lutherans wished to make certain that Chalcedonian Christology was clearly reaffirmed by the Reformation. God is *in, with,* and *through* Christ. His majesty is hidden in the humanity of Jesus of Nazareth. It is God's Incarnation in Christ that consoles troubled consciences. Christ can neither be "materialized" (as the Romanists did in their sacramental theology) nor "spiritualized" (as the Reformed did in their dualistic Christology). The Lutheran affirmation of the tradition about Christ and their additions to it had one purpose: to achieve a Christology that would carry "justification by grace through faith."

The argumentation can be examined at two places in the Formula of Concord: Epitome VII, The Person of Christ, and Solid Declaration VIII, The Person of Christ. The wording of each section varies, but the teaching is constant. Both sections state that the chief question is that because of the personal union in the person of Christ, do the divine and human natures, together with their properties really share with each other? And how far does this sharing extend? The three *genera* are taught. The analogy of incandescent iron is used to describe how both natures are united personally. In Christ God is man, and man is God because of a real and true communion. Mary is indeed *Theotokos*. Christ is able, and it is easy for him, to impart to us his true body and blood which are present in the Holy Supper not according to the mode or property of the human nature but according to the mode and property of God's right hand. The human nature in the person of Christ is neither abolished nor is one nature changed into the other. A series of antitheses rejects the teaching of Nestorius, Eutyches, Arius, Marcion, and Zwingli. On the other hand, the teaching of Cyril of Alexander about the hypostatic union, as defined in 451, and the teaching of the Council of Ephesus in 431 are affirmed.

The intention of the teaching of the Formula is perhaps best expressed in the section of the Solid Declaration, Article VIII, which states:

> Hence we consider it a pernicious error to deprive Christ according to his humanity of this majesty. To do so robs Christians of their highest comfort, afforded them in the cited promises of the presence and indwell-

ing of their head, king and high priest, who has promised that not only his unveiled deity, which to us poor sinners is like a consuming fire on dry stubble, will be with them, but that he, he, the man who has spoken with them, who has tasted every tribulation in his assumed human nature, and who can therefore sympathize with us as with men and his brethren, he wills to be with us in all our troubles also according to that nature by which he is our brother and we are flesh of his flesh.

The Lutheran tradition sought to be apostolic and catholic in its teaching about Christ. It deliberately affirmed the traditional Christology of the early church and the great councils. At the same time it insisted on freedom and flexibility to maintain the intent of this apostolic and catholic Christology that transcended formulations. As Martin Chemnitz declared:

> There is clarity among us as to the teachings but not as to the terminology. But when people can agree on the substance, they should be tolerant about the terms which only serve doctrine. Thus it is worthy of effort on the part of all pious and learned men for the sake of harmony that we use the well accepted terms, especially those used by the early church when they are proper and meaningful and not unsuitable.[10]

Such commitment to the gospel and flexibility about formulation should allow Lutherans to be open to genuine ecumenical advance. As an official statement of the Lutheran Church in America describes it:

> Ecumenism is not merely a pooling of disparate gifts but proceeds from agreement in the Gospel. The Gospel is a living reality to be asserted in new situations with meaning and authority for today. The centrality of the Gospel, affirmed by the Lutheran Confessions, allows for a considerable variety in many aspects of ecclesial life and organization, doctrinal expression, and ethical assertions.[11]

This position then becomes a resource for Lutherans as they are requested to speak from their tradition to the unofficial agreements on Christology between Eastern and Oriental Orthodox Churches, and between Oriental Orthodox Churches and the Roman Catholic Church.

In regard to the convergence in Orthodox Christology, it is probably useful to give some Lutheran reaction to the four Agreed Statements and then to the selected essays in *Does Chalcedon Divide or Unite?* The ratio-

---

[10]Martin Chemnitz, *The Two Natures of Christ*, § 12, J. A. O. Preus, trans. (St. Louis: Concordia Publishing House, 1971) 167.

[11]*Ecumenism: A Lutheran Commitment* (New York: Lutheran Church in America, 1982) § 4.

nale for this approach is that the Agreed Statements have a greater authority than individual articles.

Lutherans probably would take little exception to the contents of the Statement of Aarhus in 1964. They would affirm the teaching of Cyril of Alexandria and reject the view of Eutyches and Nestorius. They would acknowledge that Chalcedon must not be viewed in isolation from Ephesus 431 or Constantinople 553. The role of political, sociological, and cultural factors in theological controversy would be readily acknowledged.

Likewise the Bristol Statement of 1967 would be approved for the following reasons: the importance of soteriology as a framework for a discussion of Christology; the recognition of the legitimacy of different theological vocabularies to confess a common faith in Christ; the insistence that the human will is neither absorbed nor suppressed by the divine will in the incarnate *Logos,* nor are they contrary to one another; and the acknowledged value of a joint declaration in which the churches express together the same formulation their common faith in the One Lord Jesus Christ as perfect God and perfect man.

In the Geneva Statement of 1970, Lutherans would affirm the points made in the "Reaffirmation of Christological Agreement" and the goal of Eucharistic sharing. They would also endorse the idea that mutual agreement ought not be merely verbal or conceptional. The wider implications of Christological agreement as reflecting agreements of understanding about the Trinity, the Incarnation, the person and work of the Spirit, and eschatology would be acknowledged. Lutherans may raise questions about the agreement on the nature of the church with its ministry and sacraments as implied in these documents, but this is difficult to pursue because little is actually said on this topic. Lutherans would have little problem with assigning a priority to the first three Ecumenical Councils. They would support the view that a common understanding of Christology is the fundamental basis for the life, orthodoxy, and unity of the church. The importance of practical steps would be acknowledged.

The final Agreed Statement, Addis Ababa of 1971, deals with the lifting of anathemas. Lutherans would be sensitive to this issue but would probably take the point of view that condemnations of the past which are no longer relevant are no longer an obstacle to church fellowship and thus not of critical importance.

Thus, to these Agreements the Lutheran reaction would be that here is an articulation of the apostolic faith with which they can agree and which they would see in conformity with their own tradition's expression of the faith. They would welcome the centrality of Christ and the firm commitment there with freedom in other areas. In developing the wider implications of this basic agreement on Christology, Lutherans would hope in their understanding of the apostolic faith, especially as seen in the understanding of the gospel as justification by grace through faith, to see expression of a theology of the Word and the related concept of *ecclesia semper reformanda est.*

Given the above estimate of the four Agreed Statements, it is not surprising to find Lutheran approbation of some of the key papers underlying the statements. For example, John Romanides' "St. Cyril's 'One Physis or Hypostasis of God the Logos Incarnate' and Chalcedon" is a helpful historical summary.[12] As Romanides states, his article is neither an uncritical defense of Chalcedon nor a defense of the non-Chalcedonian position. Rather he seeks to show how the two traditions survived the complexities of history while always maintaining essentially the same faith. The article traces clearly how the confusion of language contributed to the controversy. The article defines Nestorianism as seen by Cyril, examines the Tome of Leo and its use by Chalcedon, looks at the crypto-Nestorianism of Theodoret and demonstrates the continuity of the Fifth Ecumenical Council with Ephesus 431 and Chalcedon 451.

This clear recital, revealing the critical issues of faith and numerous secondary issues, obviously allowed the dialogue to make considerable progress. Historically and theologically, Lutherans would confront no problems accepting the conclusions of the essay:

> In light of this it would be wise to make allowances in terminology while none whatsoever in faith. I would suggest that serious consideration be given to the Fifth Ecumenical Council, not as one which modified Chalcedon, but as one which interprets it correctly. If we agree on the meaning of Cyril's Christology, we should be as pliable as he on terms. In this regard the non-Chalcedonians should accept all of Cyril, including 433, and the Chalcedonians must stop overemphasizing the Cyril of 433.[13]

The article by V. C. Samuel surveys the scene from the perspective of an Oriental Orthodox theologian. Entitled "One Incarnate Nature of God the Word," it is a valuable counterpiece to the article by Eastern Orthodox theologian Romanides.[14] Both articles reflect a convergence. Samuel declares that no formulation is adequate to describe Christ. Whatever the exact teaching of Eutyches, the non-Chalcedonian churches reject the ideas

---

[12]In *Does Chalcedon Divide or Unite?* 50-70.

[13]Ibid., 70.

[14]Ibid., 76-90.

read into Eutyches at Chalcedon. The erroneous ideas read into a key phrase of Christological discussion, "one incarnate nature of God the Word,"—namely, the tendency to ignore the manhood of Christ and human properties in Jesus Christ, and to maintain that the manhood of Christ was incorruptible—all are rejected by the Oriental Orthodox churches. The teaching of Severus on this key phrase is reviewed. Severus had three main emphases: (1) God himself became incarnate; and (2) he individuated manhood in union with himself and made it his very own; and (3) the incarnated Word is one person. These points could all be affirmed by Lutherans. With their freedom to use various theological vocabularies, Lutherans could accept the reasons for Severus' refusal to use the phrase "two natures"—the Nestorian school adopted the phrase to assist a doctrine of two persons. The article by Samuel shows that the real differences between the Chalcedonian and non-Chalcedonian positions is terminological. Behind both groups' terminology was a desire to exclude the the same heresies. Lutherans could appreciate this and affirm a kinship with the Oriental and Eastern Orthodox

George Florovsky's article, "The Christological Dogma and Its Terminology," makes several important points.[15] A distinction must be made between the *kerygma* of the church and the philosophical terminology in terms of which it is apprehended. There is a close relationship between salvation and Christology. The concepts of "anthropological maximalism" are useful. There is a need to move beyond terminology to the life of the churches. Chalcedon represents a fundamental intuition. It states that Christ is one being perfectly divine and perfectly human. In regard to all these statements, Lutherans would not take exception.

If this is a possible Lutheran response to the unofficial conversations between Eastern and Oriental Orthodox, it is necessary to see what response could be made by Lutherans to the four Communiqués issued from the unofficial conversations between Oriental Orthodox and Roman Catholics and to several selected essays.

The First Communiqué of 1971 would present no difficulty for Lutherans. They would agree to the confessions of faith of Nicea, Constantinople, and Ephesus. The teachings of Nestorianism and Eutycheanism would be rejected. The Christological confession of the Communiqué would be acceptable. Lutherans would acknowledge that there are different ecclesiastical and theological traditions which can be interpreted along the lines of the faith of Nicea and Ephesus. They would join in a commit-

---

[15]Ibid., 121-24.

ment to the search for a common language of the mystery of salvation, although they would not see this common language as a necessity for expressions of unity.

The Second Communiqué of 1972 begins with agreement on a common basis in the one apostolic tradition affirmed in the Nicene-Constantinopolitan Creed. Acceptance of the teaching of this creed would be no problem for Lutherans. They would likewise agree with the Christological confession of this communiqué, which is fuller than that of the first communique, especially the recognition that every formulation of the Incarnation is inadequate and that both Cyril's phrase "one incarnate nature of God the Word" and the definition of Chalcedon can be correctly understood to affirm respectively the full and perfect humanity of Christ and the unity of persons. Lutherans would recognize the problems of terminology and their dangers. They would agree that there is a need to reinterpret our faith in relation to modern problems, while maintaining the meaning behind the ancient terminology. They would acknowledge that the anathemas need not be formally lifted and that there is a need for new educational materials and education carried out in ecumenical understanding and love. Lutherans would accept the priority of the first three Councils, and the conclusion that the relation between the ministry of St. Peter and ecumenical councils is still a matter for ecumenical discussion.

The Third Communiqué of 1976 deals with the unity of the church and councils. Lutherans would see the one, holy, catholic, and apostolic church in the local and universal church. They would affirm unity in fundamentals. Lutherans would concur that councils and their reception are unresolved topics on the ecumenical agenda. They would applaud the practical steps called for at the conclusion of the communiqué.

The Fourth Communiqué of 1978 does not deal directly with our topic of Christology. Rather, it is concerned with the nature and scope of primacy. Lutherans have addressed this topic in their dialogue with Roman Catholics.[16] Lutherans would agree with the statement of the Communiqué that to overcome differences and find mutual agreement and understanding, new ways of thinking and fresh categories of reflection and vision will be required.

The article by Wilhelm de Vries, "The Reasons for the Rejection of the Council of Chalcedon by the Oriental Orthodox Churches," indicates that true dialogue did not occur at Chalcedon. It states that agreement be-

---

[16]*Lutherans and Catholics in Dialogue*, vol. 5: *Papal Primacy and the Universal Church*, Paul C. Empie and T. Austin Murphy, eds. (Minneapolis: Augsburg Publishing House, 1974).

tween the pope and emperor determined the outcome of the Council from the start. The article concludes that all wanted to say the same thing at Chalcedon: there is only one Christ who is true God and true man at the same time. The dispute arose from the inability of persons at that time to believe that the truth may be expressed in different words, which may even be apparently contradictory. Lutherans would agree with all the points: the lack of dialogue, political motives at Chalcedon, and the problem of terminology. Thus they would also agree that Chalcedon was a failure in terms of maintaining the unity of the church, but not as an attempt to articulate an adequate Christology.

Lutherans would concur with the general views of councils described in the article by Tiran Nersoyan, "Problems of Consensus in Christology." They have not tended to think of the Christian life as centered and manifested in the Eucharist. They would agree that Christology is fundamental in the teaching function of the church, and that the results of the Christological controversies of the fifth and later centuries need to be reevaluated and newly understood in the language of today. They would acknowledge the limits of all language to describe Christ, and that the terminological instruments were not totally adequate to do the task. They would see that both monophysites and duophysites had legitimate concerns and fears. The solution proposed by the article would be commended: new fixed formulations and definitions will not solve the problem but rather an ongoing dialogue on the basis of theological pluralism is needed.

The short article by M. V. George, "The Christological Problem," raises many critical points that cannot be covered in this paper. It is sufficient to say that Lutherans today would not play off Scripture and tradition. They do not understand *sola scriptura* as a rejection of tradition. Many Lutherans would affirm modern historical criticism as a useful tool for biblical study. They also would believe that it can be misused. It is certainly not the supreme arbiter of biblical study for Lutherans.

Paul Verghese's article, "The Relevance of Christology Today," is an extremely useful presentation. Lutherans would have no difficulty with the close relation that he draws between trinitarian and Christological doctrines and the statement that both are tests of the Christian gospel. The description of secular Christology today would be seen as an accurate reflection of much current thinking, although the caricature of Protestant scholarship about Christ would not be viewed as entirely fair. If it were, Lutherans would not agree with such scholarship. The understanding of Chalcedon as acceptable within limits and not solving the Christological debates would find Lutheran acceptance. Likewise, Lutherans would agree that many of the problems are located in terminology; the issue of "one nature" or "two natures" is not of great substance. The conclusion of the article that terminological differences need not separate Christians if they agree on the substances of the church's faith and tradition would be compatible with Lutheran thinking.

Aloys Grillmeier's paper, "The Understanding of the Christological Definitions of Both Traditions in the Light of the Post-Chalcedonian Theology," is a helpful paper on the historical context to which little exception could be made. After Chalcedon the "Formula" was not the main issue, but the unmistakable assertion of the reality of the Godhead and the manhead in the one Christ. The paraphrasing passages in the conciliar definition were to aid in understanding the more abstract formula. Concentration on the more abstract Chalcedonian formula at the expense of the *kerygma* of Christ can be traced to Timothy Aelurus.

The second part of Grillmeier's article traces the antecedents of the formula of Chalcedon, the definition of terms at the Council, and what the post-Chalcedonian theologians could assume on the basis of the Council. Grillmeier's appeal to use the possibilities of theological reflection and his conclusion that Chalcedonian Christology makes possible the dialectic that in Jesus Christ we really encounter the one and consubstantial Son of God, though in his truly human existence which is sustained by his divine *hypostasis,* would be seen by Lutherans as in harmony with their own confessional teachings.

I have tried to describe somewhat hypothetically how Lutherans would react to the Agreed Statements and supporting papers from these two dialogues. I believe that my intuition is sound. Lutherans would have little difficulty in accepting what is there. This would not result in an attitude of compliancy. There could be general affirmation. The Lutheran question would probably be not so much with what is in the dialogue materials as with what is not expressed. In other words, is this claimed convergence on Christology supported by a paradigm of the gospel that is at least compatible with the continual Lutheran proposal to the church catholic: the gospel understood as justification by grace through faith?

Our survey of Lutheran teaching about Christology and of the two unofficial conversations involving Orthodox theologians makes at least some tentative conclusions possible:

1. Confessional Lutheranism, with its acceptance of Chalcedon, should not find itself divided from Eastern Orthodoxy on the topic of Christology. The implications of this consensus and its wider application for the church are topics needing further agreement between Lutherans and Orthodox for fuller expressions of unity.

2. Confessional Lutheranism and Roman Catholic theology have been in basic agreement about Christology since the sixteenth century.
3. Lutheranism, with its tendencies at times toward monophysitism, should have an appreciation for the intention and witness of Oriental Orthodoxy.
4. If two major groups with which confessional Lutheranism is in agreement about Christology—Eastern Orthodoxy and the Roman Catholic Church—have been able to identify a convergence in Christology with Oriental Orthodoxy, there seems to be no reason why confessional Lutheranism cannot claim this same convergence.

Lutherans may wish to say more, but they should have no difficulty in saying as much as the Agreed Statement of Aarhus, Bristol, Geneva, and Addis Ababa and the four communiqués organized by *Pro Oriente*. They should see these convergences as corresponding with their understanding of the apostolic faith and use them in their own communions as an example of a growing ecumenical convergence. Perhaps an official response should be made by some Lutheran churches, noting that although they have not been members of either unofficial conversation, they are nevertheless able to affirm the convergence claimed by both dialogues. Such an action could be of assistance to the Faith and Order Commissions of both the National Council of Churches and the World Council of Churches.

Oriental Orthodox Christology:
A Southern Baptist Perspective

E. Glenn Hinson

Baptists are probably not a good choice to comment on highly technical points of theology from an earlier day, particularly from the patristic period. Although on occasion they have affirmed traditional statements of faith such as the Nicene-Constantinopolitan or Chalcedonian Creeds, they have favored orthopraxy and looked with considerable suspicion on creeds of any kind. In their 140-year history Southern Baptists, for instance, have framed only two "confessions of faith," a term preferred over "creeds" because it is thought to suggest a less binding character. Many Baptists will echo their forebears' cry, "No creed but Christ!" or "No creed but the Bible!"

This antipathy to exacting theological formulation is deeply rooted in Baptist history. For one thing, from the beginning, in England, North America, and virtually everywhere they have been, Baptists have belonged to a socioeconomic stratum which could not have appreciated the kind of precision demanded by the debate between dyophysites and monophysites. Fifteen years ago, I taught a survey of church history in the church in which my family and I have held membership for years. About sixty persons enrolled and attended faithfully until I came to to the section on doctrinal development. "You've got to get this," I said. "This is the essence of Christian understanding of apostolic faith." Well, these laypersons showed me they didn't have to "get this." Only half of them came until I finished this segment of the course. The other half turned when I returned to other things.

In this you may see a second factor at work. Like their Puritan forebears, Baptists have perceived faith in personal and relational terms. Faith is an affair of the heart rather than the head. Behind this, I think, lies a strong Calvinist conviction that faith is mystery. No one can express in words the mystery of the Godhead or the conviction that "God was in Christ reconciling the world to Himself" (2 Cor. 5:19).

More basic still for Baptists, however, born as dissenters in an age of conformity, was a powerful stress on individual liberty, what they called "soul competency." "To be authentic and responsible," they never tired of saying, "faith must be free. Obedience, if true, will be voluntary or it is not obedience at all."

Fueling this concern was the Enlightenment. Baptists were born during the Enlightenment and quaffed deeply at its emphasis on individual liberty. In America especially they shared the impact of Enlightenment attitudes on the culture. A small sect until after the American Revolution, they threw themselves wholeheartedly into the effort of this society to conserve liberty by separation of church and state.

Southern Baptists on the Convergences on Christology

When Southern Baptists are asked to assess whether the convergences on Christology arrived at in these consultations correspond to their understanding of apostolic faith, therefore, I'm afraid most will respond with limited comprehension. Baptist summaries of what they perceive apostolic faith to be lack anything even closely resembling the theological subtleties of the Nicene and Chalcedonian formulas. A few confessions,[1] none of which has affected Southern Baptist thinking significantly, allude to those creeds affirmatively or quote them extensively. But confessions drafted by Baptists uniformly strive for strict adherence to the Bible even in language. They are usually documented heavily with Scripture references and avoid the sometimes abstract terminology of the early creeds. Accordingly, the Christological article of The Baptist Faith and Message adopted by the Southern Baptist Convention in 1963 weaves together numerous scriptural phrases and appends the supportive references as follows:

> Christ is the eternal Son of God. In His incarnation as Jesus Christ he was conceived of the Holy Spirit and born of the virgin Mary. Jesus perfectly revealed and did the will of God, taking upon Himself the demands and necessities of human nature and identifying Himself completely with mankind yet without sin. He honored the divine law by His personal obedience, and in His death on the cross He made provision for the redemption of men from sin. He was raised from the dead with a glorified body and appeared to His disciples as the person who was with them before His crucifixion. He ascended into heaven and is now exalted at the right hand

---

[1]For instance, the "Orthodox Creed" published by General Baptists against the Hoffmanite Christology of Matthew Caffyn in 1678. This confession, however, has never exerted influence in the United States.

of God where He is the One Mediator, partaking of the nature of God and of man, and in whose Person is effected the reconciliation between God and man. He will return in power and glory to judge the world and to consummate His redemptive mission. He now dwells in all believers as the living and ever present Lord.

Gen. 18:1ff.; Psalm 2:7ff.; 110:1ff.; Isa. 7:14; 53; Matt. 1:18-23; 3:17; 8:29; 11:27; 14:33; 16:16, 27; 17:5; 27; 28:1-6, 19; Mark 1:1; 3:11; Luke 1:35; 4:41; 22:70; 24:46; John 1:1-18, 29; 10:30, 38; 11:25-27; 12:44-50; 14:7-11; 16:15-16, 28; 17:1-5, 21-22; 20:1-20, 28; Acts 1:9; 2:22-24; 7:55-56; 9:4-5, 20; Rom. 1:3-4; 3:23-26; 5:6-21; 8:1-3,34; 10:4; 1 Cor. 1:30; 2:2, 8:6; 15:1-8, 24-28; 2 Cor. 5:19-21; Gal. 4:4-5; Eph. 1:20; 3:11; 4:7-10; Phil. 2:5-11; Col. 1:13-22; 2:9; 1 Thess. 4:14-18; 1 Tim. 2:5-6; 3:16; Titus 2:13-14; Heb. 1:1-3; 4:14-15; 7:14-28; 9:12-15, 24-28; 12:2; 13:8; 1 Peter 2:21-25; 3:22; 1 John. 1:7-9; 3:2; 4:14-15; 5:9; 2 John 7-9; Rev. 1:13-16; 5:9-14; 12:10-11; 13:8; 19:6.[2]

Baptist theologians, of course, review and affirm the great Christological formulas of early Christian history.[3] In the way they review the councils as history, however, they too reflect typical Baptist preference for essentially biblical rather than other formulations. Lay persons with limited training in theology will have an even stronger preference for simple biblical concepts.

As a specialist in patristics, of course, I can appreciate what the Fathers were trying to do in both sides of the debate up to Chalcedon and after, but few other Southern Baptists will have equal training for that. No one will object to the teachings of the Fathers. Indeed, we may be a little like Teve in "Fiddler on the Roof." One person said one thing. Teve said. "I agree." Someone contradicted this. Teve said, "You're right." A third person said, "But you can't agree with both. They contradicted one another." Teve replied, "You're right." From the Protestant reformers Baptists inherited an attitude which informs their outlook here. The major question they will ask is: "Is this faithful to the Scriptures? Does it say about God and Christ what the Scriptures say?"

---

[2]*The Baptist Faith and Message: A Statement Adopted by the Southern Baptist Convention* (adopted 9 May 1963) (Nashville: The Sunday School Board of the Southern Baptist Convention, 1963) 8-9.

[3]Significant examples from the writings of Southern Baptist theologians would include E. Y. Mullins's *The Christian Religion in Its Doctrinal Expression* (Philadelphia: Judson Press, 1917) 176-82; and Dale Moody, *The Word of Truth* (Grand Rapids MI: Wm. B. Eerdmans Publishing Company, 1981) 408-15.

By virtue of language alone the ancient creeds will be highly suspect among Baptists. More critical still, the questions they deal with come from the Hellenistic rather than the Hebrew environment and thus emit strange sounds to ears which have heard very little apart from the prophets and the apostles. The more subtle the nuances, the less likely will they be caught by Baptist ears. "One nature" or "two natures in one *hypostasis*" will not register at all, simply because these will seem to the average Baptist to be far removed from biblical outlook and concern. In the controversy that followed Nicea, I suspect Baptists would have sided with those who favored the term *homoios* simply because it was literally biblical. The argument that *homoousios* represented what Scriptures taught would have flowed right past them.

The chief Baptist objection, however, has to do much less with content than with the way creeds were used in early Christianity. Subtle theological formulations may have safeguarded the faith in some way, but they came at an exceedingly high price—more division, exile, imprisonment, torture, and death. The question is whether such consequences do not negate any good the formulas do in protecting faith; indeed, whether they do not act directly contrary to the love which is supposed to be the heart of the apostolic faith. The reason Baptists have always stressed individual freedom is that they are more concerned about faith as a way of life than as a set of propositions.[4]

If Southern Baptists were sophisticated enough to understand what the post-Chalcedonian debate was all about, they would probably lean toward the monophysite understanding. Most Southern Baptists have a fanatical concern for assurance of salvation. For them, then, the central concern would be whether God was really and truly united with the humanity of Jesus Christ, for only so would the salvation of humanity be possible. Most Southern Baptists emphasize the deity of Christ. They would rather have

---

[4]I say this, recognizing that, among Southern Baptists, this outlook is changing as we become the "catholic" church of the South. A fundamentalist group in the Southern Baptist Convention has been emphasizing creeds as an absolute test for persons who teach in seminaries or work for denominational agencies. In the main they accentuate belief in the inerrancy of the Bible. During his term as president of the convention, Jimmy Draper set out four new fundamentals, one of which was the hypostatic union of the two natures of Christ. Here, Southern Baptists might show wisdom if they opted for the historic creeds rather than the truncated version we have here. At least in Nicea, Constantinople, and Chalcedon the Fathers dealt with what belonged to the very essence of faith rather than something on the periphery. The issue was whether we believe in God or in some lesser being who has shared our existence fully.

a docetic Christ than a purely human Christ. A crucified man cannot save anyone. God has to do that.

More sophisticated Baptist thinkers, however, can appreciate the objective of dyophysites at Chalcedon from one point of view in particular: the issue of voluntary response of the human to the divine. Baptist obsession with the issue of voluntary and uncoerced response should carry over to their Christology, as it certainly does to mine. As I would view christology from a soteriological standpoint, the restoration of human relationship with God necessitated a voluntary obedience by humankind. In our state of sin and alienation—"fallenness" if you will—we human beings could not obey voluntarily. Out of love God did for us what we could not do for ourselves. In Christ the human obeyed the divine. Thence, I would lean toward the *Logos-anthropos* Christology of Antioch and Chalcedon rather than the *Logos-sarx* Christology of Alexandria. Like the Fathers, I would reason backwards from the church's conviction about God's rescue operation in Christ to an understanding of the interaction of human and divine in him. Salvation demanded a union of human and divine natures which would take nothing away from either. For such a union I suppose we would have to say that the human nature had to abandon itself fully and completely but nevertheless voluntarily and without coercion. How that could happen is pure mystery. Maybe the point at which we should fault the Fathers on both sides in the debate is in trying to go too far. Can anyone explain how the human and the divine could possibly be united in one person? Or how the whole of the Godhead could dwell at one and the same time in all three persons of the Trinity?

Southern Baptist Responses to Papers

You may get as many different responses from Baptists as there are Baptists, but I am inclined to think that most will feel much affinity with Archbishop Nersoyan's conclusion regarding "Problems of Consensus in Christology." We would do well, given "the exigency of our time," he has said, "to leave the councils and their definitions where they are, stop making them shibboleths for the determination of the orthodoxy or otherwise of one side or the other, and try to arrive at a new consensus on problems that the world is thrusting at us." The decision to leave Chalcedon in the background and focus instead on the more generally accepted Niceno-Constantinopolitan Creed of 381, which the Fathers at Chalcedon sought to affirm anyway, would seem to agree with his viewpoint. It would certainly be in line with the Baptist tradition to dismiss theological hairsplitting and get on with the task at hand.

Most Baptists, certainly Southern Baptists, will define this task in a radically different way than the archbishop has, however, and I don't think many will be attracted to this dialogue unless it can be shown to be related integrally to their major concern. The flame which burns bright in the heart of Southern Baptists is to discharge the Great Commission of Matthew 28:19-20. Right now, they are in the midst of a massive worldwide missions program called "Bold Mission Thrust," the aim of which is to witness to every human being on the planet by the year 2,000. Christology, to be sure, is integrally related to this mission, but I am not sure whether Southern Baptists can explain, or whether they even care to explain, how. At no point, I suspect, would there be a more fruitful area for dialogue with this denomination than to engage its connection of apostolic faith to "winning the lost to Jesus Christ as Lord and Savior." More balanced and holistic perspectives can be cited here, but Southern Baptists will not think any theology relevant which does not point toward the world mission of Jesus Christ.

To "try to arrive at a new consensus on problems that the world is thrusting at us," I am sorry to say, will cause most Southern Baptists to skitter away as quickly as possible unless we tie the attempt to their mania in mission, and to the Scriptures. In promoting peacemaking, those of us who have been involved in the publication of the *Baptist Peacemaker* have made both connections with purpose aforethought, for the vast majority of Southern Baptists will give even this critical issue their serious attention only if it has some import vis-à-vis their main concern. The fact is, as Jürgen Moltmann pointed out several years ago, theological issues are not as divisive today as social issues, and a denomination set on evangelizing the universe, as Southern Baptists are, does not want to divert attention from the center by controversy over other matters.

The question Southern Baptists will put to persons engaged in this Oriental Orthodox/Greek Orthodox/Roman Catholic dialogue, therefore, is: What bearing does your Christological discussion have on the fulfillment of the Great Commission? Does it have any bearing? In *The Evangelization of the Roman Empire* (Mercer University Press, 1981) I have tried to show that the creeds and Christology have much to do with the churches' effecting of the mission. Representing the covenant, as it were, *in nucleo,* they were critical in the establishment and preservation of the church's identity as it incorporated the diverse peoples of the Roman Empire. Without them the church might easily have gotten caught up in a game of religious craps with the competing cults and lost altogeher its identity as a covenant missionary people. As super salespersons of God's saving plan, Southern Baptists should realize how critical it is, then as now, to get the message right.

Father Verghese poses the question that Southern Baptists should wish to claim the center of attention: "How does the event of the Incarnation become effective in our time for the salvation of the world?" (*Wort und Wahreit,* 174). The Baptist tradition, stemming as it does from Puritanism, would place the greatest stress on embodiment of the Gospel in human life. Some speak of "lifestyle evangelism," by which they mean witness through the way one lives in the context in which one lives. That, surely, is what incarnation signifies. And here some discussion of "one nature" or "two natures" may assume some relevance it could not have in any other context.

Not many Baptists would emphasize the sacraments as Orthodox or Roman Catholic Christians would; our tradition tends to be sacramentally and liturgically poor. There may be a fruitful place for ecumenical engagement here, however, as the baptism, Eucharist, and ministry studies (BEM) and the apostolic-faith studies intesect with one another. Many Southern Baptists find communion with others to be enriching for their religious lives today. As the Southern Baptist Convention continues its evolution toward the catholic phase of its history, the necessity of symbolic expressions will grow. My own experience in Roman Catholic or Orthodox worship has convinced me that, in the experience of the sacraments, the Christ who is both God and man does become vividly present in the experience of those who participate not just in bread and wine but in the whole corporate experience of communion in the body of Christ. Yet, sad to say, we will not fully grasp that until we have full Eucharistic communion, a reality that points up to our dilemma.

Before we have full Eucharistic communion, we must arrive at a common expression of apostolic faith, but we will never arrive at that until we share the full communion!

Looking to the Future

The selection of the Nicene Creed for the focus of the study in The Faith and Order Commission of the World Council of Churches was a self-conscious one which followed in the wake of these dialogues between Oriental Orthodox, Greek Orthodox, and Roman Catholics. Although the Creed poses problems from other sides—for instance, vis-à-vis the nonconfessional traditions or the churches in the Third World—it has the advantage of acceptance by all of these groups. I have not heard complaint among Greek or Russian Orthodox that Chalcedon was not chosen. We may help in the integration process by continuing to keep the Nicene Creed near the center.

The papers to which we are responding have addressed the issue of relevance which has constantly surfaced in the Apostolic Faith Study. The diverse constituency of the Apostolic Faith Study Group is asking: How does the Nicene Creed serve to express apostolic faith today? How does it not do so? What more must be said to express apostolic faith today? From what I have heard thus far, many in this group would agree with Archbishop Nersoyan when he concedes that terms like *ousia, hypostasis, prosopon* "have almost become philosophical fossils and they should be taken as such." Expansion of this subject should help to integrate the studies.

Strong Protestant commitment to the Scriptures as their rule of faith and practice would commend further exploration together (perhaps in another consultation) on New Testament aspects of the Christological problem along lines laid out by M. V. George. Earlier the Apostolic Faith Study Group of the NCCC engaged in dialogue over "Creeds and Scriptures" in five major traditions—Roman Catholic, Orthodox, Lutheran, Anglican, and Free Church. Neither the Nicene nor any other creed will mean much unless it is *understood* to be solidly based on the biblical revelation. People of the Free Church tradition especially will have difficulty perceiving how the debate about Chalcedon matters unless they view it under the spotlight of scriptures. Consideration of scriptures in relation to these issues opens out into a larger one of tradition and Scripture. Although it would not be wise to spread discussion too thin, it might not be good to narrow so much as to neglect basic and often divisive issues either.

More important still from a Southern Baptist perspective, ecumenical dialogue needs to be tied to the world mission of Christianity in a more direct way. Southern Baptists will ask again and again about priorities. Have the mainline churches not abandoned their commission to evangelize as they have occupied themselves with the quest for unity and thus begun to lose members? Is the main task not to proclaim Christ rather than to debate the subtleties of Christology? Does the ecumenical movement not need continually to return to its roots in the modern missionary movement and the vision of William Carey in which a larger task of conciliation takes top priority? Southern Baptists would answer yes to all three questions.

Post-Chalcedonian Christology: Some Reflections on Oriental Orthodox Christology from a Mennonite Perspective

Thomas N. Finger

At first glance, the Mennonite Churches would seem to be about as different from the Oriental Orthodox Churches as any Christian group could be. While the latter stem from the earliest Christian centuries, the Mennonites arose during the sixteenth. While the latter differentiated themselves from Greek Orthodoxy, which was to break from Roman Catholicism in one direction, the former protested against Protestantism, which broke from Rome in quite a different direction. And Mennonites, largely Swiss, German, and Dutch in origin, have retained close ethnic ties wherever they have gone—which has seldom been anywhere near the "Orient."[1]

An initial glance at the life of both groups solidifies this impression. Oriental Orthodox Churches emphasize sacraments. Their worship is deeply marked by ritual, liturgy, vestments, sometimes even icons. The focus of their faith is apparently "mystical." Mennonites, on the other hand, have seemingly emphasized the "ethical." How one lives has been more important than how one worships. And worship has been very nonliturgical. Even the use of musical instruments has been rare. Many Mennonite groups have celebrated Holy Communion once or twice a year.

The paths of the Mennonites and the Oriental Orthodox, in fact, have been so diverse that the two groups know almost nothing of each other. My own acquaintance with the rich Oriental traditions has been recent. Accordingly, I will not attempt to speak as an authority on them. I will concentrate on explicating the Mennonite heritage at points where I strongly

---

[1]According to Mennonite World Conference statistics, there are presently 7,200 Mennonites in Ethiopia and 44,048 in India. The Mennonite Central Committee has workers in these countries and in Egypt.

suspect that similarities with the Orientals lie. I expect clarification as to what similarities and differences really exist to emerge during the process of our dialogue.

Historical Similarities?

What kind of church-historical and theological movement are the Mennonites? At least two major interpretations of our heritage exist. Each has very different implications for our potential relationships with Oriental Orthodoxy.

Interpretations of Anabaptism

Mennonites began with the Anabaptist movement of the Reformation era. The first line of interpretation regards Anabaptists as the Reformation's "left wing"; as Protestantism taken to the extreme. On this view, the Anabaptists pushed certain Protestant reactions against Roman Catholicism—the priesthood of all believers against ecclesiastical hierarchy, individual faith against sacramentalism, religious experience against creeds, Jesus' humanity against his divinity—to radical conclusions. Somewhat in this vein, Mennonite apologists have argued that we are more consistently Protestant than Lutherans, Presbyterians, or Anglicans.[2]

This argument has often been extended. Anabaptists—so it runs—were the forerunners of the Enlightenment and of the "modern" Western world. In turning from ecclesiasticism, sacraments, and creeds, they made religion a matter of individual conscience and of practical action. They left discussion of Christ's person and natures behind, and made him a model for ethics and for human self-development.[3]

If this interpretation is correct, Mennonites are more distantly removed from Roman Catholicism than are other Protestant bodies. They are even

---

[2]E.g., J. C. Wenger, *The Doctrines of the Mennonites* (Scottdale PA.: Herald Press, 1950). For a discussion of the issues, see Robert Friedmann, *The Theology of Anabaptism* (Scottdale PA: Herald Press, 1973) 17-26.

[3]According to Ernst Troeltsch, Anabaptism (later followed by Quakers, Baptists, and other "Free Churches") helped spawn a civilization where religious authority rests not on doctrines but on an ideal's or a subjective experience's "inherent capacity to produce conviction." Cf. *Protestantism and Progress* (Boston: Beacon Hill, 1958) 18; 48-50; 121-27. Recently, A. James Reimer has argued that Mennonite theology views humanity primarily in ethical and historicist terms. This trend is traceable "to the left wing of the Reformation, which, in turn, can be linked with the rise of the modern spirit." *Conrad Grebel Review,* 1:1, 52. As an antidote, Reimer recommends substantial incorporation of creedal and trinitarian themes (p. 54). See also his "Mennonite Systematic Theology and the Problem of Comprehensiveness" in Willard Swartley, ed., *Explorations of Systematic Theology* (Elkhart IN: Institute of Mennonite Studies, 1984).

further afield from Greek Orthodoxy and not even within shouting distance of the Orientals.

Recent scholarship, however, has shown that Anabaptists drew on some different sources, and drew differently from some similar sources, than did Protestants. Their efforts to recover primitive Christianity discovered and emphasized different themes. According to a common current view, Anabaptism is best described as "neither Catholic nor Protestant."[4] But if so, it is at the same time closer to Roman Catholicism than has usually been suspected. And the possibility arises that this novel and many-pronged effort to restore the early church may have discovered themes preserved in Greek and even Oriental Orthodoxy.

We can best explore this possible convergence by first considering:

Historical Similarities with the Orientals

Many of the difficulties of evaluating Anabaptism arise from the nature of the movement itself. Anabaptists were rejected and persecuted by the dominant religions and states of their times. While Protestants and Roman Catholics wrangled bitterly over most things, they joined forces in suppressing the Anabaptists. Rejection of Anabaptism was written into Lutheran and Reformed creeds.[5] Like Armenians, Syrians, Egyptians, and Ethiopians, the Anabaptists experienced creeds as tools used to convict them of religious and civil treachery.

From the beginning, then, Mennonites knew themselves to be a distinct and threatened minority. During the first decades, most were wanderers, driven from place to place and having "no continuing city." By 1572 the Dutch Mennonites were granted religious toleration. But elsewhere Anabaptists survived only by escaping to extremely remote areas (as the Swiss Jura), by farming depopulated territories (as the Rhineland), or by colonizing new ones (as the southern Ukraine). In many cases, they were allowed to settle only on condition that they not propagate their faith. In this way, the radical wandering apostles of Reformation times, their ranks severely thinned by persecution, became "the quiet in the land"—closed, withdrawn, ethnic communities.

Nevertheless, wandering has repeatedly marked our history. Exhausted by France and Germany's repeated wars, droves of Rhineland

---

[4]Walter Klaassen, *Anabaptism: Neither Catholic nor Protestant* (Waterloo, Ontario: Conrad Press, 1973).

[5]E.g., The Augsburg Confession, Articles IX and XVI, in John Leith, ed., *Creed of the Churches* (Atlanta: John Knox Press, 1982) 71, 73. Cf. also The Second Helvetic Confession, chs. 20, 30, in Leith, 169, 191.

Mennonites made their way to America's Eastern colonies in the early eighteenth century. Other Mennonites removed to Russia later in that century, only to be uprooted by the troubles sweeping the land during the twentieth. In North America, different Mennonite groups can often be identified roughly with different migrations from Europe. Elsewhere, some 10,000 Mennonites, mostly Russian refugees, have successfully colonized the virtually uninhabitable scrub wilderness known as the Paraguayan "Chaco."

Recently, a *National Geographic* writer spoke of the Armenian people as follows:

> Many times as I traced the journey of Armenia, I was to wonder if worse trouble had ever afflicted any other people, or whether any other people persecuted down the centuries had persevered more nobly. Armenians have gone forth into the world and multiplied. Peaceful, hardworking, intelligent, religious, family oriented, they have become a great, though little-known, success story.[6]

Virtually the same words could describe the Mennonites. Doubtless, other Oriental Orthodox groups have experienced similar things. In many ways, the experiences of minority ethnic groups from very different historical and geographical roots might be closer to each other than to majority groups which are racially and culturally much more like them.

I have suggested at least two parallels between Mennonite and Oriental Orthodox experience. First is the use of creeds as ecclesiastical and political weapons against us. When considering any creed, then, an historically alert Mennonite will not only ask *what* it says (will not only be concerned with its specific theological affirmations) but also *how* it *functions*. Why was it written? What was it intended to accomplish? Against whom was it directed? Mennonites will ask the same questions when anyone proposes a verbal affirmation of "the Apostolic Faith today."[7] To some extent at least Oriental Orthodox churches seem to be concerned with the same questions.

But despite this similarity, I also sense a difference. Mennonites rarely recite the Apostles' Creed. The Nicene Creed sounds uncomfortably ab-

---

[6]Robert Jordan, "The Proud Armenians," *National Geographic* 153:6 (June 1978): 851.

[7]For a fuller discussion, see Thomas N. Finger, "The Way to Nicea: Some Reflections from a Mennonite Perspective," *Conrad Grebel Review* 3:3:231-49.

struse.[8] The language of Chalcedon (though not necessarily its meaning) seems quite foreign. And the post-Chalcedonian debates—of which we know almost nothing—appear to inhabit an altogether different cosmos.

Historically, however, the Oriental Orthodox have often disputed in detail the concepts found in a Creed. Even in recent discussion they often use the kind of language that creeds employ.[9] Yet most Mennonites would find the Oriental objections to Chalcedon extremely hard to follow. Again and again, we would wonder what really is at stake amidst the extremely complex argumentation. Do the fine verbal distinctions really get at anything essential? Or do they confuse the matter further?

This does not mean that Mennonites are wholly unconcerned about confessing their faith verbally. At various times, Mennonite groups have found it helpful to set down their major beliefs with precision. This has sometimes been necessary for drawing Mennonite groups together, and for defining ourselves for others.[10] Nevertheless, church unions or splits have seldom occurred due to exact wording. They have far more often been occasioned by issues of practice. Were anyone to insist that church identity and unity depended on precise theological terminology, Mennonnites would want to know what difference it would make in practice. If it made little or none, most Mennonites would wonder why anyone thought it so important.

Recently, Oriental Orthodox spokesmen seem to be considering Chalcedon from somewhat the same perspective. Tiran Nersoyan, for instance, argues that since Greeks and Orientals are not divided over Eucharistic practice, they need not be over doctrines. For Nersoyan, the permanency of the post-Chalcedonian divisions was largely due to sociopolitical fac-

---

[8]Currently, *The Mennonite Hymnal* (Scottdale PA: Herald Press, 1969), selections 720-23, contains the Apostles' Creed, the Nicene Creed, "An Affirmation of Faith from the Writings of John," and "An Affirmation of Faith (Contemporary)." I have never heard the Nicene Creed used in a Mennonite gathering. The Affirmation from John's writings is a compilation of Scripture quotations. The "Contemporary" Affirmation was apparently selected by the committee that composed the hymnal, without the approval or authorization of any other body. Such is the informality with which Mennonites often approach "Creeds."

[9]This is true of many articles in *Does Chalcedon Divide or Unite?* (Geneva: World Council of Churches, 1981); e.g., the well-written articles by John Romanides (50-75) and V. C. Samuel (76-92).

[10]See Howard Loewen, *One Lord, One Church, One Hope and One God* (Elkhart IN: Institute of Mennonite Studies, 1985). The Mennonite Church approved a "Mennonite Confession of Faith" (Scottdale PA.: Herald Press, 1963) in 1963. Currently The Mennonite Church and The General Conference Mennonites are considering writing a new confession, and have invited smaller Mennonite groups to participate in the process.

tors.[11] Mennonites would welcome discussion with Oriental Orthodox representatives who are concerned not only with *what* a creed asserts, but also with *how* it *functions*. And such discussions might help us think more carefully as to exactly *what* creeds and Christologies assert.

The second parallel between the Mennonites and the Oriental Orthodox is their experience as (largely ethnic) minorities. Their faith is integral to their overall way of life. The opposition of "orthodox" majorities threatens to destroy them as a people.

Nevertheless, an important difference seems to exist here also. From the very beginning, Mennonites have clearly distinguished the church from the compulsory powers of the state. Though they might occasionally ask rulers to protect them, they have never regarded Christianity as something to be established, propagated or defended by the sword. Political leaders, by virtue of their office, have neither position in nor authority over the church. The faithful have never been virtually identical with a national population, but only with (usually small) groups of adults deeply committed to believing in and following Jesus.

To be sure, some Mennonite colonies have operated much as small states, handling most civil and legal matters themselves. The Mennonites in the Paraguayan Chaco do so today, with the support of a highly militaristic government. Nevertheless, even if they occasionally fall short in practice, Mennonites have always believed in living peacefully on this earth, neither promoting nor profiting from the use of even "defensive" violence, and rejecting the establishment and the shaping of the church by political means.

As far as I can tell, through most of their existence the Oriental Orthodox Churches have accepted the view that the state must protect and promote the true religion, while the church must support the state's main purposes.[12] In defending the church, the state may wield the sword and the church should support all violent activities associated with this aim. As I trace the history of Christology in, say, ancient Armenia, it seems to be

---

[11]"Problems of Consensus in Christology," *Wort und Wahrheit*, 70-82. See also Wilhelm de Vries, "The Reasons for the Rejection of the Council of Chalcedon by the Oriental Orthodox Churches," 54-60.

[12]I express this view in general terms which characterize the traditional European perspective as well. According to W. H. C. Frend, the East, including the monophysite kingdoms, granted the state even more authority in defining and enforcing religious doctrine than did the Latin West. Despite a few exceptions, the oriental orthodox territories held this Eastern perspective. Cf. *The Rise of the Monophysite Movement* (Cambridge: Cambridge University Press, 1972) 50-68.

part and parcel of the nation's overall struggle with Nestorian Persia and the Chalcedonian Byzantines. Christology seems to be a dimension of national policy in a way which Mennonites could never accept. (However, I am only beginning to learn about these histories. I am open to correction by my Oriental friends.)

These historical remarks are not merely folksy introduction to the issues of Christology and creeds. Mennonites, as I have said, can discuss neither without asking how they *function* in church and social life. We can neither meaningfully contribute to nor significantly learn from discussion of "the Apostolic Faith today" unless these dimensions be explored.

"Alexandrian" Christology

Mennonites seldom discuss the ancient Christological controversies. But at first glance it would seem that we would come down strongly on the "Antiochene" side. For this Christology emphasized Jesus' role as a human model and example.[13] On the other hand, in "Alexandrian" christology Jesus' humanity was allegedly absorbed into his deity. His distinctive human characteristics, teachings, and actions were supposedly blurred.[14]

Underlying this conjectural preference for Antiochene Christology are assumptions about Mennonite soteriology. Since Mennonites so often stress "following" Jesus as an "example," they would appear to conceive salvation in largely ethical terms. Salvation would seem to consist in an increasing alignment of wills between Jesus and the disciple; in gradual approximation to Jesus' teachings and behavior. The union between Christ and Christians would be moral, not ontological. It would be salvation through imitation, not through participation.

These conjectures as to where Mennonites might stand on Chalcedonian and post-Chalcedonian Christology correspond with the view of Anabaptist soteriology put forward by their Reformation critics. The mainline

---

[13]Though these elements are undoubtedly central to any Anabaptist Christology, opinions differ as to how compatible they are with the concerns of the ancient Councils. Robert Friedmann, for instance, finds them quite dissimilar: "The Chalcedonian doctrine was accepted without further ado. . . . But one feels that this is not the center, the decisive element. . . . What truly mattered was both the model of the life of Christ and the fact of his death on the cross. . . . All speculative, basically 'hellenic' sophistication of partistic theology is left behind" (*The Theology of Anabaptism*, 55-56).

[14]This seems to be the evaluation of John H. Yoder in *Preface to Christology* (Elkhart IN. Cooperative Bookstore, 1981) 149-56. For instance, he speaks of Alexandrian and monophysite Christology "swallowing up" the humanity of Jesus (152-53).

reformers frequently accused them of "works righteousness," and of reducing Jesus to a mere human example.[15]

Mennonite Soteriology

This understanding, however, was more influenced by the reformers' assumptions about soteriology than by what Anabaptists actually taught. Reformation polemics tended to divide all soteriological perspectives into two: salvation by works, and salvation by grace. The latter was largely forensic in character. "Grace" was not so much a transforming, ontological power as it was a declaration of pardon and favor. The reformers stressed that Christians remain *simul justus et peccator*. Even the works of Christians are sullied by sinful dispositions and motives. They are "righteous" primarily because God, on the basis of Christ's atonement, regards them as such—not because of their ontological character.

Anabaptists, however, were always challenging this forensic notion of salvation. Christians, they argued, must not only be *declared* righteous; they must also *be* righteous. But since Anabaptists were protesting the way in which the Reformation understood salvation "by grace," the reformers argued that they must be teaching what they felt to be the only other possible soteriology: salvation "by works."

In reality, however, most Anabaptists held quite a different view. They insisted that salvation was based on grace and faith. But its essence was probably closer to the Orthodox notion of "divinization" than to either the Protestant or Roman Catholic perspectives.[16]

Protestants have had difficulty with this notion. "Divinization" seems to suggest that human beings actually become all that God was, is, and will be. This apparently denies the crucial distinction between creature and Creator. Moreover, Protestants have often objected that "divinization" soteriology depersonalizes grace. It reduces the Incarnation, they have argued, to a "natural fact": to the mere penetration of human substance by divine substance. It conceives the sacraments as the more-or-less auto-

---

[15]See Alvin Beachy, *The Concept of Grace in the Radical Reformation* (Nieuwkoop, The Netherlands: B. De Graaf, 1977) 6-33.

[16]Ibid., 28-29, 67-79. "Divinization" was explicitly taught by Hans Denck, Melchior Hofmann, Menno Simons, Dirk Philips, and Peter Ridemann. While not using such a term, Balthasar Hubmaier and Pilgram Marpeck emphasized that salvation makes an ontological change in human nature.

matic "infusion" of the latter. But, Protestants have argued, salvation must be conceived in moral terms rather than in quasi-physical ones.[17]

How accurate are such criticisms? The Oriental Orthodox can respond for their traditions better than I can. But these objections cannot be sustained against the Anabaptists. For example, while Dirk Phillips insisted that salvation is divinization, he also insisted that it does not mean becoming wholly identical with God:

> Now although men become participant in the divine nature, gods and children of the Most High, they do not yet become in being and person what God and Christ alone are. Oh no! The creature will never become the Creator, and flesh will never become eternal Spirit, which God is, for this would be impossible. But believers become gods and children of the Most High through the new birth, the impartation and fellowship of the divine nature, righteousness, glory, purity, and eternal life. They will be glorified as God is glorified, shine as God shines, and live as God lives eternally. And even as God is a spirit, so they will become spirit and spiritual. . . . But men are and remain there as creatures, and God alone [is] creator and ruler. Nevertheless, they are one and God is all and in all.[18]

Moreover, divinizing grace, for the Anabaptists, was hardly impersonal. For the Dutch at least, grace was primarily the "creating love itself, which is the essence of God."[19] Grace did not first come into play to save humans from sin. Creation itself was grounded in grace. Grace is God's personal act of creating *ex nihilo*. It requires no mediating conditions or means for its operation.

Now if salvation comes into being through acts of such grace, we can understand why Anabaptists protested the Reformation denunciation of their soteriology as "works righteousness." If salvation is a new, creative act of God, no human dispositions, works, or merits can possibly earn it. Humans can in no way build the foundation, nor provide the proper cooperating activity, necessary to bring it into operation. Since grace can create apart from any conditions or presuppositions, it can neither be earned by, nor be a product of, human "works."

---

[17]A classic expression of this critique was made by Albrecht Ritschl, *The Christian Doctrine of Justification and Reconciliation*, 1:8-21. For a challenge to this interpretation from a Protestant perspective, see Emil Brunner, *The Mediator* (Philadelphia: Westminster Press, 1948) 249-64.

[18]*Van der Menschwerdinghe Jesu Christi*, as quoted in Beachy, *Concept of Grace*, 74.

[19]William Keeney, "The Incarnation, a Central Theological Concept," in Cornelius Dyck, ed., *A Legacy of Faith* (Newton KS: Faith and Life, 1962) 82.

On the other hand, if salvation is not merely forensic—not merely something declared or imputed to one—but if it is the impartation of a new nature . . . then it obviously must express itself in actions (in "works") of a new quality. The Anabaptists emphasized ethical behavior not because they wanted to be saved, but because they believed that they already were saved. For if salvation involves a change of one's nature, it will inevitably manifest itself through visible fruits. In this way, "works" become not a means to salvation, but an inevitable outflow and visible indication of salvation.[20]

This is why Anabaptists were so critical of Reformed and Lutheran communities which, they felt, manifested so little change in behavior. If salvation involves divinization, the absence of behavioral change shows that one has not been saved. And then the Reformers' insistence that salvation is forensic sounds like an excuse for this—like a way of insisting that salvation has occurred when it really hasn't.

Mennonite Christology

What does all this imply for Anabaptist Christology? At the very least, if salvation is divinization, then Christ must be fully divine in order to impart it. To be sure, with their emphasis on Jesus as model, Mennonites of recent generations can—and sometimes have—inclined towards a humanistic Christology. But the early Anabaptist writers clearly and repeatedly affirm Christ's full deity.[21] In fact, when they depart from Chalcedon, it is not in the direction of Nestorianism, but of monophysitism.

This brings us to the "heavenly flesh" Christology. The Dutch Anabaptists insisted that although Jesus was fully human, he did not derive his human nature from Mary. Though he was born "out of" Mary, he was not born "from" her. Instead, his human nature was created *ex nihilo* by the Holy Spirit, and then housed and nourished within Mary.[22] In defending

---

[20]J. A. Oosterbaan, "Grace in Dutch Mennonite Theology," in Dyck, *Legacy,* 64.

[21]See the selections in Walter Klaassen, *Anabaptistism in Outline* (Scottdale PA: Herald Press, 1981) 23-40. Except for the Dutch, all writers quoted are quite orthodox, except for Hans Denck. Denck perhaps taught something of an "adoptionism" whereby the human Jesus "became one with God and his Word" (26). But Denck's major emphasis was plainly on the divine Word, not on a humanistic Jesus. Several of Pilgram Marpeck's statements sound more like Leo's Tome than Alexandrianism: e.g., "The divinity is testified to and known through power, and the humanity through weakness in death. . . . " (34); "He is two natures, one Man, two natures, one God, divine and human in one . . . " (32). But it is probably impossible to enlist Marpeck on one side or the other in the post-Chalcedonian debates.

[22]See Keeney, "The Incarnation"; Beachy, *Concept of Grace,* 79-86.

this view, Menno Simons could occasionally sound like an Alexandrian. He argued that his opponents err when they say

> there are two sons in Christ—the one the Son of God without mother, and not subject to suffering; and the other the son of Mary without father, and subject to suffering. I think this may be called . . . pointing us to a divided Christ. . . . [23]

John Calvin devoted a scathing chapter of the *Institutes* to this view.[24] Since the seventeenth century, most Mennonites have accepted his and similar criticisms. The "heavenly flesh" Christology has become a skeleton in our closets. Mennonites writing on Christology often fail to mention it.

Nevertheless, even though this perspective was peculiar to Dutch Anabaptists, other groups did not always summarily reject it. In 1555, the Swiss and South German Anabaptists—who did not hold this Christology—acknowledged that some Scripture passages could be interpreted in support of it. Instead of refuting it, they desisted "from speaking outside of the clear Scripture, over how far or near, high or low Christ has become flesh. . . ."[25] In any case, no matter how we may evaluate the "heavenly flesh" theory, dialogue with Oriental Orthodox churches prompts Mennonites to take it back out of the closet. For it was closely related to the notion that salvation involves divinization. And even should we disagree with *what* it asserted, we must ask afresh *how* it *functioned.*

Why did Menno Simons and others insist that Jesus' human nature was created by the Spirit, and not derived from Mary? Partly because of the way they understood the fall. Adam's sin resulted in more than the imputation of his guilt to his posterity. It imparted corruption and death to human nature as such.[26] Mary's flesh, then, was also mortal and corrupt— as would be the flesh of anyone born from her. But if the human nature inseparably united with the *Logos* were inherently corrupt and destined towards death, how could Christ make us partakers of incorruption and immortality?

---

[23]"The Incarnation of Our Lord" in J. C. Wenger, ed., *The Complete Writings of Menno Simons* (Scottdale PA: Herald Press, 1956) 801; also 334, 401, 420, 437, 764-65, 884.

[24]*Institutes of the Christian Religion,* bk. 2, ch. 13.

[25]Keeney, "The Incarnation," 55.

[26]Beachy, *Concept of Grace,* 35-38. While all reformers mentioned these ontological consequences of the Fall, with the Dutch Anabaptists they attain a centrality similar to that which hold in Greek and Oriental Orthodoxy.

In general, for the Dutch Anabaptists as for the Greek and Oriental Orthodox, Christ's saving work reversed the process of incarnation. God became human so that humans might become divine. But if the human nature which God took on were irreversibly headed towards corruption, this process could never be completed.

The "heavenly flesh" Christology is often criticized for failing to make Christ fully human. From the Anabaptist perspective, however, this theology need not carry such an implication. For God's grace creates *ex nihilo*. Why could God not create a new human being all at once, just as God once created Adam? Such a person would possess a full human nature—an unfallen nature, just like Adam's.

Similar arguments arose during the post-Chalcedonian controversies. Julian of Halicarnassus, for instance, argued that Jesus' body was free from corruption from the moment of union, and *homoousios* with that of Adam before the fall.[27] To be sure, this position was refuted by Severus of Antioch and others—perhaps largely because Julian seemed to deny the reality of Jesus' humanity in many other ways. In any case, however, this issue can arise naturally when one pursues the implications of the belief that Christ became incarnate in order to permeate our entire nation with incorruption.

Implications for Christological Dialogue

The "Heavenly Flesh" Christology

What shall we make of this unusual teaching? Like most Mennonites, past and present, I regard *what* it says theologically erroneous. I agree with Calvin when he stressed that Jesus came from Eve's "seed" (Gen. 3:15), from Abraham's (Gen. 12:2-3, Gal. 3:16), and from David's (Acts 2:30, Rom. 1:4). Certainly this means more than that God instantaneously created a humanity in outward, visible continuity with theirs. It affirms a far deeper solidarity between our Lord and the whole human history from which we come.

A theology which affirms too great a contrast between the new nature which Christ brings and the old one in which we all were born can posit too wide a gulf between the church and the world. It can place unrealistically high behavioral demands on its members, who are thought to possess such an exalted nature. Mennonites have done these things. A Christology which stresses Jesus' incarnational solidarity with all people—not just with the saints—can help resist such tendencies.

---

[27]Frend, *The Rise of the Monophysite Movement*, 253-54; Jaroslav Pelikan, *The Emergence of the Catholic Tradition* (Chicago: University of Chicago Press, 1971) 271-76.

I also doubt whether the early Dutch Christology would satisfy the Oriental emphasis on Mary as *Theotokos*. For it seems to make Mary a mere container, and not the true mother of our Lord.

Nevertheless, a proper Mennonite approach to Christology will ask not only *what* particular theories *assert*, but also *how* they *function*. It will penetrate to the ethical, ecclesiastical, and social interests which accompany any Christology. When we raise such questions about the "heavenly flesh" Christology, especially in dialogue with Oriental Orthodoxy, we can be rewarded with numerous insights.

It becomes apparent that one need not to be "Antiochene" to emphasize ethics and discipleship. In fact, one begins to wonder whether Christian discipleship needs not only a fully human model, but also the guiding conviction that *God* has truly come into and transformed our nature. A Christology that confines Jesus too narrowly within human limits might not inspire the sort of radical, self-sacrificing, agapaic discipleship that is truly Christian. For this, one might need to be persuaded that a uniquely *divine* possibility for transformed living has entered the world.

Consideration of the "heavenly flesh" Christology also challenges the common distinction between worship and "mysticism" on one hand, and discipleship on the other. Modern Mennonites may feel instinctively repelled by "Alexandrian" tendencies because they were so often championed by monastic groups. And monks—so our stereotype runs—are those who escape from society and its challenges to pursue some sort of "mystical" experience.

Yet if we scratch the surface of monasticism's history, monks appear far less often as escapists and far more often as the radicals of their day. The monks of the early Christian centuries, much as the Anabaptists of the sixteenth century, were inflamed with longing for holiness in thought and deed. This engendered deep dissatisfaction with the nominal Christianity of their times. Literally or figuratively, they left society behind, seeking for forms of daily living and daily worship which, in close communion with others of like mind, could begin to embody God's kingdom more fully on earth.[28]

Once such parallels are recognized, Mennonites may begin to see that "Alexandrian" Christology also stressed Jesus as model and example. For this orientation, much as for Dutch Mennonites, it was through increasing

---

[28]See Gerhart Lardner, *The Idea of Reform* (Cambridge MS: Harvard University Press, 1959) 35-122. Connections between monasticism and Anabaptism, and between Alexandrian and heavenly flesh Christology were first pointed out to me by Dennis Martin of the Associated Mennonite Seminaries.

participation in Christ's divine nature that one's thoughts and actions were continually conformed to his.[29]

Possibly, then, within the apparently far-distant Oriental traditions, Mennonites might find resources to help us rediscover the importance of "mysticism" and worship today. Many of us have long forgotten how to truly worship. We grope toward various kinds of liturgical renewal, increasingly realizing that our resources for action will dry up without it. Yet our recent history gives us little help.

Moreover, these surprising parallels should lead us to explore more fully the impact of mysticism on our own early tradition. If Anabaptism was not merely a radicalized version of Protestantism, this may be because it drew more fully on certain mystical traditions than did the mainline reformers.[30] Even Anabaptism's strong ethical emphasis may owe more to an ascetic tradition stretching back to the desert Fathers than to any Renaissance humanism.[31] Anabaptism, in short, may owe much of its distinctiveness to the recovery of themes long minimized in the West but still much alive in Greek and Oriental Orthodoxy.

The Significance of Chalcedon

Although Mennonites would probably be initially inclined towards "Antiochene" Christology, the Oriental criticism of it offers much food for thought. As I understand it, Oriental Orthodox Christians reject Chalcedon largely because, at least according to the interpretation of Leo's Tome, it tends towards speaking of Christ's human nature as a distinct, separable reality. Chalcedon seems to leave open the possibility of speaking of a human Jesus as a complete reality, separable from his divine person.[32]

As one surveys Western Christology's recent history, one wonders if there might be much truth in that. Western theology, after all, has produced "the historical Jesus": a man who has often seemed explicable in scientific terms, and quite distinguishable from "the Christ of faith." But, our Oriental friends complain: if the church has only this human Jesus to offer, it has entirely cut its links with the divine. For modern humanity has exalted "the realm of *sarx*"; yet this process "has been devoid of any ad-

---

[29]Ibid., 110-11.

[30]Beachy, *Concept of Grace*, 187-217; Werner Packull, *Mysticism and the Early South German-Austrian Anabaptist Movement, 1525-1531* (Scottdale PA: Herald Press, 1977).

[31]Kenneth Davis, *Anabaptism and Asceticism* (Scottdale PA: Herald Press, 1974) esp. 41-54.

[32]Paul Verghese, "The Relevance of Christology Today," *Wort und Wahreit,* 174.

equate basis in reality and without any ultimate reference.''[33] And if modern Christology cannot rise above the level of *sarx,* it will really have nothing to give to our modern secular world.

This ''Nestorianism'' could even appear in neoorthodox theology—a movement which sought with all its might to reassert God's transcendence. For Emil Brunner, Jesus' deity was ''the secret of his person, which as such does not enter into the sphere of history at all.''[34] Despite all of his talk about the divine initiative, then, Brunner may still have left open the way to conceiving Jesus in strictly immanent, historical terms; and may have left Jesus' deity a series of assertions hovering in the upper stratosphere.

Many other recent Christologies move methodologically ''from below.'' They begin, that is, with Jesus' earthly ministry, and move from there toward the assertion of his deity.[35] This general approach may be sound. But in light of the Oriental challenge, one has to ask: How often does it really leave us with a human Jesus, somehow adopted and glorified by God?

Modern theologians might counter that a preexistent Son who descends from heaven and takes on flesh is far too mythological for our modern era. Moreover, such a supernatural being seems irrelevant to concrete human concerns. Yet once we reexamine Oriental and Anabaptist christologies in their contexts, such assertions cannot be so easily made. Whatever their conceptual problems, such ''Alexandrian'' emphases could inspire discipleship of a most energetic and concrete sort. And perhaps radical discipleship today will be best undergirded by the conviction that God was not only once revealed through a man, but that God has taken up and continues to take our human nature into fellowship with his own.

---

[33]M. V. George, ''The Christological Problem: Some New Testament Aspects,'' *Wort und Wahreit,* 92.

[34]Ibid., 88. The quotation is from Brunner, *The Mediator,* 343.

[35]A classic example is Wolfhart Pannenberg, *Jesus: God and Man* (Philadelphia: Westminster Press, 1968).

The Meeting of Oriental Orthodoxy and United Methodism

ROBERTA BONDI

To love [Jesus] is near and revealed,
*   and he stands like the day;*
But from the controversy of the knowers
*   he is really far away. . . .*
Oh, you wise, [you cannot interpret him]. . . .
Oh proud scribe, know yourself and see yourself.
And not in pride will you speak the account of Immanuel.
In the simplicity of faith, in perfection, in humility speak
*   the account when it is spoken.*[1]

. . . Although a difference in opinions or modes of worship may prevent
an entire external union [of Christians of different traditions], yet need it
prevent our union in affection? Though we cannot think alike, may we not
love alike? May we not be of one heart, though we are not of one opinion?
Without all doubt, we may. Herein all the children of God may unite, not-
withstanding these smaller differences. . . . [2]

The work of this consultation as I understand it is to bring together two
major Christian traditions which have not had much contact with each other:
Oriental Orthodoxy, which has its distinctive roots in the fifth century in
the East, and Protestantism, whose beginnings lie in sixteenth-, seven-
teenth-, and eighteenth-century Europe and England. There are great differences between us. Oriental Orthodoxy seems to be a single mighty river,

---

[1]From Homily 40 of the metrical homilies of Jacob of Saroug, *Homiliae selecta Mar-
Jacobi Sarugensis*, ed. P. Bedjan, 5 vols. (Paris, 1905-1910) 1:191; translation mine. Cited
hereafter as *Homilies*.

[2]From "Catholic Spirit," a sermon by John Wesley, in *John Wesley*, ed. Albert Outler
(New York: Oxford University Press, 1964) 93.

a strong and unified tradition through history. Protestantism is far from being unified; it is a river divided into many branches and estuaries to form a great delta before it flows into the sea. Protestantism and Oriental Orthodoxy have traditionally defined ourselves over against other groups that also identify themselves as Christian. Now we sometimes feel we have moved so far away from each other that we cannot always even have confidence that our waters have the same source. Yet they do.

In the sixth century, when Jacob of Saroug (some of whose words introduce this paper) was an old man, he became a bishop in the Syriac-speaking church which resisted Chalcedon. He was a great theologian in the Syriac style of theology, and he served a congregation that was composed of a mixture of Chalcedonians and Oriental Orthodox, who apparently worshiped happily together. He was a gentle man, a poet, and a wonderful preacher. Against his will he was forced by his own church to declare his faith in such a way that there should be no doubt of his Christological position within the context of fifth- and sixth-century controversies. But he felt betrayed; he hated these controversies because he saw them to be a real breach of Christian love founded upon a human love of argumentation rather than upon the Jesus who is revealed to us in the simplicity of our hearts.

John Wesley, who is the founder of my own branch of Protestantism, had a strong ecumenical dream, though he was also a great controversialist. He wrote essays and sermons and pamphlets in astounding volume over the course of his long lifetime, and a large number of them were written to refute theological positions that were repugnant to him. Like Jacob, Wesley's theology was both complex and unsystematic. He never, however, confused confessions of faith with Christianity of the heart. His concern was to preach the gospel for human salvation, and all that he wrote and did was directed toward that end. Furthermore, like Jacob, Wesley was sensitive to the splitting of the church. While he was alive the people called Methodists were never permitted to separate from the church of England. He even set up his services in such a way that the Methodists would have to rely on the Church of England for communion, which they were to attend frequently. For Christians who were separate from the Church of England, Wesley also felt great care. He did not expect identical thoughts (though he was very firm in his own theological positions) or a single manner of worship in all Christian congregations. Underneath a real crotchetiness lay an even more tender ecumenical concern.

In the ecumenical spirit, then, of Jacob of Saroug and John Wesley, I hope that in our work and time together we may bring our various strands of Protestantism and Oriental Orthodoxy together to grow in the knowledge of each other, for the benefit of our mutual love within the community of Christ. I desire that we be able to be honest about what we have in common, but also about where our real differences seem to lie, because it is only in this way that we will ever be able to move forward to genuine reconciliation at the level of congregational life. We need verbal agreement; just as much as we want a sense of understanding and liking each other, we need to know where we are different as well as where we are the same. Otherwise, our work will go on only at the most superficial level.

United Methodism:
Its Origins in John Wesley and His Beliefs

Methodism's founder, John Wesley, began his life in an Anglican parsonage in 1703, a child of two very strong-willed and talented people. His father, an Anglican clergyman, was a loyal subject of the king and violently opposed the Dissenters who represented a religion opposed to that of the Church of England. His mother, on the other hand, was the daughter of a Nonconformist clergyman; there were frequent arguments about religion in his household as he grew up. His mother, who was very well educated herself, was his first and best teacher of theology.

In his years of growing up, John Wesley enjoyed a good upper-class education, concluding its formal aspect in Christ Church, Oxford. In 1726, he became a fellow of Lincoln College; in 1728, he was ordained to the priesthood. All of this was suitable to a not-well-off member of an ecclesiastical and aristocratic household. While he was still at Oxford, from about the year 1729, he belonged to a "semi-monastic" group of young men which included his brother Charles.[3] This group devoted itself to Christian discipline, Bible study, and a study of the desert fathers as well as ancient liturgical texts. The dedicated young men were often ridiculed. Two of the nicknames given to them stuck—The Holy Club and the Methodists. Wesley himself accepted the name "Methodist" for himself and his group. During this period he began the serious work on patristic literature that was so influential on his theology the whole of his life and which is the source of so much that Wesley's theology shares with Oriental Orthodox theology.

In 1735, Wesley, his brother Charles, and two others went as missionaries to Georgia, in what is now the United States. The trip was a disaster, but it did bring him into close contact with some German Moravians, whose warm personal piety appealed to him very strongly. It was partly under their influence that Wesley was for the first time able to combine a faith of the head with a faith of the heart. This enabled him to come for himself to "an

---

[3]Ibid., 3.

assurance of faith,'' which he understood to be from the Holy Spirit which bears witness with our spirit that we are the children of God (Rom. 8:16). This he understood as ''justifying, saving faith, a full reliance on the blood of Christ shed for me, a trust in him, as my Christ, as my sole justification, sanctification, and redemption.''[4] This faith he knew to be a ''free gift,'' and not the result of our own hard Christian work. After struggling toward this faith for a long time in vain, finally as he began to understand what it was he wanted, he attended a worship service held by a group of Moravians in Aldersgate Street, London, where they were reading Luther's preface to the book of Romans. It was during this reading that, Wesley said,

> while [Luther] was describing the change which God works in the heart through faith in Christ, I felt my heart strangely warmed. I felt I did trust in Christ, Christ alone for my salvation; and an assurance was given me that he had taken away *my* sins, even *mine* and saved *me* from the law of sin and death.[5]

Whether this famous experience at Aldersgate brought about a sudden conversion, or whether it was only a part of a very long drawn-out process, is debated by Wesley scholars. But what is indisputable is this: up until this time Wesley had been obsessed with the acquiring of Christian holiness by his own hard work. External acts of charity and piety continued to be important to him. Indeed, his own understanding of the way in which Christian activity and God's grace work together synergistically to bring the Christian to sanctification is a peculiarly distinctive feature of his theology. Nevertheless, in his mature theology which he preached in the revival, ''works'' were counted as nothing without this justifying faith in the work of Christ.

In October of 1738, Wesley went through another important crisis when he read Jonathan Edwards' accounts of his revival in New England. At the same time, disenchanted with the Moravians, whom he felt were undermining the importance of Christian behavior in favor of ''quietism,'' he took up far more of the theology of his own Anglican tradition which itself had a great deal of continuity with patristic theology. In this way Wesley's theology, a combination of a Protestant emphasis on justification by faith and a Catholic emphasis on synergism and sanctification, came to be.

In April of 1739, he preached to crowds of working-class people in Bristol, and his great revival was begun. It continued until his death in 1791. During the first ten years, the distinctive pattern of Methodist organization was set up.

---

[4]Ibid., 65.   [5]Ibid., 67.

With their organization of societies, classes and bands, the brothers Wesley provided their converts with a unique program of association and involvement, which included Christian nurture, discipline and pastoral care.[6]

Wesley himself, as we have already said, did not write systematic theology. He wrote in the service of the revival, both for his Methodists and against their opponents. The vast literature that survives by him includes Notes on the Old and New Testaments; hundreds of sermons, forty-four of which, along with the Notes on the New Testament, have a special, binding quality for Methodists; hymns, journals, letters, condensations of the Christian classics for his Methodists' education, pamphlets, and so forth. Though his theology is not set out in a systematic fashion, nevertheless, through all these writings a very distinctive theology is visible. Albert Outler identifies and discusses its three distinctive doctrines and the peculiar way they fit together: original sin, justification by faith alone, and holiness of heart and life.[7]

Original sin meant for Wesley that we all find ourselves in such a state that we are not able to *choose* simply not to sin and thus achieve our own salvation by hard work. Like the Eastern churches, Wesley did not think of our basic sinful state as the erasing of the image of God, but as a corruption of it. Nevertheless, erased or corrupted, Wesley had to learn the hard way, experientially, that no amount of Christian discipline can bring about human salvation.

The second doctrine, justification by faith alone, follows from the first. This is, of course, the great doctrine of the Protestant Reformation. We have met one of Wesley's first significant experiences of it in his description of what happened to him at Aldersgate. Within this context Wesley understood justification as God's pardon of our sins, which precedes all our own good works. This faith by which we are justified is "a sure trust and confidence that Christ died for my sins, that he loved me, and gave himself for me."[8]

It is the third doctrine, "holiness of heart and life," as Wesley understood it in relation to the other two, that creates the distinctive Wesleyan theology. If justification by faith was the beginning point of the Christian life, sanctification was the goal of it. Out of his own Anglican tradition from the time he was a boy, Wesley had understood the importance of

---

[6]Ibid., 18.

[7]Outler, *Theology in the Wesleyan Spirit* (Nashville: Tidings, 1975).

[8]Ibid., 55.

"holiness of life" for the Christian. From the Eastern patristic tradition, I believe especially from the Macarian Homilies, however, he knew that Christian perfection or sanctification was not a goal at which one arrived all at once. It did not mean that the Christian came to be a finished product, static and unchanging from that time on. It had nothing to do with being unable to make errors of judgment or knowledge. It meant, instead, a continuous movement into the life of God until the Christian was entirely filled with love of God and thus of neighbor. (Gregory of Nyssa, whom there is no actual evidence Wesley read, explains that perfection is a constant movement into the love of God which is unending even after death, because God's love itself is unlimited.) Sanctification depends on the continuous gift of God's grace coupled with Christian discipline. It was not a state from which a person could not fall; indeed, backsliding always remains a possibility. Wesley himself believed that this perfection is possible to the Christian, not in the distant world of heaven, but in *this* life. He was not naive, however. Most people, he thought, would achieve this state of perfect love only at death, but he did not rule out its possibility sooner.

Wesley and Christology

A church theologian in eighteenth-century England did not have to face the same Christological issues as the theologians of the East in the fifth and sixth centuries. Wesley most definitely has a Christology, but he does not have to argue for it in the same way that he must argue for his understanding of Christian salvation. This means that he leaves undiscussed issues that were of burning importance in the early Christological controversies. He simply takes the church's conclusions for granted, assuming that his christology is both scriptural and in keeping with tradition. Wesley recognized four sources of authority which together make up what is now known as the Methodist quadrilateral: Scripture, tradition, reason, and experience. Of these four, Scripture had the priority; in this Wesley was Protestant. His respect for tradition, however, was very deep. I believe that he would have understood his Christology to be Chalcedonian.

One of Wesley's documents for his Methodist Societies was an abridgment of the Thirty-Nine Articles of the Church of England. This abridgment still stands in the United Methodist *Book of Discipline* as a standard of doctrine. The second article, on Christ, is essentially as it was in the Anglican Church.

> The Son, who is the Word of the Father, the very and eternal God, of one substance with the Father, took man's nature in the womb of the blessed virgin; so that two whole and perfect natures, that is to say, the Godhead and Manhood, were joined together in one person, never to be divided;

whereof is one Christ, very God and very Man, who truly suffered, was crucified, dead, and buried, to reconcile his Father to us, and to be a sacrifice, not only for original guilt, but also for the actual sins of men.[9]

Note that this summary is worded in Chalcedonian language insofar as it speaks of "two natures in one person." Wesley himself understood this language to affirm the full humanity and divinity of Christ within the union. But whatever may have been the original intent of Chalcedon, Wesley did not intend by this that there were two subjects in Christ, the Man and the Word, and to my knowledge, he never speaks in this way. He is intent on understanding God to be the subject of the incarnation, and the source of our salvation, God in Christ, who redeems human beings by the forgiveness of their sins (justification) and by bringing them to perfection (sanctification.) At this point, Wesley stands with the Oriental Orthodox and the rest of the Orthodox tradition in finding it fundamental to our Christian salvation that it is God in Christ who is the source of our salvation.

Wesley does not speak of the mode of the union. His own Christological concerns, however, and his respect for the Christian tradition, suggest that he would have found nothing alien in the language of hypostatic union. Certainly he did not wish to affirm that the humanity of Christ could not have had any independent existence apart from the Word. Due to the importance of eighteenth-century English deism and its view that Jesus was only a very good man and moral teacher, Wesley was hypersensitive about the need to understand Christ as God. Indeed, within the context of his own time, it could be argued that the doctrine of justification by faith in Wesley's theology and the doctrine of the one nature in Christ in Oriental Orthodoxy serve the same function almost exactly: they put at the very heart of what it means to *be* Christian an absolute dependence on the work of God in Christ—such absolute dependence that no amount of human effort, including the human obedience of Christ, can bring about human salvation.

The Christology of Oriental Orthodoxy

As I understand the Christology of the great founding Fathers of Oriental Orthodoxy, Severus of Antioch, Philoxenus of Mabboug, and Jacob of Saroug, two fundamental Christological assertions were made. First, Jesus Christ is held to be both fully divine and fully human; and second, the second person of the Trinity, God the Word or God the Son, is the sole subject of the Incarnation. These Fathers made these assertions because they believed that this had been the teaching of the church from the New Tes-

---

[9]*The Book of Discipline,* 1984 edition.

tament times until their own, and because they believed that unless the assertions were true, we would be left without salvation. God would not have
taken our collective, sinful, and death-ridden human condition upon himself to transform it, and we would be left without the life-giving sacrament
of the Eucharist.

Among these Fathers, however, there was no unanimity about how our
humanity was united with the Word. Severus is the best known of the three
among those who are not Oriental Orthodox, and in the conversations which
have gone on between the Oriental Orthodox and other groups, he is most
often discussed because of the importance of Cyril of Alexandria, his theological predecessor, for East and West, Oriental Orthodox and Orthodox. In
the following pages I would like to summarize my own understanding of Severus, and then present something about the Christology of the second of these
great theologians, Philoxenus of Mabboug. Philoxenus, though far less well
known than Severus, is a wonderful theologian in his own right, and I believe
may offer us some real resources for unity in the future. Then, in the small
space we have left, I should simply like to share some passages from Jacob
which enrich our picture of Oriental Orthodoxy without a discussion of Jacob's very complex system of images. Very little of Jacob has been translated
from the Syriac even now, and he is hard to find to read in English, so I offer
this little bit which I have translated as a kind of foretaste of what I hope will
someday be available: an English edition of Jacob's hundreds of metrical
homilies, as well as his collected volume of letters.

Severus of Antioch was a Greek-speaking theologian and bishop of
Antioch from 512 to 518. In 518, under the Chalcedonian emperor Justin,
he was removed from his see and went into hiding in Egypt. In 531 or 532
he was invited to Constantinople by the Empress Theodora who, over
against her Chalcedonian husband Justinian, favored the Oriental Orthodox. Theologically, Severus situated himself within the Alexandrine tradition. He understood his own theology of the Incarnation and the hypostatic
union to be the only possible explication of the theology of Cyril of Alexandria. Cyril had been the archenemy of Nestorius and the Antiochene
school of thought exemplified by Theodoret of Cyrhus and Ibas of Edessa.

As Severus understood it, Antiochene Christology had no satisfactory way
of speaking of the union of humanity and divinity in the person of Christ. In
Severus' view, the Antiochene position, which he believed was the dominant
one at Chalcedon, allowed only for a kind of partnership between a human
being and God the Word, similar to the way in which Peter and Paul are united.
Thus the whole of our human nature could not be redeemed through the Incarnation, and the Eucharist could only be a kind of cannibalism.

The hypostatic union of the Word and his humanity avoided these problems. He used the analogy of the way soul and body are joined in one human being to explain this hypostatic union. A human being is a nature or a composite, self-subsistent *hypostasis,* a single, "freestanding," "concrete" entity made of two parts which cannot exist without each other, soul and body. Because they cannot exist on their own they are called "non-self-subsistent *hypostases.*" To go to the Incarnation, then, the Word as the second person of the Trinity is a "non-composite, self-subsistent *hypostasis,*" by which Severus means a single identity which does not have that identity as a result of being combined with something else. Logically, a self-subsistent *hypostasis* cannot be joined in a real way with another; you cannot combine Paul and Peter into one identity. Futhermore if the Word had joined himself only with a single human being (should that have been possible), only that human being would have benefited. Instead, due to the fallen condition of the whole human race resulting from the fall of Adam, God needed to take for his own all our own collective human characteristics and conditions by joining to himself a human *hypostasis* which was not self-subsistent. This means humanity without its own, separate identity apart from the Word. Then, as through Adam we all come to participate in death, through Christ as Second Adam we could all be able by means of the gift of God's grace in church and sacraments to come to share in our new life in Christ. But all this depends upon the whole of our humanity being truly united to God in Christ.

Philoxenus of Mabboug was an older contemporary of Severus. Like Severus, and following Cyril, he also speaks of the hypostatic union of humanity and divinity in Christ. Unlike Severus, however, he was not a Greek speaker; he spoke Syriac as his native tongue, and he resented the way in which the very old Syriac tradition of theology had to fight for its existence alongside Greek theology. As he, therefore, spoke of his understanding of Christology, he used different images and analogies than Severus, though it is important to note that he did not seem to feel that his dominant images were competing with those used by Severus, but rather were alternative ways of understanding the same truths. Still, where Greek theologians in general, including Severus, wanted to spell out the actual mechanics of the Incarnation, Philoxenus, as a representative of his Syriac-speaking tradition, affirmed it and used analogies for the understanding of it, but finally insisted that its "how" must remain a mystery, always essentially incomprehensible.

Philoxenus' basic analogy to explain the union of divinity and humanity in the one incarnate nature of God the Word is taken from human life and experience, as Severus' is. For Philoxenus, however, the parallel to this union is the way in which a baptized believer is both human by nature on the one hand, and a child of God, a truly new human being in Christ, by a miracle, on the other. Jesus Christ is God by nature, and very truly human at the same time by a miracle. "Nature" as Philoxenus uses it here, is what makes a person or thing inalterably what it is in such a way that to lose the nature means to lose the identity. We retain our human nature in baptism; our new status or mode of being is something added on by God "unnaturally," by a miracle, and if we lose our newness of life in Christ, our human nature continues to remain. In the same way, Christ is God "by nature"; his humanity is added on by act of God "by a miracle." The Word is still the Word whether or not the humanity is his, but if the divinity, the nature, were to be gone (which is impossible) then God would cease to be God altogether:

> If a person should try to ask how God is born a human being from a woman, he will learn what is set next to it [in John's gospel], how each one of us, when one is by nature a human being, is born a child of God by baptism. And the explanation will be incomprehensible how the Word was born flesh from the Virgin, and how a bodily human being is born a spiritual person from the waters and the spirit.[10]

This double mode of being in both cases is not something visually available to anyone happening along; it is only visible to the eyes of faith. And even with the eyes of faith it is beyond human comprehension, as Jacob of Saroug also says in the quotation with which this paper begins.

Jacob, "the Flute of the Holy Spirit," draws upon the wonderful imagery of Ephrem Syrus and the rest of the Syriac tradition of theology to speak of Christ. (Centuries later, John Wesley read Ephrem many times, and spoke of him as "that man of a broken heart.") Unlike Severus, who, for the sake of the theological battles he had to fight, makes the language of the union of divinity and humanity as precise as possible, Jacob points us to the mystery of the Incarnation and allows that mystery to burn in our hearts.

I would like to share three representative passages from Jacob. He speaks, for example, of the original relationship between the Word and the human race:

> *The image of the Son, the Only One, [God] gave to Adam,*
> *While he was its creator, he took [the image] from him*
> *when he visited him . . . .*

---

[10]From Philoxeni Mabbugensis, *Tractatus tres de Trinitate et incarnatione*, ed. A. Vaschalde, *Corpus Scriptorum Christianorum Orientalium* (CSCO) 9 (Louvain, 1955); translation mine. Cited in Roberta C. Chesnut, *Three Monophysite Christologies* (New York: Oxford University Press, 1976) 60

While he was its creator, he was related to him
* who gave him the image. . . .*
To his own he came; in his own image he dwelt
* in the daughter of Adam,*
Who was formed in his image, and because of this,
* he was related to him.*[11]

Jacob also speaks of the way in which God entered the world at the Incarnation in a kind of disguise for the purpose of hiding himself from the powers of evil, the "rulers of the dark world." Note that he is speaking figuratively; he is a poet, and he does not mean to be taken literally. At his birth,

[Jesus] astounded them; he made them err. . . . he hid his riches in his poverty, his divinity in his humanity, his hiddenness in the revelation of his coming, and he was in our world as one of the sons of the world, and the rulers did not know him, and the seizers of the dark world did not discover him.[12]

In another place, Jacob describes the reality and power of Jesus' heavenly identity as he stands before Pilate. He addresses Jesus:

The country of your Father is your country;
* you do not go astray with us.*
Your Father in heaven is the one whom you serve
* among earthly beings;*
Your country is hidden; why are you oppressed
* in the countries?*
Above the archons, the upper beings are to you a country . . . .
* Hidden worlds, and those revealed in their circuits;*
The shining country of the ardent crowds of the house
* of Gabriel. . . .*
These are your countries, Son of God. . . .
You wished, my Lord, and you came from the high buildings
* of your Father. . . .*
Heaven is your country; why are you oppressed
* in the countries?*[13]

In all of this, Jacob's imagery is powerful and moving, and it seems to be far from the affirmations of Severus. But the affirmations are the same (though they are not always apparent in these quotations). Jesus Christ is one: one Son, one number, one *hypostasis*, one nature, one God who was

---

[11]Jacob of Saroug, Homily 94, *Homilies* 3:90; my translation.

[12]Ibid., Letter 13 in *Epistulae quot quot supersunt*, ed. G. Olinder, CSCO 110 (Louvain, 1937); my translation.

[13]Jacob of Saroug, Homily 53, pt. 5, *Homilies* 2:527-28.

enfleshed from the holy Virgin, one of the Trinity who was seen in the flesh.[14] "He is the one who is from the Father and from us. . . . He is God with his Father, and the same one, with us, the Son of Man."[15]

The Character of Modern American United Methodism and the Potential Contribution of Oriental Orthodoxy

This is the most difficult section for an American United Methodist to write, for here I must try to give a sketchy picture of United Methodism not so much as it officially is, but rather as it is at the practical level of parish life.

If we look back at Wesley we will see that American United Methodists at present are mostly very far from the theology of John Wesley as well as the kind of life he envisioned his Methodists leading. We still recognize the fourfold authority of Scripture, tradition, reason, and experience, but our major emphasis is on Scripture and experience. On the whole, our congregations do not have the same respect for tradition as Wesley did; it is inclined to be taken seriously only in the seminaries. This tendency, I suspect, has something to do with the nature of American religion more than it has to do with United Methodism itself. But tradition is not the only member of the quadrilateral to suffer. Among many people reason is also given short shrift. And even Scripture has a different significance for modern American United Methodists than it did for Wesley. The loss of a knowledge of the content and authority of Christian tradition, coupled with the undermining of the authority of reason, has left us sadly without two of our four major resources for the Christian life.

In many ways the structure of the church is more or less unchanged (though Wesley never approved of bishops in his lifetime) as congregations relate to each other through the Conference. Still, strict discipline within a local congregation as Wesley envisioned it has been permanently lost among mainline Methodists. The system of classes and societies is gone. We have ceased to see ourselves as a kind of semimonastic order within the church, working to renew the church. In most parts of the United States we are instead the church of the status quo which itself stands in need of renewal. United Methodism in this country now finds itself containing an enormous spectrum of theological positions from the extreme left to the extreme right. It is hard to make many true statements about what all United Methodists believe except that little of it is actually directly from Wesley.

---

[14]Letter 3, CSCO 110:19; my translation.

[15]Ibid.

But whatever American United Methodists have forgotten or trans-
muted of Wesley's theology in our two centuries of existence, we do retain
a sense of Wesley's emphasis on "holiness of life and works," a knowledge that salvation is a matter of both faith *and* works. United Methodists
for the most part, do not know about Wesley's doctrine of perfection, but
they do want to learn, and it makes real sense to them when they hear about
it. When they misunderstand it, they go in the direction of failing to understand the way in which it is not something we do by our own effort. In
other words, United Methodists have a hard time taking in the notion of
salvation by faith. In this, again, however, they are in line with American
nonevangelical Christianity.

As for Christology, though the Book of Discipline spells out our official position, which is Wesley's, unofficially we also range across the
whole spectrum. Some United Methodists believe that Jesus was so divine
he could not even have been tempted by ordinary human temptations. Others believe that Jesus was an especially good human being and moral example for the rest of us. In this we suffer because we have lost not only a
sense of the ongoing authority of the Christian tradition but even what the
content of that tradition is.

But United Methodists are still enthusiastic about the importance of the
religion of the heart—so much that when it comes to our dealings with other
non-United Methodist Christians, it eclipses any need for a common theological confession. It is the heartfelt conviction of most United Methodists
that praying and singing together are more important than theology. In our
worship life, this translates into a practice of "open communion": if you
are a Christian, no matter what church or denomination you belong to, you
are invited to our table. This may be the living out of a watered-down version of Wesley's "Catholic Spirit" with its interpretation of "if your heart
is as my heart, give me your hand," but it is distinctly Wesleyan, and it is
very attractive. The other side of it, however, is that our congregations have
a hard time understanding groups like the Oriental Orthodox who take a
need for theological orthodoxy very seriously.

In other words, United Methodism now appears to be very impover-
ished. Nevertheless, there is a movement afoot in our midst at this very
time, and I do not believe it would be unfair to call it a groundswell. There
is a liturgical revival going on among us as we try to recover some of the
ancient form, content, and meaning of the sacraments. We know we are
hungry for this, and we intend to satisfy our hunger. We are also very aware
of what we have lost of our own Christian tradition. Fifteen years ago we
were like an amnesia victim who does not even know he is suffering from
amnesia. Now we not only know it; we are beginning to struggle to recover

our own history, our personal history as United Methodists, and our larger family history with the Christian church.

To use only one example, the work I am at present doing on the spirituality and theological content and context of the first two centuries of monasticism in Egypt, Palestine, and Syria has great appeal for groups of United Methodist laity. It is what we need, and we are excited to rediscover it—*rediscover* rather than "discover" because all this was such an important part of Wesley's original theological synthesis. United Methodists are still like Wesley in this way: we have a great deal of energy and if we choose to, we can accomplish these tasks. Obviously we can not go back and live in the fifth century, or return to the eighteenth century to be the Methodists Wesley wished us to be. Our thought world is different. Certainly our sense of authority is different. We are not about to become a small religious order working toward renewal in a larger church, since we are the larger church. We have to rethink who we are, using all our resources from Scripture, tradition, reason, and experience. I suspect that to a greater or lesser degree this holds true for most Protestant denominations in the United States. In a short time I think, hope, and pray, we will be open in a new way to seek out our ancient heritage, and with God's grace we will be able to lay aside our centuries of separation from each other to share the theological riches of our heritage.

My own work on these Oriental Orthodox fathers as well as my reading of the conversations between the Orthodox and the Oriental Orthodox make it very clear that there is no discrepancy between the intent of the Oriental Orthodox to affirm the one subject of Christ as God the Word, fully human and fully divine and the intent of Chalcedon, including the Tome of Leo. There is nothing within the theology of John Wesley at odds with the affirmations of Oriental Orthodoxy. There is a lack of education among United Methodist laity and clergy about the content of Oriental Orthodoxy, but this need not be permanent. The animosity and suspicion of centuries is being replaced at last with mutual respect and affection as the careful work of scholarship and the healing of the Holy Spirit brings the divided church together again. The whole church is in need of renewal, perhaps mainline American Protestantism most of all. The theological tradition of the founding fathers of Oriental Orthodoxy is an amazing treasure house of riches for the whole church if only we are able to rediscover it.

Does Chalcedon Divide or Unite?
A Disciples of Christ Perspective

Michael Kinnamon

Members of the Christian Church (Disciples of Christ) share with other Christians the belief that "God was in Christ reconciling the world to himself" (2 Cor. 5:19), that Jesus is "the Christ, the Son of the Living God" (Matt. 16:16). Unlike most other Christians, we reject the idea that specific formulations of this belief (beyond the simple biblical affirmations) are necessary for determining the conditions and limits of Christian fellowship. There is no distinctively Disciples Christology; indeed, we would disavow the very notion. Our distinctive contribution to the ecumenical church comes at the level of foundational theology. Unlike most other confessing communities, in other words, Disciples are defined less by doctrinal affirmations than by affirmations we make about the very bases of Christian faith, thought, and community. Thus, this paper will not attempt to dissect the debate stemming from Chalcedon (that would be a most un-Disciple approach) but to reflect, from a Disciples perspective, on the place of Christological issues in our common life.

It is a pleasure for me, personally, to be involved in this dialogue and an important opportunity for my church to learn more about the faith and witness of the Oriental Orthodox churches. It is in the best spirit of the Disciples of Christ, a spirit I will try to summarize in this paper, to begin by acknowledging that American Protestants *need* to understand better the great Oriental traditions if we are to become more faithfully and fully the church God wills.

No Creed but Christ

When Disciples are asked about the founders of our particular movement (now denomination), we usually give the names of two American church reformers of the early nineteenth century: Alexander Campbell and Barton Stone. It is important to realize, however, that Disciples do not relate to these figures in the way that Lutherans relate to Luther, Presbyterians to Calvin, and Methodists to Wesley. The reading list for a course on Christology at a Disciples seminary would probably include Cyril, Augustine, Luther, Calvin, Schleiermacher, Barth, and Rahner; it would seldom, if ever, include Campbell or Stone. These early Disciples did write treatises on the nature of Christ and salvation, but today's Disciples, if they are aware of these writings at all, regard them as no more significant than the opinions of other nineteenth-century Christian thinkers—and in some cases less. Barton Stone, for example, argued that the incarnation of the Son of God occurs primarily in the preexistent soul of Christ, which then becomes embodied in the Jesus of history! The more orthodox Campbell thought Stone's views were strange in the 1830s, and contemporary Disciples would generally concur with that judgment.

What we have retained from these men are not their systematic reflections but their commitment to the unity of the church, coupled with an insistence on freedom from ecclesiastical coercion on matters of faith. Since Christian unity has historically been sought on the basis of broad doctrinal consensus and hierarchical patterns of authority, this passionate concern for unity on the basis of the right (and duty) of each believer to interpret Scripture without ecclesiastical interference was quite novel.

The classic statement of this position is the *Declaration and Address* written by Alexander's father, Thomas Campbell, in 1809. The church, he argued, "is essentially, intentionally, and constitutionally one." Division among Christians is thus a "horrid evil"—"anti-Christian," since it visibly divides the body of Christ, and "antiscriptural," since it denies the expressed vision of that most authoritative witness. Campbell contended that the one church consists of those who profess their faith in Christ and obey him according to the Scriptures. " . . . nothing ought to be inculcated upon Christians as articles of faith, nor required of them as terms of communion, but what is expressly taught and enjoined upon them in the word of God." Creeds and doctrinal systems may be important as teaching tools, as aids for interpretation, "yet as these must be in a great measure the effect of human reasoning, and of course must contain many inferential truths, they ought not to be made terms of Christian communion."[1] All human interpretations of God's self-revelation in Christ are inevitably partial. Thus, to make any such statement normative for the church is not only presumptuous but, as Chalcedon demonstrates, divisive. That most "Disciple" of all twentieth-century theologians, H. Richard Niebuhr, ex-

---

[1]Thomas Campbell, *Declaration and Address* (Indianapolis: International Convention of Disciples of Christ, 1949).

pressed Campbell's insight in more contemporary language when he identified the tendency to absolutize that which is relative as the greatest source of evil in the church and the world.

As a result, Disciples have maintained to this day that the only genuine "test of fellowship" is what we call, following 1 Timothy 6:12, "the good confession" (drawn from the biblical confessions of Peter and Thomas): "I believe that Jesus is the Christ, the Son of the living God, and I take him as Lord of my life." Through this public confession, writes Disciples historian Ronald Osborn, we are saying that "in the deepest issues of our experience, in our purposes and hopes, in our needs and fears, in our loyalties and dreams, in life and death, we trust completely in Jesus. We will follow where he leads us, and we will try to do his will in the world."[2] No one who makes this confession knows fully what it means, just as Simon Peter only partially comprehended his own statement of faith. With the apostles, we affirm that Jesus deserves the highest of titles—he is Christ the Lord—but it is he who defines what those titles mean as through him we come to know God and to experience the power of divine love and forgiveness.

This is the intention behind the most representative of all Disciples aphorisms: we have "no creed but Christ." The modern Disciples ecumenist, Barnett Blakemore, once suggested that Campbell was "out-Campbellited" by his contemporary, the Anglican F. D. Maurice, when the latter wrote that "the Church is a body united in the acknowledgement of a living *person;* every sect is a body united in the acknowledgement of a certain *notion.*"[3] Christian faith, we insist, cannot be found in any set of doctrines but in the surrender of the whole self to the person of Christ. Christian faith is not belief about Christ but full commitment of life to him; the issue is not purity of conception but credibility of proclamation and loyalty through discipleship. The "truth" even of "the good confession" is not in the statement it makes but the relationship it establishes and discloses. Truth, as the New Testament understands it, is not propositional but personal. Jesus Christ is "the way, the truth, and the life" (the path we are to follow, the dependable reality that sustains us on that path, and the goal of our journey).

Areas of Convergence

It will come as no surprise, given these foundational convictions, that the Christological definition of Chalcedon plays little if any role in the corporate life of the Disciples of Christ. To give one example, the "restruc-

---

[2]Ronald Osborn, *The Faith We Affirm* (St. Louis: Bethany Press, 1979) 30.

[3]Quoted in Ronald Osborn, *Experiment in Liberty* (St. Louis: Bethany Press, 1978) 103.

turing" of the Disciples in the 1960s was carried out following much serious theological reflection done by a "panel of scholars." The more than one thousand pages of their "reports" contain, to the best of my knowledge, only two passing, and somewhat disparaging, references to the Council of 451.[4] This is certainly not to say that the fundamental issues of Chalcedon are not important to Disciples. The panel's reports contain several essays on "The Nature and Work of Christ," "The Revelation of God in Jesus Christ," and so on. The clear implication, however, is that no century but the first can be normative for the church (or better, given the interpretive responsibility of each believer, no centuries but the first and the present). Most Disciples, I suspect, would regard the fifth-century disputes as a *tragic* episode in the history of Christianity, because (1) as a result of Chalcedon the church was divided; (2) the conciliar formulations have frequently been imposed as yardsticks of orthodoxy, undermining the importance of a personal encounter with the living Christ and the witness of Scripture; and (3) these formulations have led many to conceive of faith as a matter of intellectual assent rather than self-surrender.

I say all of this as candidly as possible in order to indicate that dialogue between Disciples and Oriental Orthodox (something that leaders of my denomination would most likely welcome) must take account of some very different foundational assumptions, *even if* individuals among us were to agree entirely in their understanding of the nature and work of Christ. Having said thus, I also want to stress that the communiqués and essays from the Eastern Orthodox-Oriental Orthodox and Oriental Orthodox-Roman Catholic bilateral conversations contain many things that Disciples, as I understand us, would want to affirm. I will lift up five for our consideration.

1. We acknowledge with you the centrality of Jesus Christ in our life, corporate and individual. Our unity as Christians, obscured as it is, stems from our common faith "in the one Lord Jesus Christ, God and Savior."

2. Disciples certainly endorse the themes, running throughout the Vienna communiqués, that the mystery of God in Christ is "inexhaustible and ineffable and for the human mind never fully comprehensible or expressible," and that Christians should, therefore, be able to live with "different emphases in the theological and dogmatic elaboration of

---

[4]*The Renewal of the Church: The Panel Reports,* 3 vols. (St. Louis: Bethany Press, 1963).

Christ's mystery"[5] (though we would obviously disagree on the amount of theological diversity which the Christian community can tolerate). Disciples would be particularly at home with the spirit of Archbishop Nersoyan's remarkable paper. Especially welcome is his assertion that, while theological analysis can be helpful (and is, indeed, inevitable), it is "unnecessary and often inadvisable to make subscription to those attempted rationalizations the test of the salvation or the damnation of the believer." (This may be another case of "out-Campbelliting" the Disciples!) We will probably disagree on what precisely constitutes the essential deposit of faith around which unity grows (more about that in a moment); but we certainly agree with Archbishop Nersoyan that consensus is demanded only in essentials, while "for the rest we leave the mind of the Christian free with a freedom that may be guided but not imposed upon." It is true that the purpose of creedal and doctrinal formulations is the unity of the church. But, as he observes, when these formulations are made *de fide,* "then the enterprise will be counterproductive and will defeat its purpose inasmuch as one variable will be picked up against another, and there will be dissension among [persons] of the same period of time, or generation gap between [persons] of sequent periods of time."[6]

3. Along with the 1973 Vienna communiqué, Disciples are aware of the pressing need "to reinterpret our faith in Christ in relation to problems that confront [humanity] today," including war, racism, poverty, and injustice. As a product of the American experience, Disciples are deeply concerned with the credibility and relevance of our proclamation in the midst of a secular society. Beyond that, the "implicit theology" of the Disciples of Christ (i.e., the usually unarticulated assumptions behind our lived commitments), as Disciples theologian Clark Williamson has convincingly argued, is a "theology of sanctification" that takes as its focus "the basic issues of justice between and among human beings, between and among nations, between us and the creation, and between us and God." While this points toward other theological differences between our churches, it also underlines our common commitment to a relevant, life-giving witness to Christ through both doxology and diaconia.

---

[5]The Oriental Orthodox–Roman Catholic papers and communiqués are published in *Wort und Wahreit,* suppl. issue 1 (Vienna: Pro Oriente, December 1972). See, e.g., 235.

[6]Tiran Nersoyan, "Problems of Consensus in Christology," in *Wort und Wahreit,* 76-77.

4. We share the conviction, in the words of the 1976 Vienna communique, that "unity is Christ's gift to his church, and is not merely the result of human endeavors." The church, said Thomas Campbell, is in its essence one. The Campbells frequently spoke about the importance of unity for evangelism. Their main point, however, was not that Christian unity facilitates more effective mission, but that, according to the Scriptures, it is an essential characteristic of the church. Our task, therefore, is not to create a cooperative federation but to realize and make visible the fellowship that is ours in the Body of Christ.

5. Finally, Disciples celebrate with you the growing trust and theological convergence represented by the reports of these two bilateral conversations. As a church committed to the ecumenical vision, we contend that *any* dialogue aimed at deeper communion is an act of witness, a way of affirming that we believe in a power capable of bringing us together across the dividing walls of hostility in this very broken world.

Areas of Further Discussion

It is important to lift up common convictions, but equally important to acknowledge openly our areas of present disagreement for the sake of future discussion. This time I have four.

1. The first and most significant issue I want to address was nicely stated by the great Roman Catholic ecumenist, Yves Congar, when he said that "the prime theological problem raised by ecumenism today is that of specifying as far as possible what differences are compatible with the establishment of full communion. What diversity can authentic organic unity admit?"[7] How do we determine what is essential and what secondary when we speak about issues like Christology? How do we identify the acceptable limits of diversity, both of belief and practice, in the church? I cannot answer these questions, but I would like to suggest a framework for thinking about them (or at least for understanding the Disciples position).

A useful starting point is Willem Visser't Hooft's contention that throughout the history of the church there runs a fundamental tension between unity and renewal, between those for whom the emphasis is on *sancta* and those whose priority is to maintain the church's integrity as the *una*. My own preference is to speak about the church (or responsible ecumenism, for that matter) as a constant dialectic involving "community" and "truth." Christians are called and empowered to be a diverse community

---

[7]Yves Congar, "Trials and Promises of Ecumenism," in *Voices of Unity* (Geneva: WCC, 1981) 31.

of love *and* to bear witness, through proclamation and discipleship, to the truth of Jesus Christ. The question of the unity we seek boils down to the way one relates those two "givens" of our common life.[8]

Disciples, when true to our founding vision, fall on the community end of that spectrum. That is, there are few claims about the truth of the Christian faith for which we would be willing to break fellowship with others who call themselves Christian. It is true that the second generation of Disciples (like so many "second generations"), failing to acknowledge the relativity of their own perspective, claimed to have recovered the essential core of the biblical faith and, thus, insisted that reunion must be on the basis of their particular conception of the "ancient order of things." But, in our better moments, we have remained what some would call "minimalists." Are Disciples Antiochene or Alexandrian? More of us undoubtedly lean toward Antioch, but we would certainly not insist on any one position, giving priority instead to the preservation of a theologically pluralistic community. "We do not wish to conceal from the world," said Barton Stone in 1814, "that there are Calvinists and Armenians in many doctrines in our communion, and yet we live in the closest bonds of Christian union. *In this we rather glory,* because we see the practicability of Christians living together in love and union who differ in opinions." Stone taught that such tolerance of broad diversity was modeled for us in Scripture. "How differently did the Christians think on many subjects, even in apostolic times! Yet how far were the apostles from making this diversity of opinions a term of fellowship among these humble Christians! The fact that Jesus is the Christ, the Son of God, is believed by all Christians of every name; and if they prove their faith by their good works, their peculiar notions of his person should not be made terms of fellowship and union."[9] Modern biblical scholarship, by demonstrating that Scripture itself contains a great variety of Christological affirmations, has reinforced this point for contemporary Disciples—and others. The World Council of Churches Faith and Order Commission, for example, has acknowledged that present dif-

---

[8]A book I have written on this theme is forthcoming from Eerdmans Publishing Co. Its working title is *Truth and Community: Diversity and Its Limits in the Ecumenical Movement.*

[9]*The Christian Messenger* 5 (1831): 109. For a discussion of these themes in Stone's work, see William Garrett West, *Barton Warren Stone* (Nashville: Disciples of Christ Historical Society, 1954) ch. 7.

ferences among churches reflect "possible and legitimate interpretations of one and the same Gospel."[10]

This emphasis on diversity in communion need not, however, imply a disinterest in the truthfulness of claims about Christ. The refusal to absolutize finite definitions, said Niebuhr, is not meant to deny that Truth remains our goal. The fact that we know our concepts are not universal does not mean that they may not be concepts of the Universal. It does imply, however, that truth is seldom discovered in splendid isolation but precisely through dialogue in community. We need the perspective of those who see from a different angle, we need to expand the circle of those who interpret the sources of the faith, if we are serious about the truth of Christ. Thus, Disciples might argue, diverse "community" is an essential component of the search for truth, a contention that would make us exceedingly reluctant to press theological disagreements to the point of breaking communion or to insist on anything but a minimum of essentials ("Jesus is the Christ, the Son of the living God") as a basis for reunion.

Beyond this, Disciples would probably argue that the unity of the Christian family is itself a central truth of the gospel, taking precedence over nearly all other claims. "If we oppose the union of believers," Stone exclaimed, "we oppose the will of God, the prayer of Jesus, the spirit of piety, and the salvation of the world!"[11] At our best, in other words, we are so commited to Jesus Christ, the living Truth, that any separation from others who by their own understanding are also commited to him is really intolerable.

My reading of these papers and reports indicates that we understand the relationship of truth and community (truth as a basis of real community, community as the context for discovering truth) in quite different ways. This might prove to be a fruitful area of inquiry in any future discussions between Oriental Orthodox and Disciples.

As you might expect, given all I have said thus far, the one essay that troubled me most was that of Paul Verghese. I particularly reject his repeated assertion that "the reason why the Chalcedonian controversy appears irrelevant to some today is that they deny the reality of the Christian faith which affirms that the Son of Man is the Son of God," that our "con-

---

[10]The statement is from the report of the Faith and Order Commission's 1967 meeting in Bristol.

[11]West, *Barton Warren Stone*, ch. 7.

victions about the Person of Jesus have been fundamentally eroded.''[12] To be perfectly honest, I find this insulting. Most Disciples, I suspect, do find the Chalcedonian debates ''irrelevant,'' not because they lack faith (though some may) but because they cannot regard one hermeneutical moment as normative for subsequent centuries.

3. I appreciate the metropolitan's contention that soteriology is at the heart of the Christological controversies, but I am again puzzled by the strong implication in Verghese's essay that the terminology we use to describe the reality of God in Christ, or our conception of salvation, somehow affects our salvation itself. A typical Disciple response was voiced by Alexander Campbell: ''No [person] can be saved by the belief of any theory, true or false. No [person] will be damned for the disbelief of any theory.'' The old arguments have no *essential* bearing on salvation; God mercifully does not reserve grace for those who rightly understand—as if perfect understanding were even possible.

4. Disciples will always be uncomfortable with statements (as in the 1978 Vienna communiqué) about infallibility or inerrant teaching authority in the church. In my opinion, two things incompatible with the ecumenical vision and the principle of dialogue are (1) a literalist hermeneutic of ''infallible'' Scripture and (2) claims of an infallible teaching office in the church. If there is a Disciples ''non-negotiable'' in ecumenical conversations, it is freedom from such claims and the coercion they imply.

I should add that Disciples ecumenists have generally endorsed the World Council of Churches' vision of unity as a ''conciliar fellowship,'' but again we would agree with Archbishop Nersoyan when he speaks of councils (including Chalcedon) as teaching rather than legislative organs. Pegging orthodoxy to the authority of councils has been demonstrably divisive. ''[W]hen we seek broad agreements on the affirmations of our faith and consider the Councils as corroborative authorities rather than originative and determinative,'' Nersoyan argues, ''then our goal of unity will be better served.''[13]

Conclusion

I want to conclude with three brief observations:

1. There is much that the Disciples of Christ can learn from the Oriental Orthodox churches. Father M. V. George's discussion of tradition,[14] for

---

[12]Paul Verghese, ''The Relevance of Christology Today,'' in *Wort und Wahreit,* 178, 168.

[13]Nersoyan, ''Problems of Consensus,'' 72.

[14]M. V. George, ''The Christological Problem: Some New Testament Aspects,'' in *Wort und Wahreit.*

example, challenges Disciples to acknowledge that Christian unity is temporal as well as geographical. We need to expand the "circle of interpreters" by listening more carefully to the accumulated wisdom of previous centuries, including that from Armenia, Egypt, Ethiopia, India, and Syria. Your appreciation of teaching authority can also assist us as we face the challenge of "receiving" ecumenical documents. It must be frustrating for you to dialogue with a church representative who cannot claim, in any sense, to speak authoritatively on behalf of his fellowship. How are we to respond to a text such as *Baptism, Eucharist and Ministry?* How can we determine whether we indeed agree with the "emerging ecumenical consensus" on such issues? These questions are forcing Disciples to admit, with a sense of irony, that we may have to strengthen further our teaching and decision-making processes (so often the focus of division in the church) if we are, as Stone longed, "to sink into union with the body of Christ at large."

2. Disciples, I think, pose an important question for Orthodox churches, Eastern and Oriental. I would humbly submit that Disciples (and other Protestants) bear witness to the fact that Christ has been praised and served and the gospel proclaimed, that the apostolic tradition has been preserved, in the absence of bishops, creeds, formalized liturgies, or dogmatic definitions of the nature of Christ. We are learning through ecumenical contact that the first three at least can be beneficial for the church's unity and continuity. We would ask you to consider whether they are essential. This question is, I think, in the spirit of *Baptism, Eucharist and Ministry* with its double-edged challenge regarding apostolic succession in ministry.

3. Finally, this paper as a whole underscores my conviction that the study of the National and World Councils, "Towards the Common Expression of the Apostolic Faith Today," a study which I welcome enthusiastically, cannot afford to overlook foundational theological questions. For some of our traditions, the study will be a bit off target if it concentrates on what we can say together about various themes of systematic (dogmatic) theology without also addressing the purpose and place of common expressions of faith in the life of the church.

A Presbyterian Response
to the Orthodox Agreed Statements

Patrick Gillespie Henry

"In simplest terms, the Nicene Creed says: Whatever God is, Jesus is that; and whatever humanity is, Jesus is that too, in one whole person."[1] It could be argued that this is all Chalcedon says, too: it states the paradox baldly, boldly, and challenges us to *acknowledge* who Christ is instead of *explaining* how he is who he is. The four adverbs *asunchutos, atreptos, adiairetos, achoristos* say simply that no matter what you think about two things which come together as one—namely, that they must be confused or changed or divided or separated, either in reality or even conceptually— in this case none of those happens. In other words, the Definition of Chalcedon "explains" by dissolving our notions of what would count as "explanation" in every other situation.

Presbyterian piety, despite the intellectual toughness of its origins in John Calvin and the straining for precise definition in its seventeenth-century scholastic development, is uncomfortable with theologizing. *The Book of Confessions* (second edition, 1970), though constituting Part I of the Constitution of the (former) United Presbyterian Church in the USA, is not binding on Presbyterians, but is for our guidance and instruction. Presbyterians are in fact unaccustomed to referring to texts. Father Kilian McDonnell, OSB, much experienced in Lutheran–Roman Catholic and Reformed–Roman Catholic theological dialogues, has noted that the Lutheran theologians have the texts of their Confessions on the table and refer to them constantly, while the Reformed theologians neither have the texts readily at hand nor characteristically base arguments on them.

Theology is of course hard work, and when there are many other concerns to preoccupy us, the hard work of theologizing is left to a small band

[1] Jack Rogers, *Presbyterian Creeds: A Guide to the Book of Confessions* (Philadelphia: The Westminster Press, 1985) 55.

of professionals whose language and speculations are always in danger of floating entirely out of the ken of the people of God. Pastors are caught in the middle, between scholars whose understanding of "humanity" is conditioned by their own experience of tenure in the midst of students who share (more or less) their own intellectual commitments, and laypersons who, in a desperately uncertain and untenured world peopled by all sorts and conditions of men and women, are hungry to know what it means to them that they are the sisters and brothers of Christ. Christology is first and foremost a *pastoral* issue, and the pastors do not seem to be getting much help from anywhere.

It is the pastoral nature of the Agreed Statements that seems to me most appealing to and instructive for Presbyterians. I doubt the drafters of the Agreed Statements set out to write pastoral documents, but there are at least two features of Orthodox tradition that make such concerns almost inevitable in any Orthodox theologizing: the centrality of the Eucharist and the concept of divinization (*theosis*).

For Orthodox, Roman Catholics (especially since the reforms of the Second Vatican Council), and Lutherans, the Eucharist is a constant reminder and reinforcer of the mystery and reality to which Chalcedon points. Whether attention is focused on the transforming power of the Holy Spirit by whom Jesus was conceived of the virgin Mary and by whom the eucharistic elements are now consecrated to become the body and blood of the Lord, or on transubstantiation, or on the real presence, the message the faithful receive is this: the sharp distinctions we make between this world and the next, the human and the divine, the material and the spiritual, are fundamentally illusory.

It is not easy to figure out just what Presbyterian Eucharistic doctrine is. Anyone visiting a typical Presbyterian church gets the immediate impression, however, that Eucharistic doctrine is probably not all that critical, since the action of gathering around the table is so obviously secondary to the action of hearing the sermon. If the sermon has increased while the Eucharist has decreased, the aim of John Calvin has been distorted, for he held the right preaching of the Word and the right administration of the sacraments to be coordinate functions of the church. In terms of eucharistic doctrine, modern Presbyterianism owes more to (or can blame more on) Zwingli than Calvin. But in Calvin's terminology there is an opening for a Zwinglian attenuation of Eucharistic mystery, for Calvin's chief concern was the *administration* of the sacraments: "How does God intend us to do it?" rather than "What is God doing in it?" Orthodox, Catholics, and Lutherans, if asked why they celebrate the Eucharist, would probably say it is because the Eucharist is how God comes to us. A Presbyterian would probably say it is because Jesus, who is God, told us we should. For Presbyterians, unlike the others, Sunday morning regularly poses the Chalcedonian problem instead of reaffirming the Chalcedonian solution.

If the Eucharist gives Orthodox and Presbyterians a different sense of what is possible in the world, the Orthodox doctrine of *theosis* provides an understanding of the world that accounts for those different possibilities. "By his infinite grace God has called us to attain to His uncreated glory"[2] The Presbyterian would characteristically say that by grace God has called us to repent of our sins and acknowledge his sovereign glory. The function of Christ's divine nature is not the essentially pastoral one of showing us what we can become, but the specifically legal one of assuring Christ's authority to judge.

Underlying this distinction is what I have come to believe is the most profound difference between Eastern and Western Christian spirituality: which is the holier mountain, Tabor or Golgotha? The transfiguration, which plays such a large role in Eastern piety and art, simply does not appear in the Presbyterian spiritual landscape. In the 1,521 pages of the Library of Christian Classics translation of Calvin's *Institutes of the Christian Religion* there is only one indexed reference to the story. It is when Calvin is talking about the nature of the body present in the Eucharist, and says about the glorified body, that Christ "intended by that splendor to give them a foretaste of immortality" (4.17.17). He says nothing about the transfiguration as a foretaste of possibilities *in this world*. The Agreed Statements echo the famous aphorism of Athanasius, "God became by nature man that man may become by grace God." Calvin would say that "God became by nature man that men might know definitively and without excuse just how far from God they are."

The Presbyterian would have no problems affirming the next sentence in the Agreed Statement: "The manhood of Christ thus reveals and realizes the true vocation of man." But the next sentence reveals a vision fixed on Tabor rather than on Golgotha: "God draws us into fulness of Communion with Himself in the Body of Christ, *that we may be transfigured from glory to glory*" (italics added). The Orthodox looks to Mount Tabor, where the face of Christ "shone like the sun, and his garments became white as light" (Matt. 17:2), as the primary evidence for the two natures. But the Presbyterian, like most Western Christians, looks to Mount Golgotha

---

[2]Agreed Statement Bristol 1967, published in Paulos Gregorios, William H. Lazareth, and Nikos A. Nissiotis, *Does Chalcedon Divide or Unite?: Towards Convergence in Orthodox Christology* (Geneva: World Council of Churches, 1981) 5; originally published in *Greek Orthodox Review* 13:2 (Fall 1968): 133-36.

and the cry of dereliction, "My God, my God, why have you forsaken me?" (Matt. 27:47). If you want to know what it means for a human being to be God, you look to Tabor; if you want to know what it means for God to be a human being, you look to Golgotha.

For Presbyterians (and, I suspect, most Protestants), the divine and human natures are harder to bring together than they are for Orthodox. An understanding of creation and fall that emphasizes slipping away from an original, very close affinity with God, veering off the true path—an understanding rooted in the Christian Platonism of such Fathers as Gregory of Nyssa and Basil the Great—establishes a less drastic separation between "human nature" and "divine nature" than does an understanding rooted in the Augustinian conviction that we were creatures who were essentially different from God from the beginning and who immediately rebelled against God. As Dostoevsky's Grand Inquisitor puts it, the human being is by nature a rebel.

Indeed, I should think that for most Presbyterians the toughest problems is not the acknowledgment of two natures, but the doctrine of two wills. Human will is almost by definition opposed to divine will; our will becomes human in the very act of rebellion and defiance. Speaking of the monothelete and monenergistic controversies of the seventh century, the 1967 Agreed Statement (p. 6; italics added) says:

> All of us agree that the human will is neither absorbed nor suppressed by the divine will in the Incarnate Logos, *nor are they contrary one to the other*. . . . The position of those who wish to speak of one divine-human will and energy united without confusion or separation does not appear therefore to be incompatible with the decision of the Council of Constantinople (680-81), which affirms two natural wills and two natural energies in Him existing indivisibly, inconvertibly, inseparably, inconfusedly.

The difficulty for a Presbyterian comes in understanding how these two positions can be interpreted to mean the same thing. Given the generally pessimistic view of human will in the Calvinist tradition, it is hard to see how "one divine-human will" could be anywhere close to equivalent to two natural wills, one divine and one human.

The point in these Agreed Statements at which the Presbyterian feels most at home is the point at which practical, procedural steps for making the doctrinal agreements real in the life of the church are discussed. Presbyterians are famous (notorious?) for their concern about process and good order, and when problems leave the realm of natures and wills and come down to how you lift anathemas and whether it really matters whether everyone acknowledges the authority of the same number of Councils, the

Presbyterian is in familiar territory. The conclusion of the Third Agreed Statement and virtually all of the Fourth are devoted to practical questions, many of which show an appreciation for the power of changed patterns of spiritual formation to make a whole new context for theological discussion. For instance, greater cooperation between seminaries, the rewriting of church history, investigation of the fundamental ecclesiological question, "Who is a saint?"—all these are essential if the agreements reached in intimate, intense consultation on the part of a small group of articulate theologians are to have pervasive and lasting impact in the churches. And the link between the theological and the practical is made clear by the question whether lifting an anathema imposed by a council calls in question the infallibility of the church, a question which is phrased this way in the Fourth Statement: "What are the specific limits within which the infallibility of the Church with her divine-human nature operates?" The analogy between "the divine-human nature of the church" and "in him the two natures are united in the one *hypostasis* of the divine *Logos*" is not exact, but it is close enough to be suggestive, and certainly worth pondering.

In conclusion, here are some points I believe the consultation needs to discuss:

(1) Why did it take fifteen centuries to discover that all the animosity and anathematization was the result not of substantial disagreement (which everybody thought it was), but of semantic, terminological confusion? What happened during all those centuries to the example of Basil and Athanasius, both of whom, within their own lifetimes, came to understand that there could be different, prima facie incompatible ways of saying the same thing?

(2) The Agreed Statements refer frequently to "the tradition of the one undivided church." Is the pre-Chalcedon church "one undivided" as a historical reality, or is its "oneness" and "undividedness" discerned by the eye of faith (or through the lens of later orthodoxy)? For instance, Origen was not officially excluded from that one undivided church until a century after Chalcedon. If one Orthodox church is willing to lift an anathema against someone who is treated as a Father by another Orthodox church, is there any chance that two Orthodox churches might together lift an anathema that they have both pronounced against someone? If theologians were to be persuaded by the arguments of historians that "Nestorius was not a Nestorian," would there be *in principle* an insurmountable hurdle to the rehabilitation of Nestorius? Another way of putting this question: Are there some predetermined limits beyond which the scholarly investigations and re-

writing of church history called for in Agreed Statements Three and Four
will not be permitted to go? In light of the surprising discovery between
1964 and 1971 that differences treated as fundamentally dogmatic for
a millennium and a half were after all merely semantic, how could pre
determined limits on other questions be justified?

(3) If it has been determined that the different terminologies used by the
various Orthodox churches all really mean the same thing, is it necessary to press for the formulation of a common statement? Isn't it a
more genuinely ecumenical move to acknowledge the common meaning of the different words than to try to find one form of words that will
almost certainly lose some of the nuances preserved in a variety of formulas? (There is an analogy here with Irenaeus's argument that it takes
four Gospels, each with its own special emphasis, to convey the fullness of the truth of the Incarnation; I imagine we would all agree with
Irenaeus, against Tatian's effort to blend everything into a single account.)

(4) The discoveries of the 1964-1971 Orthodox discussions create an agenda
not only for the Orthodox, but also for Protestants and Catholics, who
must also understand the rewritten history. For instance, the Second
Helvetic Confession, one of the components of *The Book of Confessions,* says in chapter 11 (5.068):

> And indeed we detest the dogma of the Nestorians who make two of
> the one Christ and dissolve the unity of the Person. Likewise we thor-
> oughly execrate the madness of Eutyches and of the Monothelites or Mo-
> nophysites who destroy the property of the human nature.

Presbyterians will have to learn that adherence to Chalcedon does not
require denouncing those historically known as "monophysites."

Appendix 1

Communiqué
of the first nonofficial ecumenical consultation between theologians of the Oriental Orthodox and the Roman Catholic Churches, organized by the Foundation *Pro Oriente,* in Vienna, 7-11 September 1971

The Roman Catholic and the Oriental Orthodox theologians, gathered together in Vienna, 7-11 September 1971, for an unofficial ecumenical consultation at the invitation of the Foundation *Pro Oriente,* have agreed on the following statement:

"We, as Christians, feel united in a spirit of brotherhood in our faith in the one Lord Jesus Christ, God and Savior, and recognize equally the commission and prayer of our Lord that we may all be one in him in order that we may bear common witness to him that the world may believe (John 17:21).

"We find our common basis in the same apostolic tradition, particularly as affirmed in the Niceno-Constantinopolitan Creed; we all confess the dogmatic decisions and teachings of Nicea (325), Constantinople (381), and Ephesus (431); we all agree in rejecting both the Nestorian and Eutychian positions about Jesus Christ. We have endeavoured for a deeper understanding of the Chalcedonian and non-Chalcedonian Christologies which have separated us until now.

"We believe that our Lord and Savior Jesus Christ, is God the Son incarnate; perfect in his divinity and perfect in his humanity. His divinity was not separated from his humanity for a single moment, not for the twinkling of an eye. His humanity is one with his divinity without commixtion, without confusion, without division, without separation. We in our common faith in the one Lord Jesus Christ regard his mystery inexhaustible and ineffable and for the human mind never fully comprehensible or expressible.

"We see that there are still differences in the theological interpretation of the mystery of Christ because of our different ecclesiastical and theological traditions; we are convinced, however, that these differing formulations on both sides can be understood along the lines of the faith of Nicea and Ephesus.

"Realizing that there can be different emphases in the theological and dogmatic elaboration of Christ's mystery, we wish to encourage common efforts for a deeper and more comprehensive understanding of this mystery in harmony with our different ecclesiastical traditions.

"We have also discussed generally the problem of the Ecumenical Councils, their authority and reception, and we urge that these problems be extensively studied on both sides. We commonly submit ourselves to the witness of the Holy Scriptures of the New Testament and thus to the apostolic *kerygma* and express our intention not to get tired in the search for a common language of the mystery of salvation in our Lord in a brotherly spirit . . . 'until we all attain the unity of the faith and of the knowledge of the Son of God' (Eph. 4:13). We wish to see the mystery of the compassion of God translated into a life of Christian compassion.

"All of us have experienced how fruitful this consultation has been, and we pray that God who brought us together may bless us and guide our future efforts in such helpful discussions."

* * * *

Communiqué
of the second nonofficial ecumenical consultation between theologians of the Oriental Orthodox and the Roman Catholic Churches, organized by the Foundation *Pro Oriente,* in Vienna, 3-9 September 1973

1. Once again we give thanks to God who has brought us together here in Vienna for the second non-official ecumenical consultation between theologians of the Oriental Orthodox Churches and the Roman Catholic Church, at the invitation of the Foundation *Pro Oriente,* 3-9 September 1973.

We have come together in order to become more deeply aware of the fundamentally common faith in the mystery of the Incarnation in an increasingly interdependent world with all its problems which are also our own, and to make our common faith more meaningful to modern man. We reaffirm what was said in the first non-official consultation (Vienna, 7-11 September 1971). We have in an increasing measure experienced the same spirit of fraternal unity in the faith in one Lord Jesus Christ, God and Savior as we did two years ago. We were impelled by the same loyalty to the prayer of our Lord that "they all be one." Our common basis is the same one apostolic tradition, particularly as affirmed in the Niceno-Constantinopolitan symbol which all of us confess.

2. Together we confess our faith that he who is the Second Person of the Trinity came down for us and for our salvation, became man like us in all respects except sin. The Son of God was incarnate and became the Son of man, so that we the children of men may become the children of God by his grace. Great is the mystery of the God-man; no created mind can fully comprehend the mystery of how Godhead and manhood became united in the one Lord Jesus Christ. Neither can human words give adequate utterance to it. We recognize the limits of every philosophical and theological attempt to grasp the mystery in concept or express it in words. If the formulas coined by the fathers and doctors of the churches have enabled us to obtain an authentic glimpse of the divine truth, we recognize that every formula that we can devise needs further interpretation. We saw that what appears to be the right formulation can be wrongly understood, and also how even behind an apparently wrong formulation there can be a right understanding. We understand that when our common father in Christ, St. Cyril of Alexandria speaks of the one incarnate nature of God's Word, he does not deny but rather expresses the full and perfect humanity of Christ. We also believe that the definition of the Council of Chalcedon, rightly understood today, affirms the unity of person and the indissoluble union of Godhead and manhood in Christ despite the phrase "in two natures." We all agree that our Lord Jesus Christ, who is consubstantial with the Father in his divinity, himself became consubstantial with us in his humanity. He perfectly unites in himself perfect Godhead with perfect manhood without division, without separation, without change, without commixture. The flesh possessing a rational soul did not exist before the union. The flesh remained flesh even after the God-befitting resurrection and ascension. Though the body of God, it has not been changed into the Godhead. We are partaking in the holy Eucharist the life-giving flesh of the Lord which he united with his divinity.

3. The problem of terminology remains with us. For those of us in the Western tradition, to hear of the one nature of Christ can be misleading, because it may be understood as a denial of his humanity. For those of us in the Oriental Orthodox Churches, to hear of two natures can be misleading because it can be misunderstood as affirming two persons in Christ. But both sides are agreed in rejecting Eutychianism and Nestorianism. We all agree in our confession of the one Lord Jesus Christ, very God of very God, begotten before ages from the Father; who was born of the virgin Mary, grew in wisdom and stature as a full human being, suffered, died, was buried, rose again on the third day and ascended into heaven, and is to come again as judge and ruler of the living and the departed.

Our common effort to clarify the meaning of the Greek terms *hypostasis* and *physis* in the trinitarian and Christological contexts made us realize how difficult it was to find a satisfactory definition of these terms that could do justice to both contexts in a consistent manner.

4. Furthermore we realize our common need to reinterpret our faith in Christ in relation to problems that confront man today—the disunity of mankind; the presence of poverty and injustice; and attitudes toward people of other religions, races, and cultures towards unbelievers and despisers of the church, and toward all those for whom it has become increasingly difficult to enter into the the world of faith. While the meaning behind the ancient terminology remains valid, this terminology itself is hardly relevant for an adequate solution of these problems. There is urgent need to interpret in contemporary terms how the Son of God becoming one with us in the Incarnation affects the life of man today. And there we feel we can find a common approach and express our hopes that all of our churches will work together with zeal and courage to meet this challenge.

5. In the question of anathemata now being pronounced by one side on the teachers and Fathers of the other, we were of the opinion that it was not necessary to insist on the acceptance of these as teachers and Fathers by those who formally condemned them. A formal lifting of the anathemas also may not be necessary. It may be possible for the churches simply to drop from the liturgical corpus anathemata of saints and teachers of the other side, as some churches have already begun to do. It would then also be necessary to attempt writing new church history books and catechisms in which we seek to be more fair to one another by instructing and educating the faithful and our future priests, teachers, and church leaders in a spirit of tolerant ecumenical understanding and love.

6. We also studied the question of Ecumenical Councils, especially the difference in number (three, seven, or twenty-one). Though no consensus is easily attainable in this issue, we agree that the first three Ecumenical Councils had, because of their more general acceptance in the church, a greater degree of fullness, which the later Councils do not have. We look forward, however, to future regional and ecumenical Councils with larger representation as the reunion of churches is hastened by the working of the Holy Spirit. As regards the relation between the ministry of St. Peter and the Ecumenical Councils, as the Roman Catholics understand it, we have not reached a consensus on it though the principle of collegiality emphasized by the Second Vatican Council is appreciated as a move in the right direction according to which the role of the bishop of Rome is seen within the Council and not above it.

7. We appeal to all men of good will everywhere to pray that the scandal of divisions within the one church of Christ be done away with, and that the churches be brought to the full union as and when Christ wills it, that the whole world may see it and believe in him.

* * * *

Communiqué
of the third nonofficial ecumenical consultation between theologians of the Oriental Orthodox and the Roman Catholic Churches, organized by the Foundation *Pro Oriente*, in Vienna, 30 August–5 September 1976.

For the third time we have gathered together as a non-official consultation of Oriental Orthodox and Roman Catholic Theologians, here in Vienna, 30 August–5 September 1976, upon invitation of the Foundation *Pro Oriente*.

On the basis of the wide area of Christological agreement in the first two consultations, which we reaffirmed here, we sought to enter into the question of an understanding of the nature of the church, and the structure of its unity. Unity is Christ's gift to his church, and is not merely the result of human endeavors. While this unity allows for a multiplicity of traditions, the diversity has to be held together by basic unity in fundamental matters.

One of our concerns in this third non-official consultation has been to discuss the notions "local" church, the "universal" church, and the church catholic. We confessed that it is the same mystery of the one, holy, catholic, apostolic church, the Body of our risen and ascended Lord, that is being manifest both in the "local" church and in the "universal" church. One and the same church, for there cannot be more than one, is manifested both locally and universally as a *koinonia* of truth and love, characterized by Eucharistic communion and the corporate unity of the episcopate. The unity of the church has its source and prototype in the unity of the Father, the Son, and the Holy Spirit, into which we have been baptized.

Today all our churches are spreading worldwide. As a consequence, more than before, we experience today in many places both our sharing of much in common of the Christian faith and life, and also our disunity insofar as we are unable to manifest fully the unity of the church in truth and love, in Eucharistic communion and unity of the episcopate.

We have studied together the notion of conciliarity—the understanding of the church as a *koinonia*, so essential to the nature of the church as the Body of Christ, and so clearly visible in the structure of its life and leadership from the very inception. It is the Holy Spirit who leads us into all truth and all unity through councils and other means; it is to him that we look in hope for a council in which the unity of the one church in truth and love, in Eucharistic communion and episcopal unity can be publicly affirmed and manifested.

In our discussions we distinguished between the council or synod as an event, and the synod as an aspect of the continuing structure of the church's life. As for the council as an event, we could not agree on how and by whom such a worldwide council of our churches should be convoked and conducted, nor could we agree completely on the procedure for the reception of past or future councils. We also took note of the fact, that while the Roman Catholic Church regards many of the councils held after the Ecumenical Council of Ephesus 431 as "ecumenical," although in a differentiated sense, the Oriental Orthodox Churches are unable to so regard them.

We wished to affirm the right of the churches to convoke a council whenever found necessary and possible though there is no necessity to hold Ecumenical Councils at given intervals as a permanent structure of the church. We recognize the need of structures of coordination between the autocephalous churches for the settlement of disputes and for facing together the problems of tasks confronting our churches in the modern world.

* * *

As an unofficial consultation, we are not in a position to act as official representatives of our churches or to make decisions in their name. We offer here to our churches the results of our experience, out of which we make the following proposals:

1. *Pro Oriente,* to which we owe so much, should be requested to take the necessary steps to prepare a fourth unofficial consultation in Vienna in the nearest possible future which will focus mainly on two issues:

    (a) Papal primacy and jurisdiction—theoretical consideration and practical implications; and

    (b) the status of the Catholic Churches of Oriental Rites—ecclesiological and practical considerations

2. The churches should be requested to set up a Joint Commission composed of bishops, theologians, and canonists, in order to:

    (a) look more closely into the agreements and disagreements in the unofficial consultations and present them to church authorities and people for study;

(b) examine more closely the issues and actions which continue to ir-
ritate our churches and harm relations between them—prosely-
tism, practices regarding marriages and other sacraments, the use
of outside resources for objectives not in harmony with the good of
our churches—and to make specific recommendations for changing the situations;

(c) look into the possibility of convening assemblies of representatives
of the various churches in the different nations and regions, in order to make people in our churches more aware of the unity that
now exists;

(d) make recommendations to the churches regarding further steps that
need to be taken along the road to full unity, such as the withdrawal
of anathemas; and a more systematic organization of the exchange
of students and professors, and mutual visits by prelates; and inter-
church aid projects.

* * *

Once again we acknowledge with grateful hearts the guidance of the
Holy Spirit in our work here, which was throughout characterized by genuine openness and desire to understand each other. As theologians we join
fervently in the prayer of our Lord and of the church that the day may soon
come when the unity of all will be more manifestly seen and experienced
bearing fruit in truth, love, joy, and peace.

* * * *

Communiqué

of the fourth nonofficial ecumenical consultation
between theologians of the Oriental Orthodox
and Roman Catholic Churches
organized by the Foundation *Pro Oriente*,
in Vienna, 11-17 September 1978

A. Background

1. The fourth unofficial Vienna consultation between theologians of the
Oriental Orthodox Churches and the Roman Catholic Church, convened
by the Foundation *Pro Oriente* 11-17 September 1978, had as its primary
topic the nature and scope of primacy in the exercise of ecclesiastical authority. As a related minor topic, the role of the Oriental Catholic Churches
was also given some consideration.

2. Sixteen Roman Catholic theologians and sixteen Oriental Orthodox theologians attended; three representatives of the Oriental Catholic Churches were also present. The meetings were cochaired by Vardapet Dr. Mesrob K. Krikorian of the Armenian Apostolic Church (Etchmiadzin) and by Fr. John F. Long, SJ (Rome). In the absence of the latter on the first days, Prof. Ernst Chc. Suttner of the University of Vienna took the chair on his behalf.

3. The consultation was held in an atmosphere of cordiality and openness and was characterized by common prayer and mutual assistance at each other's liturgical celebrations. Each day was begun with liturgical prayer celebrated according to one of the traditions represented at the consultation. A pilgrimage was made to the shrine of Mariazell, to the Carmelite Convent there, and to the Cloister of the Canons Regulars at Herzogenburg. The participants also assisted at the worship services of the local Coptic, Armenian, and Roman Catholic communities.

4. Seventeen scholarly papers on the historical canonical and theological aspects of primacy were presented and discussed. The principle was clearly recognized that the historical context in which decisions were made and formulas were enunciated in the churches has often had a crucial impact on the content of those decisions and formulations.

B. Areas of Agreement

1. There was general agreement that in all of our churches three elements were integrally related to each other: primacy, conciliarity, and the consensus of the believing community, though their relative importance has been differently understood in different situations.

2. While in the Roman Catholic Church, primacy of the bishop of Rome is regarded as of universal scope, the Oriental Orthodox Churches historically practiced regional primacy; but these have exercised and continue to exercise primatial jurisdiction also over a national diaspora widespread in many continents of the world.

3. In the view of the Oriental Orthodox Churches, primacy is of historical and ecclesiological origin, in some cases confirmed by Ecumenical Councils. In the view of the Roman Catholic Church, the historical development of the primacy of the bishop of Rome has its roots in the divine plan for the church. In both cases conviction about the continuing guidance of the Holy Spirit was the basis for these views and yet provides the common ground for coming to mutual agreement in the future and for a common understanding of the Scriptural witness.

4. In the Roman Catholic Church there is a specific tradition concerning the basis and scope of the primacy of the bishop of Rome, which has received conciliar exposition and sanction. These formulations, especially

those of the First and Second Vatican Councils, are to be understood in the context of their historical, sociological, and political conditions and also in the light of the historical evolution of the whole teaching of the Roman church, a process which is still continuing. The Oriental Orthodox Churches have not felt it necessary to formulate verbally and declare their understanding of primacy, though it is clearly implied in the continuing life and teaching of their churches. However, in the light of the newly emerging global perspectives and pluralistic tendencies in the world community, all of our churches have to undertake afresh a common theological reflection on primacy with a new vision of our future unity. In this respect the discrepancy between theory and practice in all churches was commonly recognized. Efforts should be made to overcome misunderstandings in this regard and to arrive at common conceptions.

5. There was agreement that infallibility or, as the Oriental Orthodox Churches prefer to say, dependable teaching authority, pertains to the church as a whole, as the Body of Christ and abode of the Holy Spirit. There was no complete agreement as to the relative importance of the different organs in the church through which this inerrant teaching authority is to find expression.

C. Goals for Communion

1. We were agreed that we should work toward a goal of full union of sister churches—with communion in the faith, in the sacraments of the church, in the ministry, and within a canonical structure. Each church as well as all churches together will have a primatial and conciliar structure, providing for their communion in a given place as well as on regional and worldwide scale.

2. The structure will be basically conciliar. No single church in this communion will by itself be regarded as the source and origin of that communion; the source of the unity of the church is the action of the triune God—Father, Son, and Holy Spirit. It is the same Spirit who operates in all sister churches the same faith, hope, and love, as well as ministry and sacraments. About regarding one particular church as the center of the unity, there was no agreement, though the need of a special ministry for unity was recognized by all.

3. This communion will find diverse means of expression—the exchange of letters of peace among the churches, the public liturgical remembering of the churches and their primates by each other, the placing of responsibility for convoking general synods in order to deal with common concerns of the churches, and so on.

4. The Oriental Catholic Churches will not be regarded—even in the transitional period before full unity—as a device for bringing Oriental Orthodox

Churches inside the Roman Communion. Their role will be more in terms of collaborating in the restoration of Eucharistic communion among the sister churches. The Oriental Orthodox Churches, according to the principles of Vatican II and subsequent statements of the See of Rome, cannot be fields of mission for other churches. The sister churches will work out local solutions, in accordance with differing local situations, implementing as far as possible the principle of a unified episcopate for each locality.

5. We were agreed that the primates of all the sister churches have a special responsibility for witnessing to and promoting the manifest unity of the church. No consensus was reached on the special responsibility which the Roman Catholic Church believes the bishop of Rome has in this regard or on the special office of Peter in the church. It was recognized by the Catholic participants, however, that the future exercise of such an office is not identical with the present practice which has developed without contact with the Oriental traditions. Therefore, this role of the bishop of Rome needs further mutual discussion and elucidation among the sister churches as well as within the Roman Communion itself on the basis of the Nicene Canons and the further developments which have taken place and are continuing to take place in all churches.

6. The consultation recognized the need for further studies and development of our understanding of such fundamental ideas as the nature and function of authority in the church, the shape of our future communion, the meaning and degree of autonomy in the church and the reception of conciliar decisions after the separation. Of particular importance is a fresh study in common of the whole New Testament with its witness to the nature and mission of the church and to its various ministries.

D. Recommendations

1. Taking into account the fact that the work of the four Vienna consultations is not yet officially assessed by our churches nor widely known to many even in the clergy, not to mention most of the laity, the following recommendations are made:

2. The results of the four Vienna consultations should be presented by the participants to their respective churches for evaluation and assessment, so that these evaluations can be a basis for further steps to be considered by an official commission of the churches taking into account especially the recommendations of the Third Consultation.

3. It would be useful to bring together in one volume the main conclusions of the four consultations with selections from the more significant papers. This could be published for use by theologians and theological students as well as others interested.

4. A series of more popular and briefer publications and articles in various languages could be published for bringing the members of our churches into the discussion. Other mass media presentations would also be useful.

E. Conclusion

1. The differences between the Roman Catholics and the Oriental Orthodox have grown out of their mutual estrangement and separate development in the period since the Council of Chalcedon. Differing historical experiences of the past fifteen centuries have made deep marks on the thinking and convictions of both traditions. In order to overcome these differences and to find mutual agreement and understanding, new ways of thinking and fresh categories of reflection and vision seem to be required, so that the sister churches may together fulfill their common responsibility to the Lord and carry out their common mission in the light of the present situation and for the sake of future generations.

2. The Holy Spirit who guides the church, will continue to lead us to full unity. And all of our churches have to be responsive to the divine call in obedience and hope.

Vienna, 17 September 1978

Appendix 2

A Working Paper from
the Consultation of the Commission on Faith and Order
with the Oriental Orthodox Churches
on Christological Concerns and the Apostolic Faith,
26, 27 April 1985, New York, New York

To the Apostolic Faith Study,
Commission on Faith and Order, NCCCUSA

Introduction

During the past twenty years, four dialogues have taken place between the Oriental Orthodox Churches and the Eastern Orthodox Churches. In addition during the 1970s a series of four consultations took place in Vienna at the *Pro Oriente* Foundation between Oriental Orthodox theologians and Roman Catholic theologians. In these unofficial Agreed Statements and communiqués, remarkably, the divisive issue of the christological statement of Chalcedon is apparently resolved. In these documents Oriental Orthodox, Eastern Orthodox, and the Roman Catholics agree that ancient differences dividing the church following the Council of Chalcedon in 451 have more to do with terminology as well as other disaffections than with theological substance. In each consultation, participants agreed that in Jesus Christ, the invisible Godhead became visible and fully human.

For this consultation, seven representatives of the Reformation traditions were asked to study these documents and to produce working papers for the consultation looking for points of *contact* and points for further exploration between their own communions and Oriental Orthodoxy. The Oriental Orthodox participants were asked to respond to these papers. These papers, along with the communiqués, Agreed Statements and selected papers from the earlier discussions, became the basis of the dialogue.

I. Christological Issues

All groups participating in the New York meeting agreed that in Jesus Christ we encounter God the Word become truly human. Furthermore, it was recognized that historically, for the Oriental Orthodox, it is God the Son who is the subject of the Incarnation, for it is only God who can save us. Some time was spent discussing whether this affirmation of the importance of the single divine subject in Christ was parallel in function to the Reformation churches' insistence upon "justification by faith alone": both deny that human beings are capable of saving themselves by their own efforts; both insist that salvation comes as the free gift of God who loves us and gives us eternal life.

Of the members of the Reformation groups presenting papers, the participants from the Presbyterian Church (USA), Lutheran Church in America, United Methodist Church, and the Episcopal Church stated that their christological traditions were in agreement not just with the content but also with the manner in which the early church councils affirmed them. The Southern Baptists, Disciples of Christ, and Mennonites, while they agreed with the content affirmed by the Councils, found that the way in which the questions were posed, and in which the creeds and their language were used, was significantly different from their way of experiencing and expressing Christian truths. At other points in the discussions, however, the Reformation groups found themselves in different constellations of agreement and difference. All groups participating agreed that, while we are grounded in the past, our work be directed toward the life of the church in the modern world, with our vision on the future.

The conversations raised important issues that were only briefly touched. While these may not be church-dividing problems, they can be profitably discussed in the Apostolic Faith Study, should participants in the study see fit. These issues include: (1) What does it mean to speak of Jesus Christ as "fully human"? What are the necessary elements of this humanity? How does this way of seeing him challenge the common American understandings about what it means to be human? (2) What does it mean to speak of Jesus Christ as "fully divine"? How does divinity act in the person of Jesus Christ? What does it mean to be God? (3) What is the relation of Christology to soteriology? (4) Is there a substantive issue (and if so, what is it) behind the reluctance of the Oriental Orthodox to speak of Jesus Christ as "fully God and fully human" rather than "fully God and fully man"? (5) What does all this mean for the life and witness of the church?

II. Methodological Considerations
Related to the Search for Church Unity

During the course of the discussions, the participants became increasingly aware that they approach issues such as Christology from different ecclesiological perspectives, and that these perspectives lead to different priorities in ecumenical dialogue. Some of the participating churches give priority to the preservation of a theologically pluralistic community, while others give priority to the preservation of the tradition as historically articulated. It also became apparent, however, that old stereotypes of these positions are inappropriate. Those concerned with diverse community and participatory authority, for example, are by no means disinterested in the truthfulness of Christian proclamation and witness but argue that truth is discovered through dialogue in community. Likewise, those concerned with fidelity to tradition are not disinterested in diverse community and the relation of revealed truth to the whole life of the church, but insist that such community must be firmly rooted in the truth revealed to the apostles and maintained in the apostolic tradition of the church. This is important since the different emphases help to explain certain "attitudes" that are frequently misunderstood. Some church representatives appear to be "suspicious" or "rigid"when their intent is to affirm the importance of tradition and teaching authority. Others appear "relativistic" (due in part to the absence of authoritative teaching instruments) when their intent is to affirm that we are already part of Christ's body.

With growing trust, some agreements about ecumenical methodology were possible. We could commonly endorse Archbishop Nersoyan's assertion that unity among Christians demands consensus only in essentials, while "for the rest we leave the mind of the Christian free with a freedom that may be guided but not imposed upon." We further agreed with his statement that the mystery of God in Christ is "inexhaustible and ineffable and for the human mind never fully comprehensible or expressible," and that Christians should, therefore, be able to live with "different emphases in the theological and dogmatic elaboration of Christ's mystery." We note with real regret that many apparent divisions have resulted from terminological misunderstandings that have obscured real identity of faith (though this in no way minimizes those genuine differences that must be addressed).

The members of the consultation were quite impressed by the recognized need and increasing willingness of churches divided for fifteen centuries to find new ways of resolving ancient discussions, ways that challenge all of the churches to seek paths towards reconciliation in the development of doctrinal formulations. Finally, Protestants would like to hear issues of church authority and structure discussed in explicit relationship to issues concerning the church's mission, and to explain how their own understandings of church structure are related to their visions for mission. We recognize the need for more study of the amount of theological diversity which the Christian community can tolerate, on our understanding of just what is essential (and therefore demands consensus) and what is secondary (and therefore admits of legitimate diversity).

These issues are treated in the *Pro Oriente* documents and relate to the World Council study of Conciliar Fellowship. The reception process of

Baptism, Eucharist and Ministry in which the churches are currently engaged should help the understanding of various modes of authority.

III. Future Directions:
Christology and Ecclesiology in the Broader Context

In the course of the consultation, the questions raised and difficulties in understanding each other often stemmed from the fact that the traditions and present lives of our various churches are very diverse, and often unknown to one another. For this reason, future discussion of issues closely related to Christology and ecclesiology might help set these areas in an appropiate context and enable us to understand the *significance* of Christological and ecclesiological affirmations that each of us makes. The purpose of raising these other issues would not be to complicate our discussions, but simply to provide the background against which the primary issues might be better focused.

It appears that Oriental Orthodox Christological concerns are linked with the concept of salvation as "divinization," a notion unclear to most Protestants. Contrariwise, the reasons why Protestants have emphasized justification seem somewhat unclear to some Orientals. Second, Protestants would have a deeper appreciation of Orthodox Christology were they to comprehend better its grounding in the sacramental life of these churches. However, it is not always clear to Protestants how the Oriental Orthodox emphasis on "sacraments" is related to the active lives of Christians in the world. Protestants may need to clarify how, for themselves, meaningful christological statements are linked to being Christ's disciples, and to hear how the Oriental Orthodox make this connection, particularly through active participation in sacramental life.

IV. Authority

Tradition, we realize, has been understood in many different ways by Orthodox, Anglican and Protestant Christians. Protestants have generally not given tradition prominence in their ecclesiology, but this does not mean that tradition is not to be found in the churches of the Reformation. One important question, we believe, is *where* tradition exercises authority within Protestant bodies. The Reformed, as well as the Anglican and Lutheran Churches, appeal to creed, confessions, and liturgies, while free churches locate tradition in commonly accepted practices, hymns, generative histories, and ethos. While many Protestant churches do not afford tradition formal authority, it is nonetheless indispensable for their faith and practice. Participants recognize the importance of examining more carefully the informal and yet powerful place of the authority of tradition in many Protestant churches. At the same time, Protestant participants were brought to appreciate the role of formal authority as found in Orthodox churches. In an age of relativism, the high regard that Orthodox Christians have for the authority of Council, ancient practice, and ministerial office may be valuable for Anglican and Protestant Christians.

We emphasize at this point that when we explore the matter of authority in respective traditions, we are dealing with something more than narrow ecclesiastical issues. At stake here is the question of the faithful proclamation of the church throughout its history and the integrity of its mission to the world. How shall we be certain that the witness of the church is true to the Lord who calls us to service? How shall we know that our acts are faithful to God's purpose? How shall we determine that the hope offered through us is no false hope? Such questions cannot be answered apart from questions of the authority of Jesus Christ as exercised through Scripture and tradition in the church. How do we speak authoritatively in a way that is consistent with the gospel we proclaim?

V. Pastoral Reflections

The convergences on the understanding of Jesus Christ, truly divine and truly human, would challenge the churches, recognizing their faith in these consultations and in the ecumenical movement, to begin to reflect in their life and mission a common witness and supportive collaboration at many levels of church life.

We recommend to the Apostolic Faith Study of the NCCC that it suggest appropriate measures to see that religious education materials be revised to: (1) recognize the measure of reconciliation among Anglican, Protestant, Catholic, Eastern and Oriental Orthodox Churches that has been achieved on the basis of ecumenical dialogue; (2) recount the nontheological factors that have perpetuated the fifth-century divisions throughout the centuries; and (3) remove the caricatures which Orthodox and Catholics may have of Protestant Christology, and which Protestants and Catholics may have of Eastern and Oriental Orthodox communities.

We encourage the Apostolic Faith Study to reflect on how its progress in common understandings of the faith among our churches may contribute to more sensitive ways of relating to one another with respect and without proselytizing. We encourage Faith and Order to suggest ways of providing common witness among these churches corresponding to the level of common faith represented in this consultation.

We recommend to seminaries and other instrumentalities of clergy/leadership education to use the *Pro Oriente-* and World Council-sponsored discussions, as well as the papers of this consultation in their published form, to enrich programs of theological education in all churches.

We recommend that the Apostolic Faith Study of the NCCC explore agreements or pastoral arrangements between various Oriental Orthodox patriarchates and Roman Catholic and Eastern Orthodox churches for models of response to the agreed statements on the pilgrimage towards full communion. Since Christ is the center of our faith, and since we can affirm in common that "God was in Christ," we feel it is encumbent upon our churches to explore through Faith and Order ways of giving greater common witness to our constituencies and beyond.

May 1985

Contributors

DR. ROBERTA BONDI, Associate Professor of Theology, Candler School of Theology, Emory University, Atlanta GA 30322.

DR. THOMAS N. FINGER, Professor, Northern Baptist Seminary, 660 East Butterfield Road, Lombard IL 60148.

THE VERY REV. PROF. G. FLOROVSKY, Professor Emeritus, Harvard University, Princeton University, Princeton NJ.

DR. PAUL FRIES, Professor of Theology, Academic Dean, New Brunswick Theological Seminary, 17 Seminary Place, New Brunswick NJ 08901.

THE REV. FR. M. V. GEORGE, Vice Principal, Orthodox Theological Seminary, Kottayam, Kerala, India.

METROPOLITAN PAULOS MAR GREGORIOS, Delhi Orthodox Center, 2 Institutional Area, Tughlazabad, Delhi 110 062, India.

PROF. DR. ALOYS GRILLMEIER, SJ, Professor of Dogmatical Theology at the Philosophical and Theological College St. Georgen, Offenbacher Landstrafe 224, d-66 Frankfurt/main, West Germany.

BROTHER JEFFREY GROS, Director, Commission of Faith and Order, NCCCUSA, Room 872, 475 Riverside Drive, New York NY 10115.

DR. PATRICK GILLESPIE HENRY, Director, Institute for Ecumenical Cultural Research, P. O. Box 6188, Collegeville MN 56321

DR. E. GLENN HINSON, David T. Porter Professor of Church History, Southern Baptist Theological Seminary, Louisville KY 40280.

DR. MICHAEL KINNAMON, Professor, Christian Theological Seminary, 100 W. 42nd Street, Indianapolis IN 46208.

HIS GRACE ARCHBISHOP TIRAN NERSOYAN, 580 West 187th Street, New York NY 10022.

THE VERY REV. PROF. J. S. ROMANIDES, Eleftheias 23 Kalamaki/Athens Greece.

DR. WILLIAM G. RUSCH, Ecumenical Officer, Lutheran Church in America, 321 Madison Avenue, New York NY 10016.

THE REV. PROF. V. C. SAMUEL, Theological College, P.O. Box 665, Addis Ababa, Ethiopia.

PROF. DR. WILHELM DE VRIES, SJ, Professor of Church History, Institutum Pontificum Orientale, Rome, Piazza Santa Maria Maggiore 7, I-00185 Rome.

Indexes

Subject Index

Proper Name Index

DATE DUE

MAR 6 '91		
DEC 13 '91		
JAN -2 '92		
APR 13 1997		
29 (10/1(99)		
JAN 12 1999		
DEC 2 1 1999		
MAR 23 2015		

HIGHSMITH # 45220